PENINSULAR GENERAL

Frederick Myatt

PENINSULAR GENERAL

Sir Thomas Picton 1758–1815

DAVID & CHARLES
Newton Abbot London North Pomfret (Vt)

British Library Cataloguing in Publication Data

Myatt, Frederick
   Peninsular general.
   1. Picton, *Sir* Thomas
   2. Great Britain. Army – Biography
   3. Generals – Great Britain – Biography
   I. Title
   355.3'32'0924   DA68.12.P/

   ISBN 0-7153-7923-2

Library of Congress Catalog Card Number: 79–56256

Typeset by Northampton Phototypesetters
and printed in Great Britain
by Redwood Burn Limited, Trowbridge & Esher
for David & Charles (Publishers) Limited
Brunel House Newton Abbot Devon

Published in the United States of America
by David & Charles Inc
North Pomfret Vermont 05053 USA

CONTENTS

LIST OF MAPS

INTRODUCTION

There can be no doubt that the greatest British military figure of the Napoleonic Wars was the Duke of Wellington, but while few will deny him his place it is an unfortunate fact that his very eminence tended, and indeed still tends, to overshadow even the most able of his subordinates, amongst whom must be included the Welsh soldier, Sir Thomas Picton.

Although Picton had no claim to be placed in the first rank of military commanders he was nevertheless a colourful character and a fine fighting soldier—perhaps one of the best that Wales, a land of warriors, had produced—and on this count he deserves a little more recognition than he has had so far.

In this book I have set out to produce a study of a distinguished Divisional Commander, a competent and reliable officer of the kind that greater generals are always pleased to have under them. The great difficulty in writing a biography of an individual who may be classed as an illustrious subordinate is that officers in this category rarely have the opportunity to distinguish themselves in every operation in which their formation takes part.

The inescapable fact places an author in danger from both flanks. On the one hand he can dwell almost entirely on the highlights and thus let the book develop into a series of more or less lightly connected episodes; this method, however, while it certainly ensures that the subject of the work is kept constantly in the reader's eye, must tend to give an extremely biased and distorted impression of the campaigns as a whole, particularly to the reader who is not already familiar with the military history of the period.

On the other hand it is easy to put in so much background material that the subject makes no more than sporadic appearances, thus converting the book to a campaign history rather than a biography. The course between the two is a narrow one and it is easy to stray from it; on balance it has seemed to me that it is desirable to present an intelligible, if very general, outline of the main events of the period as a background against which the reader can assess for himself the relative importance of the contribution made by the subject.

Another essential part of this background must be some detail of the military arrangements of the day, and because of this I have included a certain amount of general information on the Peninsular army and in particular on Picton's own 'Fighting Third' division, a formation happily still in existence and still bearing the high reputation which it established under its first permanent commander so long ago.

A NOTE ON SOURCES

The four main works on which the military background of this book is based are Wellington's Despatches, Fortescue's *History of the British Army*, Oman's *Peninsular War* and Napier's *Peninsular War*. Robinson's *Memoirs and Correspondence of Lieutenant-General Sir Thomas Picton* have also proved valuable; Sir William Napier, himself a Peninsular veteran and one without much love for Picton, often deals severely with this book but it is by no means as bad as he makes out. Its author had had no first-hand military experience but he had clearly studied the sources then available, particularly Londonderry's *Story of the Peninsular War*, which he seems to have relied on a good deal for detail.

Apart from these sources, scattered references to Picton are to be found in the numerous diaries, biographies, and books of reminiscence which appeared in the years after 1815, the most useful of which are listed. Many others, although not included in the bibliography, have provided minor background material.

The main source of information on the Trinidad affair must be the relevant volume of Howells' *State Trials*, although some of the statements on both sides have to be treated with caution, being entirely concerned with court proceedings. The books by Draper and Fullarton, though extremely interesting, are both so seriously biased (one for and one against) that they cannot be regarded as completely reliable. The Picton papers and the Trinidad papers are rather disappointing.

There appears to be relatively little other unpublished material of much value apart from the letters in the possession of the National Library of Wales, which are particularly useful in that they throw a little, though disappointingly little, light on Picton's private life. The probable reason for this serious lack of personal material is that in spite of his later military eminence Picton seems to have remained the archetypal country squire, content with his rural existence and shunning the fashionable world of gossipy memoirs. Worse still (from the biographer's point of view) he remained a bachelor, which contributed largely to the paucity of domestic material. The moral of this, presumably, is that when writing a book of this nature it is clearly desirable to select a subject with a devoted wife and a vast, letter-writing family.

CHAPTER 1

THE SUBALTERN

During the American War of Independence, the city of Bristol had been full of soldiers, because apart from its usual commercial activities the port had also been the main trooping centre for units crossing the Atlantic to fight the rebellious colonists. By 1783, however, the war was over, the triumphant rebels had gained their independence and all the British Government wanted was to get its army home and disband as much of it as it dared as quickly as possible.

The result of this was that Bristol was crammed with billeted military units, mostly infantry regiments, awaiting summary disbandment, amongst them being the 75th Regiment. This bore no relationship to a later 75th Regiment, which still forms part of the British infantry under its modern title of the Gordon Highlanders. It had been raised in 1776 as a wartime measure but had seen no overseas service, and in a few weeks at most it was to vanish without trace.

This was to be expected, for the policy was, and always had been, to keep the old corps intact and disband the newer ones. The men must certainly have known of this, and perhaps even welcomed the prospect of a respite from a hard life under iron discipline. When they were given the news on the midday parade they gave no indication of any dissatisfaction but dismissed quietly to their quarters.

Thereafter their attitude changed quickly, for, faced at last with the immediate prospect of discharge, they began to consider the bleakness of their own future. There was relatively little employment available, and what there was was unlikely to be given to soldiers, who in those days were equated in the eyes of the general public with rogues and vagabonds—which circumstances beyond their control might well force them to become. A few lucky men with trades might be absorbed back into the economy; a few strong but unskilled men might find jobs as chairmen, porters, labourers, and the like, and a very few old soldiers might qualify gratefully for the relative comfort and security of Chelsea Hospital. The bulk, however, would be driven to begging or crime, while ever living in the hope that some change in the international situation might offer them a chance to return to the Colours.

It is more than probable that agitators had been at work, for the latter half of the eighteenth century was a time of great social upheaval and it is certain that in the uneasy period between the American War and the French Revolution there were plenty of people ready to embarrass any legitimate government by preaching sedition.

Drink almost certainly also played its part. Cheap gin was one of the curses of the day and even penniless soldiers would probably have retired to the ginshops for a midday dram or two to whet the prospect of freedom. Whatever the reasons, by the middle of the afternoon the 75th was reduced to a rowdy and potentially very dangerous mob, milling wildly and shouting incoherently that they would *not* disband, that they would *not* give up their arms.

The non-commissioned officers present did what they could to pacify them but, as is often the case, the sudden, inexplicable collapse of discipline seems to have left them bewildered and quite incapable of dealing with a situation far outside their previous experience. This is not surprising for most discipline, even though backed by ferocious punishments, must remain a matter of voluntary submission by the individuals concerned; and once this voluntary submission ceases chaos must often result.

Someone soon reported the affair to the officer in temporary command of the regiment, who happened to be a twenty-five year old captain by the name of Thomas Picton—a tall burly Welshman with piercing eyes, a prominent hooked nose, and a determined chin. We do not know why such a relatively junior officer had been left in that situation; it is possible that his elders were all on leave or, and even more likely, pulling strings in London to avoid going on half-pay; it is possible that he was no more than an orderly officer responsible in the temporary absence of his seniors for the routine running of the unit. Whatever the reasons, he was to prove very capable of dealing with the problem so unexpectedly placed before him.

He can have been in no doubt as to the possible gravity of the situation. Mutiny, even if confined to a single group, must always be a grave military offence, but in this case the risks of a really serious situation were considerable. The place was full of soldiers, almost all awaiting discharge, and if they too developed similar ideas there was a very real risk that the rich city of Bristol might be given up to loot.

Nor, if this occurred, could anything much be done immediately to check it, for in the last resort there was no means of enforcing the law left to the magistrates except the use of troops. If these were out of control the result would be anarchy until such time as other units could be assembled and despatched to restore order.

Picton, thus well aware of the need for speed, snatched up his sword, clapped on his hat and hurried off to the scene of the disturbance. On arrival he wasted no time, for, having identified the ringleader (probably a known troublemaker), he plunged boldly into the crowd, sword in hand, and hauling him out violently by the collar flung him bodily into the arms of the assembled non-commissioned officers, who at once removed him to some safe place of detention.

This, as he had probably anticipated, was decisive; the men were still trained soldiers, their instinctive habit of discipline still strong, and prompt action on the part of an officer well known to them brought them to their senses—certainly to his relief and possibly to their own also.

The uproar subsided and as soon as things were quiet the young Picton addressed the meeting with some force. The men then returned peacefully to their quarters and were disbanded next day without further trouble.

It must be said that there is a curious lack of corroboration for this whole episode, which rests entirely on the account by Robinson, Picton's later biographer, who does not quote his authority. Nevertheless, it probably occurred, since Robinson, a respectable clergyman and usually accurate in other respects, can hardly have invented it, though he may have made the best of it.

Assuming therefore, as we must, that the affair actually occurred substantially as stated, it is of great interest as being the first recorded occasion for the display of certain strong characteristics which were to mark all the young officer's actions until the end of his life. They were all there—the physical courage, the self-confidence, the immediate decision in favour of direct, violent, uncomplicated action, and the equally swift execution of his resolve. Even his subsequent address to his shaken soldiers, although nowhere recorded, must surely have displayed at least the beginning of those tremendous powers of malediction which were later to arouse such awe, such anger, and such unwilling admiration in those serving under him.

Thomas Picton was born at his father's house at Pyston, Pembrokeshire, in August 1758, being one of several sons. His father was a

Welsh country squire in reasonably good circumstances, and as his mother also later inherited some money it is probable that he was brought up comfortably, though not luxuriously.

Not a great deal is known of his early life; it is likely that in the fashion of his time he ran more or less wild with the village boys and probably received much of his early education locally. Although later he was obviously a well-read man his spelling always remained somewhat erratic, and it is now quite impossible to say whether this results from early educational deficiencies or from a not uncommon blind spot in his make-up.

The boy had been determined from his earliest youth to become a soldier, a decision in which he was probably much influenced by his uncle Lieutenant-Colonel William Picton, who was then commanding the 12th Foot. The army was not at that time a profession offering much in the way of financial rewards but the circumstances of the family made this relatively unimportant. The reputation of the British army was then high; it had fought gallantly and successfully in the Seven Years War (which ended when Picton was five) and in conjunction with the Navy had laid the foundations of the new British Empire. His father apparently had no objection to it as a career for one of his sons and on 22 January 1772, therefore, the boy was commissioned as an ensign into his uncle's regiment, of which the Lord Cornwallis was Colonel.

By modern standards thirteen may seem to be an unduly tender age at which to embark on such an arduous career, but in the eighteenth century there were ample precedents for it. Commissions were purchased, or sometimes obtained free by interest, for infants a few months old, after which these literal and metaphorical babes-in-arms proceeded to draw the pay, or at least the half-pay, of their rank. By judicious purchase moreover they, or more correctly their families, could often obtain promotion into the bargain so that the nursemaid who, when asked the reason for the commotion in the nursery, replied that it was 'only the major crying for his porage' was speaking the literal if ludicrous truth.

Even at the advanced age of thirteen, however, young Thomas did not join his regiment immediately, but was first sent, possibly unwillingly, to undergo a course of study at a military academy in Chelsea run by a Frenchman by the name of de Lachée to learn at least some of the theoretical rudiments of his chosen profession. This step, which was probably suggested by his uncle, was a somewhat unusual one in its day because as a rule the young officer of cavalry or infantry joined his regiment completely ignorant of his business.

On arrival he was customarily placed in the care of some steady old sergeant who taught him some of the basics of the business in much the same way as his father's keeper had taught him to shoot.

Much of the training and daily routine of a regiment in those days was in the capable hands of the senior non-commissioned officers, usually elderly men grown grey in the service, full of military lore and jealous for the honour of the regiment, so that in times of peace the officers had little to do. The adjutant and quartermaster were indeed usually busy men; but as adjutants often, and quartermasters always, had risen from the ranks they can hardly be considered a fair exception. It was only a few years later that William Cobbett, of *Rural Rides* fame, enlisted and in two years became a sergeant-major, practically running his regiment. This was, of course, remarkably quick because he was a remarkable man, but it gives some indication of the state of affairs.

The regimental officer was thus enabled to spend much of his time in drinking, gambling, duelling and womanising, secure in the knowledge that when the regiment was put through its evolutions there would always be a capable sergeant at his elbow to prompt him in the proper words of command. His real function came on active service, when he was expected to be brave, give a lead, and if necessary die like a gentleman—which, to give him credit, he usually did.

It is, of course, grossly unfair to put all officers in this category for there were always some, frequently the sons or protégés of old and probably not very affluent officers, who were keen to learn their profession; and there is little doubt that Picton, influenced as he was by his uncle, belonged to this relatively small minority.

The scientific corps, i.e. the artillery and engineers, did of course ensure that their young officers received proper training but they were exceptional and were, if the truth be known, regarded by the army at large as very peculiar people indeed. Although the curriculum at M. de Lachée's establishment has not come down to us it was probably based fairly closely on their syllabus and would almost certainly have included mathematics, military drawing, some basic instruction in the principles of fortification, and of course French, then the military, diplomatic and social lingua franca of the civilised world. It may well have been there too that young Picton acquired the habit of systematic reading which never left him. He himself never doubted the value of a thorough early training; over forty years later he was to electrify his personal staff by asserting that French officers were much superior to British by virtue of their military education.

'Dammit, sir', he was to say in his usual blunt way, referring to British officers, 'they knew nothing, we are saved by our non-commissioned officers who are the best in the world.'

The Army which Picton joined towards the end of 1773 differed little from the one which the Marlborough had commanded so successfully sixty years before. It had fought with distinction in the Seven Years War and if thereafter it had slipped into the state of decay common to British armies in peacetime that had been a matter of deliberate policy on the part of the government. People of almost every shade of political opinion in England were firmly of the belief that a standing army in peacetime was a constant menace to the lawfully elected government, which it might at any time attempt to overthrow. This belief, which stemmed from the military rule of Cromwell, was (and perhaps still is) a justifiable one for, although nothing of the sort has been attempted in England for the last three hundred years, it is by no means an unusual event in the world today.

It is of course true that soldiers who seize power will never admit to any worse reason than disgust at the spectacle of corrupt and inefficient civil government, which by its very nature is bound to irritate military men with their passion for discipline and order.

This eighteenth-century fear of armed force naturally had an adverse effect on the efficiency of the army, since the politicians habitually resorted to certain standard, well-tried methods of keeping it in its proper place. The most important of these was rigid control of finance, the first result of which was to keep the army small, for it was argued that soldiers could be raised easily enough when a war broke out and should be discharged as soon as possible after it was over, a method which may have made for economy but which certainly did not increase efficiency. People in those days pinned their faith on the navy for home defence and considered quite seriously that all that was required in the way of land forces was some form of militia, command of which would remain firmly in the hands of the country gentlemen who then constituted the bulk of the House of Commons. On this basis therefore the function of the standing army in peacetime became largely one of garrisoning new overseas possessions and this was tolerated by the country at large, for overseas possessions meant increased trade and prosperity, while a few handfuls of widely scattered, fever-ridden soldiers could hardly constitute a menace to anyone. The army at home was only just large enough to supply reliefs to these overseas garrisons and was chiefly employed seeking recruits, most of whom were eventually destined to die in those same profitable colonies.

It was, however, also used occasionally, under strict magisterial control, to act as police in riots and other serious disturbances, which did little to increase its popularity in the country at large.

In order that no large military centres should develop (and so give officers visible proof of their collective strength) barracks were not permitted except for those in London and at a few fortresses. The bulk of the army was billeted, chiefly in ale-houses, and in order to spread the load equally, and also keep the soldiers busy, infantry units were kept constantly on the move, so that the widely used expression, 'a marching regiment', was a very fair description of the ordinary battalion of the Line.

The system of billeting had a second effect also—that it increased the already considerable public dislike of soldiers, particularly in their role, already mentioned, of internal security. A rough sort of social discipline was of course imposed by public opinion but the mob, which considered itself a collection of free-born Britons, objected strongly to government restraint based on cavalry charges or volleys of musketry, however patently necessary this restraint might be. Soldiers in billets increased this feeling because they were seen to be parasites, mere drunken brawlers who robbed hen-roosts and vegetable gardens and terrorised peaceable citizens, and this naturally suited the book of governments of the time, who stuck closely to the old adage of 'divide and rule'.

When the young ensign Thomas Picton left the academy in Chelsea he was posted to his regiment in Gibraltar, and as the regiment was for all practical purposes the highest permanent formation in the army it may be as well to consider briefly the constitution of a typical example.

An infantry regiment of the period was commanded by a colonel and consisted of one or more battalions each commanded by a lieutenant-colonel. Regiments were numbered serially and were usually known only by this number: for example, the 12th, the regiment into which Picton was first commissioned, was known simply as the 12th Foot, although the term Foot was just beginning to be superseded by the term 'Regiment'. When a regiment had more than one battalion, these were also numbered serially within the regiment e.g. 1st/12th, 2nd/66th, etc.

The colonel exercised no tactical control over the regiment, which was, indeed, a strictly administrative organisation, the tactical unit being the battalion; he had, however, considerable administrative responsibilities, for in those days, in order to reduce overhead costs, the government simply paid the colonel an annual lump sum out of which he paid, fed, and equipped his regiment—and, if he was careful, also made a modest profit for his pains. This latter was accepted as a necessity, as indeed it was: in those days there was no half-pay for general officers as such, so that when unemployed they only had the half-pay of their regimental rank to sustain them. The policy therefore was either to give them sinecure appointments as governors of fortresses or to make them colonels of regiments, which, apart from providing for their wants, also tended to attach them to the government and cause them to avoid any unfortunate adventures of the Cromwellian type.

The system was inevitably open to fraud, for even the most honest and conscientious colonel was liable to be swindled by his agent or by a dishonest contractor. Nevertheless, it lasted for a very long time, chiefly because it suited almost everybody: the only person to suffer was the soldier in the ranks, who often wore shoddy clothes and ate rotten meat and bad bread, but as he was not in a position to complain few people in authority worried much about him.

A typical battalion in 1773 consisted of probably not more than six hundred men. It was commanded by a lieutenant-colonel with a major, seven or eight captains, twenty or more lieutenants and ensigns, and about the same number of sergeants, the remainder being in the ranks as corporals and private men.

Battalion headquarters would probably have comprised the commanding officer, the major, a lieutenant and adjutant, a surgeon (sometimes with an assistant), a quartermaster, a small corps of drums and fifes, a few pioneers and possibly a clerk or two, while the remainder would have been divided into ten companies—the grenadier company, eight battalion companies and the light company.

Grenadiers were originally introduced into the British infantry in 1680 to throw the primitive grenades then in use, but although the weapon was soon abandoned the grenadiers remained as a *corps d'élite*. They consisted of the tallest and smartest men in the unit and regarded it as their function to lead any assault; they also had certain slight differences of dress, originally permitted for purely utilitarian reasons but subsequently zealously retained as a privilege long after the necessity for them had ceased.

The light company was an innovation: the operations in Canada during the Seven Years War had shown the need for light infantry, and in 1770, only three years before Picton actually joined his regiment, a light company had been authorised for each infantry battalion. They varied very much in quality, for a few years of peace had been enough in most cases to make people forget the lessons of the side-show in the forest, with the result that the army as a whole had reverted to the worship of the geometrical movement of large, well-drilled bodies of troops upon the open plains of northern Europe. As a consequence the average light company, although specially armed and clothed, received little or no specialist training and frequently became a repository for all the worst characters of the battalion. It is not known if this applied to the 12th Regiment or not; Picton's uncle, who commanded it, was a good and experienced soldier but as he had served (with great distinction) as a captain of grenadiers in Europe it is at least possible that he was on the side of the big battalions.

A battalion of the period fought and manoeuvred in line or column. The line was three ranks deep and was primarily a defensive formation which allowed every man to use his musket; a line could be advanced or retired but it was extremely difficult to maintain proper dressing over anything but the shortest distances, so that the more usual formation for manoeuvre and attack was the column, in which the companies formed up in line, one behind the other, into a compact mass.

The infantry weapon of the period was the Tower musket, a smooth-bore flintlock throwing a ball of somewhat over an ounce in weight to a lethal range of two or three hundred yards. It was however so hopelessly inaccurate that effective fire could only be produced in the form of volleys at close range. The musket was also relatively ineffective in wet weather, when recourse often had to be made to the bayonet. Uniform had not changed much for years and consisted of tricorn hats, long red coats, buff or white breeches, and high black gaiters, together with the necessary belts and equipment for the carriage of ammunition and necessaries. Hair was still worn long and was scraped into queues and powdered with flour. The men themselves were a rough enough collection: they were nearly all volunteers —although, as many of them had enlisted under the influence of copious quantities of alcohol (administered, needless to say, by the recruiting sergeant) or other means of persuasion or coercion, the term volunteer must be used in its widest sense. Once in—and it must be remembered that in peacetime they enlisted for life—and after their first misery was over, they either deserted or made the best of it; the mere fact of enlisting cut them off from civilian society, even the lowest, so that their only home was their regiment and their only company that of their fellow-soldiers. Their existence was dull—but probably no more so than their civil lives: they did a few parades and guards, and spent a good deal of time pipe-claying and polishing, but otherwise had little to do; they lived on boiled meat, and bread, and weak beer, and were herded together into the sheds and various outbuildings of the ale-houses in which they were billeted. Every spare penny of their pay, which was little enough, went on drink, and after it was spent they begged, borrowed or stole more for the same purposes. It is difficult to blame them, for their lives were dull and brutish; they played no games and few could read, even if they could have afforded books and candles. Yet in spite of this there was plenty of fine fighting material amongst them—hard disciplined veterans ready to follow their officers anywhere. A few years later these qualities were to be severely tested.

The Rock of Gibraltar had been in British hands since its capture in 1704 by Sir George Rooke and over the course of years had been so strongly fortified as to render it virtually impregnable, but it cannot have been a very exciting first posting for a keen young officer fresh from military academy. The town was small and cramped and social life strictly limited, so that once Picton had thoroughly explored the maze of tunnels and fortifications he must have become bored. Fortunately this lack of practical experience was to some extent compensated for by intensive military reading under the wise guidance of his uncle, and by the fact that he was able to make numerous excursions into southern Spain, in the course of which he learnt a great deal about the country and its people and also became fluent in the Spanish tongue, all of which was to stand him in good stead in the distant future.

In 1777 Picton became a lieutenant and in the same year exchanged into the 75th Regiment, in England as a captain; he was desperately bored with garrison duty and being by then theoretically proficient in his profession he naturally wished to put his knowledge to the test of active service. There was plenty available, for in 1775 the American War of Independence had broken out and from then until 1782 there was a great deal of fighting in progress in North America. There was also almost continuous warfare in India, but Picton seemed fated not to see any active service, for his new regiment remained in England for the whole period of the hostilities, thus condemning him to a routine which can have been but little less dull than the one from which he had escaped.

To make things even worse for him, in 1780 a strong Spanish force besieged Gibraltar, thus turning the dull station into a battle-ground; the operations lasted until September 1782 when a final combined

French and Spanish attack was decisively defeated, after which they withdrew.

The 12th, his old regiment, were of course in the thick of the fighting, and he must have been seriously disappointed at not being with them. Then came the peace, and with it the troubled disbandment of the 75th Regiment. King George III came to hear of the latter affair, and his Royal approbation was conveyed to Captain Picton through the commander-in-chief, together with the most handsome promise of a majority, but as the latter never materialised Picton went on half-pay with the rest. He had perhaps been rather unwise in leaving the safe haven of such a senior corps as the 12th for a newly-raised regiment which he must have realised would almost inevitably be disbanded. His uncle had however been appointed colonel of the 75th in 1777; and in an age when some sort of interest was essential for military advancement, he presumably had considered the risk worth taking.

He retired to his home in Pembrokeshire where, being comfortably provided for financially, he was able to follow the usual pursuits of a country gentleman of the period. He was a good shot and he also enjoyed coursing, but above all he hunted. He had been from his earliest days a good horseman and there is little doubt that these regular days out with a Welsh mountain pack did much to help improve his already excellent eye for country. It also, it would seem, gave him strong views on the type of horse best suited for hard work, for although he was a tall heavy man he showed no enthusiasm in later life for the large and showy chargers so often affected by general officers. His preference was always for 'a stout cob' or 'active horses not above fifteen hands', and all his years of campaigning never apparently gave him any reason to change his views. Little is known of his other activities during his period of half-pay but it is not difficult to guess at them: country gentlemen of the period were not famed as courtiers; they rode hard, they drank hard and they stated their opinions in no uncertain terms, and we have no real reason to suppose that Picton varied very much from the generality. He does not seem to have formed any romantic attachments with the opposite sex, although it is clear from scattered reference that his tastes in this direction were entirely normal. The most probable reason for this is that always in the back of his mind was the desire to be unencumbered and ready for active service when the call came.

He remained a keen soldier, desperately anxious for honour, glory, and professional advancement, and he still read widely. He also wrote endless letters to the Horse Guards asking for full-pay

23

employment, but such appointments were few and applications many, so that without a great deal of influence (which he did not possess) his prospects of active employment were slight.

In this way he passed eleven years; but at last in 1793 his chance came, for in that year war broke out with revolutionary France and he at once renewed his applications for employment. There was, as it happened, but little augmentation of the army in the early days of the war and he continued to be unsuccessful until quite suddenly he heard that Sir John Vaughan, an acquaintance and neighbour, had been appointed to command in the West Indies. So Picton at once settled his affairs, packed his kit and took passage on a West-bound merchantman. He had no official appointment nor, as far as can be ascertained, even the promise of an appointment, but he considered the risk well worth taking.

CHAPTER 2

THE WEST INDIES

The West Indian islands had for long been the small change of warfare amongst the nations of Europe, but although they had passed from hand to hand with some regularity this had rarely had much effect on the lives of their inhabitants. The bulk of the European population were English, French and Spanish planters who lived in feudal luxury on their estates while the hard work was done for them by thousands of negro slaves, and since most nations were interested in commerce these occasional changes of sovereignty had rarely worried them. They had simply continued to grow and export their crops, chiefly sugar, without much interference from their somewhat nominal masters of the moment.

All nations experienced great difficulty in maintaining effective garrisons in the islands, for they were unhealthy in the extreme. Although they were very beautiful, the heat and damp forest fostered all sorts of diseases, chiefly yellow fever, so that the planters, surrounded as they were by every comfort, managed to survive in a precarious way but the soldiers fresh from Europe died in their thousands. In Britain the soldier was by no means popular, and little care was expended on him in overseas garrisons. Men were recruited as best they could be, given a bare minimum of training and packed into leaky transports in which, if the winds were unfavourable, they might spend months under the most unpleasant and insanitary conditions imaginable. They were fed on bad salt meat and hard biscuit, washed down with the minimum of foul water and a little spirits, and, being crammed together below decks in conditions little better than those of a slave ship, it is small wonder that they died easily even on the voyage over. This, however, was only the beginning; they arrived weak from long periods on board ship, quite unsuitably clad, and were at once herded into rough barracks, often no more than palm shacks and usually built on the lowest and most unhealthy ground available. Their work was confined to a couple

The West Indies

of parades each day and an occasional guard, but otherwise they lay and sweated under their rough roofs until the evening cooled enough to enable them to stir out.

Even then there was little to do, so the men repaired to the nearest native village and there enjoyed themselves after a fashion with the local women of the lowest class, who dispensed both favours and disease with horrifying generosity. Always too there was the rum: no soldier need remain sober for a minute if he had but a penny in his pocket and even the penniless ones had only to hang around the plantation presses where they could soon drink themselves into insensibility on the fiery, newly distilled spirit. In this they were abetted by the negroes, who regarded men in red coats as simply a different species of slave.

Thus they lived, and thus they frequently died; at best it was accepted that forty or fifty per cent of the garrisons would die annually; at worst a single bad outbreak of some virulent fever could practically destroy whole battalions in a few weeks.

It is therefore understandable that West Indian service was hated and feared by most soldiers; officers would resign or go on half-pay to avoid it or, if they could afford the money, would bribe some impecunious half-pay officer to exchange with them and go in their place. Even so the officers survived somewhat better than the men, chiefly because they lived under better conditions, ate better food and had perhaps a little more self-control; but still they died in considerable numbers—even Brigadier John Moore, a particularly abstemious officer who had advanced views on tropical hygiene and lived a most Spartan existence, had been lucky to escape with his life.

In the circumstances it might have been thought that native troops would have provided a sensible answer to the problem, and so in many ways they would have done. It was, however, impracticable to import native soldiers from other tropical possessions and the planters were understandably very loath to agree to the raising of armed bodies of slaves, for it was slave risings that they most dreaded. They therefore continued to demand white garrisons and the government continued to supply them. Nobody knows, or ever will know, how many tens of thousands of British soldiers died uselessly in the West Indies in the late seventeenth, eighteenth and early nineteenth centuries.

The French Revolution introduced a new element into West Indian affairs: previously, the islands had passed from one nation to another without serious interference with their internal affairs or the established order of things, but the French, full of revolutionary ardour, declared that all men, black or white, were equal, and that slavery was abolished. The results were immediate; the slaves in the French islands, simple, primitive and little removed from savagery, at once attempted to possess their masters' goods and when the latter objected they cut their throats, at which the survivors, feeling this to be an extreme interpretation of equality, formed themselves into armed bands and started counter-operations. In a few months the French islands were in a state of terror with rape, arson, torture and murder as matters of daily occurrence; and very soon the French planters, who by the very nature of their lives were anti-revolution-aries, suggested that it would be an excellent thing for everybody (except perhaps the slaves) if the islands were taken under British protection. There was at first a good deal of indecision about this on the part of the British government, but when war broke out in 1793 the islands were at once seized without any difficulty, the French Navy being quite unable to protect them. These seizures were, however, by no means uniformly successful: Victor Hugues, the mulatto Commissioner of Convention for the French Revolutionary government, was an active, capable, and quite ruthless leader and in the circumstances he was able to make the British hold on these islands very precarious. The 'brigands', a delightfully general term used to describe any person in arms against the British, were both numerous and active and being moreover inured to the climate they were more than a match in the forest for the fever-ridden European troops sent against them.

A French fleet actually succeeded in eluding the British ships and landing arms, men and supplies on Guadeloupe, while all the time French agents were busy stirring up trouble amongst the negroes in the British possessions; and so successful were they that in 1794 the negroes actually rose against their masters, when the situation at once became desperate. General Grey, the British Commander-in-Chief in the West Indies, was a fine soldier and did as much, and indeed more, than might reasonably have been expected of him; he was, however, driven to distraction by wild and contradictory orders from the government at home and as he received but few reinforce-ments, and those of appalling quality, he was able to achieve very little. The last straw as far as Grey was concerned came when the government, inexcusably and out of sheer ignorance, repudiated an order regarding prize money on which he and the naval commander, Admiral Jervis, had already acted, whereupon they both resigned.

It was as a result of Grey's resignation that Sir John Vaughan was appointed to the command, and Picton at once snatched at this faint chance of a return to service. Things turned out favourably for him; on his arrival at the headquarters in Martinique he was warmly welcomed by Vaughan, who was, like all commanders in the West Indies, chronically short of capable officers, and who therefore used his influence to get him appointed as a full-pay captain in the 17th Regiment while remaining on his staff; and a few months later Vaughan did even better for his protégé by getting him promoted to a majority, still of course on the staff, and appointing him Deputy Quartermaster-General with the local rank of lieutenant-colonel.

There are but few details available of his activities for the next few months, but as in those days the department of the Quartermaster-General dealt (amongst other things) with operations, it is certain that he was kept busy. It *is* known that in March 1795 he was sent by Sir John to Barbados to meet some reinforcements which the latter proposed to employ immediately on active operations, and that when he saw their appalling quality he at once, on his own responsibility, countermanded Vaughan's orders, a change which Vaughan subsequently approved. With the fleet bearing these reinforcements there also arrived a despatch from Dundas, the Secretary for the Colonies, full of wild impracticable plans, together with a firm refusal to allow the raising of negro troops, all of which Vaughan sensibly ignored. Instead he set about dealing with a difficult situation in his capable way and in the light of his own wide local knowledge, and in spite of the known difficulties he might well have succeeded; but then in August 1795, like so many British soldiers before him, he died suddenly in Martinique.

His death put Picton in a difficult situation inasmuch as his appointment to Vaughan's staff had been entirely a personal one: the first thing that happened was that he lost his post as DQMG and with it his temporary rank, and although the actual reasons for this are not known it is not difficult to make a shrewd guess at them. Brigadier Knox, the Quartermaster-General in the West Indies, succeeded Vaughan in temporary command and it is probable that he simply seized the opportunity of thus creating a vacancy for some protégé of his own; this would have been quite in accordance with eighteenth-century custom and would have given rise to little or no comment. The other possibility is that Knox was actuated by dislike of Picton and so took the opportunity of removing him from his department as soon as he ceased to be under Vaughan's protection.

Picton therefore waited at headquarters in considerable un-certainty, fully resigned to returning home, but before he could do so one of his rather rare strokes of luck intervened.

By 1795 the British government had at last realised the gravity of the West Indian situation and had determined to despatch a strong expedition to deal with it. They therefore assembled a force of no less than twenty-four battalions which it was intended should sail in September 1795 in order to arrive in the West Indies at the beginning of the (relatively) healthy season, and to command it they appointed General Sir Ralph Abercromby. Abercromby was a Scotsman and a professional soldier of the old school who, without money or influence, had reached high rank by sheer merit. He was well-read and a deep thinker of liberal views who had refused to serve against the colonists in the American War of Independence because his conscience would not permit him to do so. In spite of these rather advanced ideas, however, he had achieved a considerable military reputation, and as he regarded the war against Revolutionary France as a just one he entered into it wholeheartedly. He was a brave, patient and kindly man, and he could be strong-willed if necessary, a characteristic he was soon to be called upon to display.

The force assembled and embarked but was delayed for a long period by contrary winds, and during this time it was discovered that there were serious deficiencies in the stores and equipment provided, whereupon Abercromby, to the great fury of Dundas, flatly refused to sail until they had been rectified. No sooner had this been done than the wind turned foul again.

These delays had a serious effect on the morale of the officers and men of the force, for none of them had in the least wanted to go to the West Indies in the first place and the long period of uncomfortable waiting on the crowded transports had not increased their enthusiasm for a task which they knew would inevitably kill most of them. Eventually, however, on 15 November 1795 the expedition sailed under the escort of a squadron of warships, only to be dispersed immediately on the 18th and 19th by a terrible storm which drove a number of ships ashore and sank others with heavy loss.

It took some time to assemble the survivors but this was at last achieved and on 3 December the expedition sailed again, only to be dispersed yet again by bad weather; more ships were sunk and a number of others, having been blown miles off their course, were captured by French privateers. This time a few ships did actually succeed in reaching the West Indies, where they arrived in ones and twos and where their tired, sickly soldiers were at once dispersed as individual reinforcements to the garrisons there.

The *Glory*, Admiral Christian's flagship on which Abercromby sailed, spent seven terrible weeks in the Channel before it finally got

30

back to port but immediately it did so the sixty-two-year-old general, although severely shaken and exhausted by the long buffeting he had received, at once sailed again, this time in a frigate. This third attempt was successful and on 17 March 1796 he finally arrived in Barbados with the rest of the convoy hobbling along behind him as best it could.

One of the officers on his reception committee was Major Picton and old Abercromby treated him with great consideration; they had never met before but the general was a friend of Picton's uncle, and it may even be that in the fashion of the day the latter had solicited Abercromby's protection for his nephew; whatever the reason, the new commander-in-chief at once took him on to his staff as a volunteer aide-de-camp, a singularly ill-defined position but one at which Picton not unnaturally jumped eagerly.

As soon as his battered force had arrived, Abercromby decided that his first objective must be St Lucia; on 26 April 1796, therefore, his leading troops landed on the island and after a month's brisk operations achieved success.

Picton does not appear to have played any particularly distinguished part in these operations, so there is no need to describe them in detail; it is of interest, however, to note that two of Abercromby's brigadiers were John Moore and John Hope, both of whom were later to achieve fame.

At the end of the campaign Abercromby was apparently sufficiently pleased with Picton to wish to regularise his position and an order was published saying that 'all orders coming through Colonel Picton shall be considered as the order of the Commander-in-Chief'. This was probably no more than routine, but Robinson concluded, naively enough, that it was intended as a high honour and this is one of the points which Napier holds up to ridicule in that part of his 'strictures' dealing with the unfortunate clergyman who was Picton's first biographer. It will be noted, however, that Picton was again a colonel and the fact that Abercromby had bothered to use his influence to obtain him that rank (in the 56th Regiment but still, of course, on the staff) is a surer mark of his approval than the order to which Napier objected.

The commander-in-chief next turned his attention to St Vincent and Grenada, which fell almost simultaneously; both these successes were incomplete since the interior of the islands swarmed with armed brigands, but they were nevertheless considerable achievements in the difficult circumstances under which they had been attempted. At this stage of the operations Abercromby, who was by no means well, decided to go home to recuperate and sailed at the end of June, taking Picton with him. Their stay in England was a short one, for January 1797 found them back in Martinique; they found that the situation had worsened considerably in their absence, for Spain, which had hitherto been a neutral, indeed a benevolent neutral, had declared war against England.

Abercromby decided after a careful appreciation of the situation that the Spanish island of Trinidad constituted the greatest menace to the British West Indies, and on 15 February 1797 he sailed with a force to attack it. The Spaniards made all preparations to resist but on the night of 16 February one of their warships lying in the harbour suddenly burst into flames; the fire spread rapidly and by next morning all but one of the vessels had been completely destroyed. This event, the causes of which were never discovered, so demoralised the Spaniards that on 17 February they surrendered without resistance.

The loss of the Spanish ships had at once removed any threat to the British colonies and there was therefore no strategic need to garrison Trinidad; Abercromby decided that it was desirable to do so, however, and it is probable that this decision was arrived at for political reasons.

Spain was weak and corrupt, and it is likely that as he saw it a firm footing in Trinidad might eventually result either in the whole of the Spanish possessions falling into British hands or else the islands cutting themselves off from Spain, whose weak and incompetent rule they despised, and setting themselves up as independent countries: in either case Spanish America would prove a rich area for British trade.

Abercromby therefore took the decision which was to have such an effect on Picton's future and appointed him governor of the island; then, having left him a thousand men and some broad general instructions (the gist of which was to do the best he could) the old general sailed away to Martinique.

Trinidad was in an appalling state, not far from anarchy, when Picton assumed his new appointment. Although it had been a Spanish colony the actual control and supervision by Spain had been slight; and the colonists, who heartily despised their mother country, had taken little notice of the few weak attempts to rule them. Unfortunately, it happened that no real substitute for the home government existed, for the better class of people, chiefly French and Spanish traders and planters, were too immersed in commerce to give much attention to political affairs with the result that such administration as there was had fallen into the hands of a little set of minor officials and lawyers who thought only of their own enrichment. This they achieved mainly by extortion and by what would now be called graft of all kinds. The bulk of the population were rogues too, for the tradition of the old Spanish Main still ran strongly there; the island had for many years been a base for pirates who had an appalling reputation for ferocity, and gradually round this hard core there had assembled a remarkable assortment of dubious characters; there were refugees from half the West Indian islands, there were fugitive negroes and criminals avoiding justice, including a great many ex-slaves who had been involved in various hideous massacres on the other islands. There were also deserters from most of the armies and navies of Europe and a considerable floating population of peons from the mainland, a class of people little removed from bandits. Over the years this reckless mixture had produced a wild and lawless community of all shades of colour and depravity. They were lazy and dishonest, fond of bright clothes and ornaments, and they fought and drank and womanised in the squalid alleys of the towns and villages. They were, however, united in a fierce hatred of law and order, which in the natural course of things meant that they particularly disliked the British—when the British fleet was approaching the island the French consul offered the Spanish governor the immediate assistance of three thousand armed men against it. A fair indication of the disrepute in which the Trinidadians were held may be obtained from a contemporary ordinance of the more law-abiding island of Grenada, which stated uncompromisingly that:

All persons coming from Trinidad shall give bond on their arrival of one thousand pounds sterling to be of good behaviour; and if such bond is not given, such person to be declared a vagabond and, without any other proof than that of usual or frequent residence in Trinidad, to be committed to jail.

Abercromby had left Picton a force of a thousand men with which he was to control this most turbulent and unruly population *and* defend the island from outside attack, and even on paper it was a pitifully small force for the task; but when one also takes into consideration the fact that about half of it (more or less) could be assumed to be sick at any one time its inadequacy becomes ridiculous. The quality and reliability of Picton's troops also left much to be desired; firstly there was the 57th, a steady enough regiment on which he must have relied greatly; then there was a body which he refers to as Hompesch's

33

detachment, which presumably was a part of Hompesch's Chasseurs, one of the numerous 'mongrel' foreign corps of mercenaries or political refugees which were raised at the end of the eighteenth century to make up for the chronic shortage of recruits; and lastly he had some three or four hundred locally enlisted negroes. The potential weakness and dangers of this mixture at once became apparent; even for the British soldiers the temptations of the West Indies were great, for it was not difficult to desert, thus exchanging a life of discipline and hard duty for one of lounging, rum-swilling, and the enjoyment of the local sirens. It was, of course, true that the combination would kill them quite quickly, but not much more quickly than they would have died anyway, and it says much for the discipline and care of the regimental officers that relatively few chose the shorter (but perhaps gayer) life. The Germans of Hompesch's were a different case; they deserted in considerable numbers to Venezuela, where they were paid twenty dollars if they had their arms with them and although this is to some extent understandable (for they were mostly pressed for the service by German princelings in exchange for hard cash, and having thus neither background nor discipline succumbed easily to the blandishments of the French agents who swarmed on the island), yet it naturally infuriated Picton. It is not therefore surprising to find him noting on a strength return to Abercromby that the detachment was composed 'entirely of foreigners' and possessed 'little of his confidence'. Nothing is known of the negro detachment except that Picton, on the same return, notes tersely that they were 'chiefly picked up on the island', which gives a shrewd enough idea of his opinion of them.

CHAPTER 3

THE GOVERNOR

In spite of his somewhat meagre resources Picton at once set about
reducing Trinidad to order, a task for which he seems to have been
well suited. He was then thirty-nine, a big, burly loud-voiced man of
commanding presence. Although a gentleman by birth he appears to
have been either deficient in, or perhaps disdainful of, the social graces
of his day, said exactly what he thought (usually with a free flow of
oaths) and was apparently supremely confident that he could deal with
the problem facing him.

It is interesting to note that his approach to the problem varied
little, except in degree, from the way in which he dealt with the
incipient mutiny in the 75th Regiment so many years before. He soon
decided, very sensibly, that his first task was to reduce his own force
to some sort of order and this he proceeded to do effectively if
somewhat drastically; the 57th gave little trouble but the Germans
were deserting in considerable numbers, taking their arms with them,
and their officers (with one or two honourable exceptions) appeared
either disinclined or unable to prevent them. Picton therefore offered
a reward for each one apprehended *or killed* and he subsequently
refers to numbers being 'brought' without going into much detail as to
their state at the time. He had fourteen of the more serious offenders
court-martialled on the island and executed out of hand in the
presence of their comrades, and at the same time arranged for the
foreigners to do duty at a place where he was able to give them some
personal supervision. This firmness (which, as he was vested with
supreme military and civil authority, was perfectly legal) soon began
to have its desired effect, and as soon as this was apparent Picton
found it preferable, in spite of his own wide powers, to despatch
subsequent offenders to be dealt with by the commander-in-chief.

The new governor's efficiency and firmness were very soon
apparent to all and gave much encouragement to the law-abiding
element in the island who, seeing that he meant business, offered him

every support; he was also much helped in his dealings with the islanders by his fluency in French and Spanish. As a result of this local co-operation he was soon able to raise an armed body of local militia which, from its local knowledge, was well equipped to police the interior of the island, thus leaving the regular force disposable for its external defence.

By the end of his first year of office Trinidad was a much improved place. Roads had been built and piracy and banditry largely eliminated, with the result that the island had a greatly increased commerce with the mainland and thus flourished accordingly. This prosperity was confined to a great extent to the traders and planters, so that the great bulk of the population, receiving no benefit, saw no reason to change their way of life; they simply remained relatively cowed by force and waited for an opportunity to resume their old and lawless habits.

This seemed likely to come fairly soon, for the first rainy season had such a disastrous effect on the health of Picton's European troops that their efficiency was gravely impaired, and as soon as this was apparent the disaffected portion of the population decided to rise. The size of this portion is not known, but having regard to the French consul's earlier offer of three thousand men it was probably considerable.

Picton was not to be caught napping, for during his brief tour as governor he had managed to establish a highly effective intelligence system—so good indeed that an exasperated spy for the other side was once driven to complain that there was not an event or a decision on the island which Picton did not know about in forty-eight hours.

The rising was thus abortive, and at the proper time the governor pounced on the conspirators and swept the ringleaders into his net. Thereafter justice was summary and swift; the chief plotter was hanged and his aides sentenced to long periods of imprisonment, which effectively discouraged the rank and file of the disaffected from any further armed action against authority.

It may be that the governor's methods of restoring law and order were harsh, but he was a rough-and-ready ruler who had no illusions regarding the nature of the people with whom he had to deal. His conduct moreover must also be examined in the light of legal conditions in England of the same period, for these were, by modern standards, extremely drastic. Criminals, some of them mere children, were hanged for numerous offences, many of which would now be regarded as minor ones, and those who escaped with their lives were often condemned to long periods in jail, or to transportation, or to severe flogging, any of which could prove just as fatal as the gallows.

Picton was also somewhat handicapped, in theory at any rate, by his complete ignorance of Spanish law, by which this island was governed, particularly as the few administrators who could have advised him were so corrupt as to be completely unreliable. In practice, however, it seems unlikely that the determined governor fussed himself too much with legal niceties. In a very real sense he *was* the law and he seems to have been ready (perhaps indeed too ready for his future security) to disregard precedent and rely on common sense backed by force.

Once his domain was more or less peaceable the energetic governor was able to turn his mind to the wider aspects of his position. Like most sensible Britons of the day he realised that England's power to resist Napoleon depended on her wealth, which in its turn depended on her trade, and that because her trade with Europe was seriously affected by the war her merchants were seeking new markets elsewhere. He therefore saw at once the opportunities offered by the Spanish colonies on the American mainland; shrewd old Abercromby had already had ideas on these lines and it is fairly obvious that he had discussed them with Picton as a matter of long-term policy. The latter now felt able to take some positive steps towards this goal; the island was quiet, the home government apparently approved his conduct, and as a result of numerous representations he now had a small but effective naval force. On 25 May 1798 therefore, judging that the time was ripe for action, he wrote a long letter on the subject to the commander-in-chief. In it he first referred to the capacity of the splendid harbour of Trinidad to command the commerce of the whole vast mainland, then went on to describe the oppressive system of government in operation there. Next came the real object of his letter, a plan to seize some central point on the coast of the mainland with three thousand troops, a sixty-gun ship, a frigate and the necessary transports. This, he emphasised, would not be a conquest but simply a preliminary to

a declaration that the intentions of his Majesty are to give the inhabitants of South America an opportunity of asserting their claim to an independent government and Free Trade.

He then explained that the expedition could be launched cheaply (an important consideration for any British government) since he proposed to arm the inhabitants as they rose in support of him and let them gain their own freedom.

37

Finally he made an interesting reference to a certain native of Caracas, an individual by the name of Miranda 'who might be useful on this occasion, not that he possesses a great local knowledge or has any considerable connections . . . but as a native of the country, who has made himself a good deal talked of, he might fix the attentions of the people and thereby make himself serviceable. For reasons very obvious, I would advise his not being consulted on the business, or acquainted with it, until the moment of execution. . . .'

The whole concept was an interesting one, and well in accord with the spirit of the age. Spain was a hostile, crumbling power; so why not wrest her colonies away from her, so combining nobility of purpose with the prospects of commercial expansion?

For various reasons nothing came of this project and the Spanish colonies remained uneasily under the yoke of Spain until they finally freed themselves under the leadership of Simon Bolivar some thirty years later. Picton however continued to make preparations to put his plan into effect and these activities (which could not of course be concealed) so alarmed the governors of the places on the Spanish mainland most threatened, Caracas and Guayana, that they went to the rather remarkable length of offering a reward of twenty thousand dollars for his head.

Picton was apparently more amused (and slightly flattered) than anything else by this offer and on 25 January 1799 he wrote to both the governors concerned in more or less identical terms; his letter to Caracas read as follows:

Dear Sir,
Your excellency has highly flattered my vanity by the very handsome value which you have been pleased to fix upon my head. Twenty thousand dollars is an offer which would not discredit your Royal master's munificence!
As the trifle has the good fortune to recommend itself to your excellency's attention, come and take it and it will be much at your service: in expectation of which I have the honour to be etc etc.

(signed) Thomas Picton

In view of the generous size of the reward it is perhaps odd that there is no record of any attempt on the part of the island's numerous desperados to enrich themselves considerably by a swift knife-thrust. Picton was hardly popular amongst them and $20,000 was a considerable offer. Possibly they doubted the good faith of the gentleman making it, possibly they simply did not care to take the risk. Picton would have been a formidable character to tackle; he was large and fearless and as we have seen (and shall see again) very ready to flourish a large sabre, to say nothing of the fact that he must also have kept a pair of pistols close to hand. In addition he was well guarded by the 57th Regiment and so, for one reason or another, came to no harm.

Towards the end of 1799 the more responsible inhabitants of Trinidad were thrown into consternation by a rumour that there was a possibility of peace, for a peace conference meant territorial adjustments and of these the one they feared was a possible restoration of their island to Spain. Their old relationship with their mother country had been characterised by a mixture of extortion, brutality and neglect on the part of their masters, and the people of Trinidad, particularly those who had welcomed and co-operated with the British, knew that they would get short enough shrift if these same old masters returned. Their every action was faithfully reported to the Spanish authorities by a host of spies and they would be certain to suffer savage reprisals, as had happened when Havana had been restored to Spain in 1793. Indeed, in so far as it was in their power, the Spaniards were already taking such reprisals as they could, and amongst many others the case of old Don Christoval Robles may be quoted as an example. He was an honest, upright man who had struggled for nearly fifty years for a decent government for Trinidad and he had co-operated wholeheartedly with Picton from the outset because he felt that here was a man who could offer what he sought. Such property as he owned on the South American mainland had already been forfeited, and if the Spaniards had returned it is certain that he would have been speedily executed; there were many others in the same unhappy situation.

As soon as this possibility was represented to Picton he at once wrote to Dundas, the Secretary for War, and also to Abercromby, to whom he sent a copy of his letter to Dundas. In his letter to the Secretary for War he pointed out that the restoration of the island to Spain would destroy for ever the faith of the oppressed Spanish colonists in the sincerity of the British, and, after detailing his apprehensions as to what might happen to the people of Trinidad, finished with an appeal that the island should not be regarded as a mere bargaining pawn. He said very much the same in his letter to Abercromby, adding however that no Spanish government could be trusted and that any assurances of good treatment to the inhabitants if the island were restored to Spain would be quite worthless.

As it turned out the island was not returned to Spain as part of the peace settlement of 1802, so perhaps his letters played their part. Apart from these apprehensions on the part of the inhabitants, the situation in Trinidad continued to be as peaceful as might have been expected in the circumstances and Picton obviously felt, as indeed he had every reason to feel, that his conduct was approved. At the end of 1799 his salary as governor was doubled and in 1801 he was formally confirmed in his appointment as civil and military governor of the island.

By this time life (apart from the natural apprehensions of many of the inhabitants regarding their future) had settled down to a relatively normal colonial existence. Picton, like his friends the planters, lived in some state, ate well, dressed well, drank a good deal of imported wine, and it is said, kept a mistress. The mulatto girls of the island were famed for their beauty and most of the planters seem to have kept one or more permanently installed on the premises, so that he can hardly be blamed for following a pleasant and long-established custom.

Picton's young woman, so we are assured, lorded it in the manner of her kind, had the fuel contract for the garrison, and wielded powers almost of life and death over those of the inhabitants who offended her. This may be true, although Picton later attracted so much scurrilous and patently untrue rumour that it is now difficult to separate truth from fiction.

His commission was accompanied by extensive instructions, the most significant in the light of later events being:

> . . . the same courts of jurisdiction which existed in the said Island previous to the surrender thereof to us, shall, for the present, be continued . . . and they shall proceed according to the laws by which the said Island was then governed; and that such judicial powers as, previous to the surrender of the said Island to us, were exercised by the Spanish Governor, shall be exercised by you our Governor in like manner as the same were exercised previous to the surrender of the said Island.

This was clear enough as far as it went, although as has already been seen the practical difficulties were well-nigh insurmountable.

One serious omission was any indication regarding the future policy of the government regarding the island. This was perhaps understandable since the period of a major war is hardly the time for considering the fate of small sugar islands; nevertheless even a broad general brief would undoubtedly have been a help. Picton, in the absence of guidance, settled for the status quo, the continuation of the island as a slave colony; and this led him into some difficulties. The whole system was an evil one by modern standards, but at the end of the eighteenth century—and indeed for a good deal longer—relatively few influential voices were raised against it.

One of the dreads of the planters, and indeed of all the free population of the West Indian islands, was the prospect of a slave rising. The negroes, many of them relatively fresh from Africa, lived a strange subterranean life in which ju-ju and magic and poison played a considerable part, and although the whole thing was outside the conception of the Europeans they nevertheless suspected enough of what went on to imbue them with a superstitious dread of the very slaves over whom they exercised complete and unfettered control. Well-behaved individuals might be treated with a sort of careless kindness, but any negro who stepped out of line was considered to merit, and invariably received, condign punishment.

The jail of Trinidad, complete with executioner and torturer, was primarily a house of correction for erring slaves, but this again, though horrifying to modern ears, was regarded as essential at the time.

There is no doubt that Picton supported the slave system, or that he rewrote the slave code in 1800. This code, which laid down the treatment and punishment of slaves, was of Spanish origin and it is a matter of regret that Picton, no doubt encouraged by the planters, saw fit to increase the severity of punishments which could be meted out with little or no reference to any higher authority.

The year also brought several other events important to Picton: first there was the death of old Sir Ralph Abercromby from wounds received during his successful assault on Aboukir on the Egyptian coast near Alexandria, an operation chiefly notable for proving that when well led in carefully planned operations, the British soldiers were well able to deal with those of France. Picton said little of this loss but he must have been deeply affected. The general had befriended him at a time when his future looked dark, had given him a position on his staff, used his influence to get him promoted and, finally, had made him governor of Trinidad; in later years he habitually referred to himself proudly as one of Abercromby's pupils.

Later, it was alleged that he had obtained his governorship by disguising his true nature from Sir Ralph or, alternatively, that the latter had 'pushed' Picton at the instigation of some powerful interest, presumably (and well in the eighteenth-century tradition) in anticipation of some suitable *quid pro quo*. Neither of these theories seem very probable, however, when examined dispassionately. Picton had been on Abercromby's personal staff, and had sailed on long sea voyages with him in the cramped conditions then prevailing, and it is impossible to believe that so shrewd a judge of men could have been deceived. The interest theory is equally unsound, for Picton seems to have been singularly lacking in that useful aid to professional advancement, and certainly the allegations never as much as hinted whose the interest might be; Abercromby was a decent old soldier and the last man to be involved in that sort of transaction. The most that one can say is that he knew and liked Picton's uncle, but although this may have predisposed him in Picton's favour it seems overwhelmingly likely that he made Picton governor of Trinidad because he believed him to be the best available man for the job.

A second event which occurred in that year was a complaint to the British government against Picton, alleging that he was exporting the produce of the colony in foreign vessels to the injury of British shipping interests and of course to his own profit.

Little else was heard of this complaint but it is not difficult to guess that other and similar charges were made; in the complicated state of affairs in the West Indies it is very probable that some individual or individuals in Trinidad who wished to injure the governor's reputation were in a position to make semi-official complaints to commercial or political interests in England. The complaint about shipping was quickly disposed of by Dundas, who expressed his complete satisfaction with Picton's explanation, and there (for the moment) the matter ended.

It is clear that by this time Picton had accumulated considerable business interests in Trinidad and had acquired plantations and slaves, and we have no real evidence as to how this happened. His salary of £1200 was generous and his various fees—a legitimate perquisite of any governor in these days—may have come, by his own admission, to twice that sum, so that he was hardly short of money. One must be careful not to confuse modern ideas of probity with those of the late eighteenth century. In those days men whose duty took them to virtual exile in remote, unhealthy places saw no reason not to make a profit if they could, and most place-holders were soon able to deal in a conveniently ill-defined zone of conduct in which fees and other trifles were regarded as legitimate. The great Clive of India who returned home enormously rich, later commented, perhaps not wholly cynically, that on looking back he was surprised at his own moderation. Even Wellington, most upright of men, returned from India with a modest fortune, a fact which gave him sufficient financial independence to enable him to state his own opinions without too much dependence on the feelings of his paymasters of the moment.

Some people scorned to take a penny while others were rapacious in the extreme; the great bulk simply took the middle course and few thought any the worse of them. The most that one can say therefore is that what now seems unedifying was then regarded as normal practice. Picton's later letters from the Peninsula make various references to considerable business interests in Trinidad, and he clearly saw no need to make any attempt at concealment of these.

The third, and from Picton's point of view almost certainly the most important, event was his promotion to Brigadier-General with effect from 21 October 1801. He was, after all, a soldier and an ambitious one and although for the moment he was required to perform the civil and vastly irritating (if not unprofitable) role of governor it is obvious that he longed, as he had always longed, for an active military command and some glory.

Early in 1801 there had been wide political changes in England. Ever since the Irish rebellion Pitt had been completing plans for the union of the British and Irish Parliaments and this he finally achieved on 1 January 1801. His next object was to revise and modify the law which forbade Catholics to sit in Parliament, but here he came against the uncompromising hostility of King George III and resigned after sixteen years in office. He was followed by most of the important members of his administration (including Dundas), so that Addington, who succeeded him, was compelled to assume his onerous duties supported by a mediocre second eleven, composed chiefly of undistinguished Tory noblemen. This government, which understandably lacked any confidence in its ability to wage war, accepted Napoleon's offer of peace as soon as it decently could and on 1 October 1801 a preliminary armistice was signed.

The peace was at first welcomed by the British people, although Napoleon had driven a hard bargain which soon gave the more thoughtful great reason to be dissatisfied. All in all Sheridan's celebrated description of it—something which 'every man ought to be glad of, but no man could be proud of'—was very apt and, after the first wave of relief, probably expressed very accurately the feelings of the country. From Picton's point of view the most immediately important aspect of the matter was that Trinidad remained in British hands, which in view of the previous fears of the inhabitants and his representations on their behalf must have afforded him, and them, much satisfaction.

One of the first results of the peace was that the government had time to think of other things than waging war, and amongst those other things decided that Trinidad would be a suitable place for white

43

immigrants. Although this was perhaps logical if the island were to become a great commercial base, it did not fit in well with the old system. Any sudden influx of relatively low-class Britons, many of a radical outlook, was bound to be a disruptive influence, and so it turned out. The governor's first reaction, as perhaps might have been expected, was to treat them very firmly indeed and threaten them with the gallows or jail if they stepped out of line, a line of conduct not calculated to endear him to the new arrivals. Perhaps fortunately, the newcomers wanted to establish a British democratic system and disenfranchise all the foreigners and coloured people, and as these views hardly pleased the disaffected inhabitants of the island Picton was able to take advantage of this to run the place on the principle of divide and rule. Nevertheless there was a good deal of scurrilous literature put about in the shape of pamphlets and broadsheets, couched in the outrageous terms usual at the time, one of the main culprits being a mysterious journalist who combined the eminently Scottish surname of MacCallum with the Christian names of Pierre Franc, and who, by his evasiveness regarding his origins, may well have been a Jacobin agent.

This decision of the home government, though mildly irritating, paled into insignificance as far as Picton was concerned compared with its decision to change the system of government of the West Indian islands. In the case of Trinidad, it was decided that it should be ruled by a commission of three officers, one civil, one naval, and one military, it being considered that 'advantages must arise which cannot be expected from the labours of any one individual . . .'. The attitude of the government is understandable; it had tolerated as a wartime necessity for many years a policy which it otherwise abhorred, namely the rule of British colonies by serving British officers who were little more than dictators (benevolent or otherwise) and now it was going to revert to a possibly more clumsy but certainly a rather more consitutional form of government. Although the fact was not specifically stated it is also clear enough by implication that they intended the civil commissioner to be the head of the administration with the two service officers as his advisers in their own particular spheres only.

The civil commissioner nominated was a Colonel Fullarton (not a serving officer) and the naval commissioner was to be Captain Sir Samuel Hood, KB; the third, and junior, commissioner was to be the erstwhile governor, Brigadier-General Thomas Picton.

Picton, very understandably, was upset by this, although the government was fully within its rights in the matter. It may perhaps have been tactless to offer him a junior position after he had held a senior one, but this is a thing which happens to soldiers often enough when wars are over; moreover it offered a post on full pay at a time when many soldiers were being placed on half-pay, so that all in all the government may have felt that it was acting generously in the circumstances.

There were however various pieces of vague but sinister evidence which suggested that Fullarton was being sent to the island for the specific purpose of investigating Picton's conduct there. According to Robinson, the Under-Secretary for the Colonies had been indiscreet enough to drop a hint of this to a Doctor Lynch who wished to practise in Trinidad. He advised him that the best person to whom he should have an introduction was Fullarton, on the grounds that '. . . Picton would be ordered to return to England before the expiration of six months, as Colonel Fullarton was instructed to investigate the conduct of Colonel [sic] Picton whilst in the island of Trinidad . . .'; and although Sullivan, the Under-Secretary in question, subsequently denied it, it seems highly unlikely that Dr Lynch would have invented it. It thus seems likely that Hobart was readier to give credence to complaints than his predecessor Dundas, and seized the opportunity of the appointment of the commissioners to have some of the old ones dragged up again.

Fullarton, the new commissioner, was of a type not uncommon in the eighteenth century. He was the son of a considerable (though not particularly wealthy) Scottish landowner and had aristocratic connections through his wife, a daughter of Lord Reay. In spite of his military rank he had never been a regular soldier, and it appears that his early military affairs were somewhat murky, due to a certain unreliability in financial matters. He had raised two regiments, one at least largely from amongst his father's tenants, and their affairs were in such a state that the Duke of York had protested vigorously against his appointment as commissioner until things had been sorted out. Fullarton however clearly had friends in high places (he had at one time been a Member of Parliament and doubtless his father-in-law also had strings to pull), so that the appointment went through. On the credit side it is but fair to say that in 1783 he had served in India and had at one time commanded an independent force south-east of Mysore, which according to Fortescue he handled with much skill and determination.

Fullarton landed in Trinidad in January 1803, accompanied by his wife, her sister, four place-hungry young men seeking well-paid government jobs, a considerable personal staff and five surveyors, plus a rabble of immigrants only vaguely connected with him. He was obviously rather a grand gentleman and came ashore ceremoniously clad in a semi-official uniform based on the Windsor dress of blue coat with red collar and cuffs. He was met by Picton, who by Fullarton's own account greeted him in a friendly manner. Almost immediately however Fullarton behaved in a manner which made it clear to the erstwhile governor that the main function of the new commissioner was to discredit him. He dashed round the island examining all sorts of witnesses who might have something to say against Picton; and within a few weeks after his arrival he proposed in council a motion that:

> There be produced certified statements of all the criminal proceedings which have taken place since the commencement of the late Government, together with a list, specifying every individual of whatever country, colour or condition, who has been imprisoned, banished, fettered, flogged, burned or otherwise punished; also specifying the dates of their respective commitments, trials, sentence, period of confinement, punishments; and of all those who have died in prison.

This astounding motion naturally left no doubt at all in Picton's mind, and as soon therefore as Sir Samuel Hood arrived in February 1803 he tendered his resignation. In these days however such things took time, due to the slowness of communications, so in the meanwhile he did what he could to work with his fellow-commissioners. Hood, a distinguished sailor who had been Nelson's second-in-command at the Nile, was no trouble. He and Picton liked each other at their first meeting and the sailor was thereafter one of Picton's loyal supporters in spite of Fullarton's attempts to persuade him to change his allegiance. Hood refused to do this, being perhaps influenced even further against Fullarton by the actions of his wife, a high-handed lady whom Hood detested.

For Picton life was rapidly becoming intolerable. Scene followed scene, there were insincere apologies swiftly withdrawn, so that he longed only for release. The culmination came when Fullarton in council read out no less than fifty-seven charges against Picton in his presence. Picton, never a very tolerant individual, at once boiled over and Fullarton himself claims that only the fact that he was wearing a sword, Picton being unarmed, saved him from immediate physical violence.

Soon afterwards Fullarton, claiming to be in actual fear of his life, fled to a schooner which he had previously hired and sailed for

Barbados, whence he despatched his charges to England by the hand of one of his young men.

Picton and Hood then met in council and declared that as Fullarton had deserted his post he could no longer be regarded as being a commissioner. This was their last decision in the affair because almost immediately Hood went off to be commander-in-chief of the Leeward Islands; he, like Picton, hated his civil post and was only too delighted that the renewal of the war with France had given him the chance to go to sea again.

Picton soon followed, for on 31 May he heard that his resignation had been accepted and 14 June he left Trinidad for the last time. Before doing so he received a deputation from the inhabitants, who presented him with a handsome sword as a token of their esteem for him during his period as governor.

He had been given the choice of either returning to England or going to Barbados, and, knowing that an expedition was about to sail from the latter place to recapture St Lucia and Tobago from the French he at once proceeded there and offered his services to the commander-in-chief, who accepted them gladly.

A few days after Picton's departure Fullarton returned to Trinidad and attempted to govern it, a task which he clearly found difficult. Like many persons of liberal views, when suddenly faced with the realities of ruling a fundamentally unruly people he overreacted and reimposed many severe measures which he had not long before persuaded his council to abolish. His stay was however a short one, for almost exactly six months after his initial arrival on the scene he sailed for England. It is perhaps a measure of his character that he took with him the balance of cash in the Treasury, said to have been about $100,000, leaving the administration penniless. He had been behaving oddly for some time. His hectoring, threatening manner towards people whom he believed hostile, his precipitate flight, his strange actions during the brief period of his return, all rather indicate some lack of mental balance.

In spite of the unfortunate circumstances Picton was glad enough to be rid of the vexations of civil government and get back to a more active military role. As it happened however his hopes of glory again came to nothing, for although there was indeed a short fight at St Lucia the reserve, which he commanded, took no part in it, and Tobago surrendered without a shot being fired. Ironically enough, Picton was at once appointed as commandant of the latter place, but although he was doubtless gratified by his new commander, General Grinfield's trust in him he by no means relished the prospect of pacifying yet another unruly island. His stay there however was destined to be short, for a few weeks later he heard that Colonel Fullarton had sailed from Trinidad for England bearing a long list of charges against him, while simultaneously a batch of private letters from friends in England arrived with the news that the home press was full of stories of his cruelties and excesses while governor of Trinidad. All advised him to return home to defend himself, so in the circumstances he at once resigned his command of Tobago and sailed for England.

It was as well that he did so, for when he arrived in October 1803 he found that the situation was even worse than he had expected; Fullarton and his friends had been busy; crude coloured prints depicting his alleged cruelties were being hawked in the streets and the press was full of horrible stories. His arrival was greeted with storms of execration and wide demands made for a government enquiry—all of which must have been bitter fruit indeed to a soldier whose only ambition was military distinction.

CHAPTER 4

THE CALDERON AFFAIR

In 1803 England was under the threat of a French invasion and Picton, in the midst of all his worries, found time to prepare a paper on the subject of the defence of the country which he sent to the Prime Minister. The matter is unimportant in itself but throws some light on Picton's character, for here was a soldier who had spent much of his thirty years' service either on half-pay or in a semi-civil capacity, who had hardly heard a shot fired, and who had returned to England with the most appalling accusations hanging over his head, calmly offering unsolicited military advice to the head of the government. It showed great patriotism; it showed deep and careful military thought, for the plan, envisaging a kind of large-scale guerrilla warfare, was a sound one; it showed considerable self-confidence; but above all it showed a quite remarkable, if very characteristic, lack of tact.

At some early stage in the proceedings Picton had an interview with Hobart regarding the accusations against him, and although nothing is known of this meeting it is certain that it was unsatisfactory from Picton's point of view. The enormous public outcry fomented by Fullarton compelled the government to take some positive action against the alleged villain of the piece and in December 1803 Picton was arrested by order of the Privy Council, which at once ordered a detailed investigation into his conduct in Trinidad. Bail was fixed at £20,000, a huge sum which indicated the Council's estimate of the gravity of the affair. It was put up by a close friend of Picton's, one Joseph Marryat, a Member of Parliament for Sandwich, Trinidad Government Agent in London, and father of the famous novelist.

Almost simultaneously an indictment was brought against him by Colonel Fullarton; the principal charge (amongst the numerous ones which Fullarton had brought home) was that Picton, while governor, had permitted the application of torture to a girl, Luise Calderon, in order to extract a confession from her regarding a robbery; and it was alleged among other things that the girl had been treated so severely that she 'fell down as one dead' and was denied medical treatment. Other alleged crimes, for which charges were also brought, included seven for illegal execution, and seven more for poisoning. There was also some suggestion that further charges, involving the hanging of German mercenaries, might be forthcoming later.

The grand jury of Middlesex found a true bill regarding the torture of the girl and as a result of this indictment a writ of mandamus was issued calling upon the new governor of Trinidad to set up a court in Port-of-Spain to examine witnesses and take such statements from them as he might consider necessary. The new governor (it will be noted that the system of rule by commissioners had quickly been abandoned), was Brigadier-General Hislop, a bibulous and wholly undistinguished individual who wanted nothing but a quiet life; he showed no great enthusiasm for the task but naturally had no option but to comply. In view of the very long delay imposed by the length of the journey from England to Trinidad a considerable period of time necessarily had to be allowed for these proceedings, and in the peculiar manner of the time Fullarton and his friends continued to inflame public opinion by a series of pamphlets and a book.

In these Colonel Fullarton, after alluding in the most handsome way to Picton's obvious qualifications for the post of governor—his sagacity, address, activity and countenance, and his acquaintance with French and Spanish—then went on to suggest that at first his naturally cruel and violent disposition was held in check by Sir Ralph Abercromby but that as soon as he had been left in an independent situation Picton had commenced a series of the most appalling and systematic atrocities against the unfortunate inhabitants of the island. Having thus however aroused the curiosity of the reader he continued by saying that he was precluded at present from detailing them—presumably a belated form of lip-service to the fact that the case was *subjudice*.

He further asserted that the late governor 'had expelled almost every Spanish and English lawyer from the settlement', stating in a letter to a private correspondent that 'lawyers were like carrion-crows which flocked round carcasses and corruption . . .'. This splendid statement (which it will be noted was made to a *private* correspondent), had an unmistakably Picton flavour, but in view of other evidence it also has a considerable basis of truth, for Abercromby's instructions to John Nichol, Picton's chief judge on the island when he first went there, contains the following indictment of the same gentry. The old general wrote:

... and as I have received serious complaints of the extortions practiced by the exactions of excessive fees, and the mal-applications of useless and unnecessary proceedings by the escrivanos, attorneys etc you are hereby required to shorten and simplify the proceedings . . . conformably to the instructions you shall receive from Lt Col Picton . . . and I also give you full power and authority to suspend from their employments all escrivanos, attorneys, or other officers, who shall be guilty of extortions, contumacy, or contravention of your decrees. . . .

Fullarton and his friends also described the various oppressive acts by which Picton had enforced a reign of terror under which he had not only prevented people from complaining but had actually compelled them by artifice to offer addresses to his vigilance and vigour. They did not however suggest the means by which this remarkable piece of cajolery had been achieved.

Without any doubt the shrewdest and most telling paragraph of all was one which compared Picton with an officer in contemporary fiction as affording

the strongest illustration of the character, so admirably portrayed in Dr Moores 'Zelucco' of an officer who could always restrain his temper in perfect forbearance and submission on the parade under the reprehension of a commanding officer of such vociferating tendencies as General Grinfield; but could never put the reins on his impetuous nature when in command, or unconstrained by the presence of a superior; and still less could curb his violence when a poor soldier or helpless victim was at the mercy of his resentment.

This novel, by the father of General Sir John Moore, was published in 1785, and in its preface the author refers to 'the unpleasant task of tracing the windings of vice and delineating the disgusting features of villainy'.

In the meanwhile, Hislop had assembled his mandamus court in Port-of-Spain, the proceedings had begun and the following principal facts gradually emerged. On 7 December 1801 one Pedro Ruiz, a Trinidad trader, complained that two thousand dollars had been stolen from a locked strong-box in his house, and suspicion immediately fell upon a young mulatto girl, Luise Calderon, who had been with him as mistress-cum-housekeeper for two or three years. She was however apparently an ardent young woman, for during the absence of her protector on business she had been in the habit of admitting to his house (and her favours) a young coloured man by the name of Carlos Gonzales.

These visits had not gone unobserved, even in the easy-going atmosphere of Trinidad where rum was two shillings a gallon, women of all kinds and colour were readily available, every tavern was a brothel, and sexual licence almost completely uncurbed. Very soon a number of its more respectable citizens, not improbably the scandalised wives of Ruiz's neighbours, came forward to state that the young man had actually been in the house on the day of the robbery. The case was at once investigated by the local magistrate, who interrogated both the accused; both denied any knowledge of the crime, so the magistrate, who was understandably by no means satisfied with the truth of the statements, then applied to the governor in accordance with Spanish law for permission to apply 'a slight torture' to the girl Calderon in order to encourage her to talk. When this application, which was in writing, was submitted to Picton he enquired of his advisers whether the request was legal and having been assured that it was he gave permission for 'the question to be applied'.

The magistrate, armed with this authority, then interviewed the girl again and explained to her the consequences of her refusal to admit her complicity in the crime. She however again denied any knowledge of the affair and the 'question' was therefore duly put.

The torture resorted to was 'picketing', in which the victim was suspended by a cord from the wrists over a pulley, the whole weight of the body being taken on one bare foot which rested on an upright wooden peg or picket with a flat top about one inch square. Picketing had been an accepted form of punishment in the British cavalry until almost the end of the eighteenth century but had eventually been abandoned, not primarily for humanitarian reasons but because it was liable to cause lasting physical damage to its victim, often in the form of rupture, and soldiers were hard to find. Under Spanish law it might be inflicted for a maximum period of one hour, and only on a person over the age of fourteen years.

Luise Calderon remained picketed for only a few minutes, after which she admitted, sensibly (and, one hopes, truthfully), that Gonzales was the thief. Gonzales for his part, while admitting that he was the girl's lover, still denied the theft but was found upon trial (after the Spanish fashion) to be guilty and was sentenced to a fine, a period of forced labour, and banishment. Calderon, who had been imprisoned for some time while awaiting trial, was judged to have been sufficiently punished and was therefore freed. Further evidence elicited the facts that the girl's feet were not injured or even swollen by the picketing, that she did not cry out, and that far from appearing dead as had been alleged she was able to walk unaided nearly a mile to Ruiz's house where she demonstrated how the crime had been committed, smoking a cigar the while.

The two vital questions upon which the whole thing hinged were clearly the age of the girl Calderon at the time of her torture and whether Spanish law was in force at the time, and not surprisingly a good deal of conflicting evidence emerged.

The matter of the girl's age reduced the whole matter, serious though it was, to the verge of farce. It had been made clear to her friends that she was required to be under the age of fourteen at the relevant time and they responded nobly if not always truthfully. Being simple souls for the most part, they calculated that the younger they could make her the more serious the offence must be, and statements were actually made that she had been as young as seven at the time. This meant by simple arithmetic that she had been the mistress of Ruiz at the age of four-and-a-half, an improbability that at once brought furious denials from her scandalised ex-protector.

The question of the law was also hotly if inconclusively debated and the court finally closed, after which the various testimonies were despatched to England. The whole thing had taken a good deal of time and it was not until 24 January 1806 that the case came up for hearing in the Court of King's Bench before Lord Ellenborough and a special jury.

It was clear from the start that the prospects of an impartial trial were faint, for public opinion had been so stirred up that the jury was probably more than half convinced before the trial ever started that it was assembled to see justice done on a bloodthirsty tyrant whose guilt was not in doubt.

The cold legal atmosphere of the King's Bench also played its part. Much of the evidence given in Port-of-Spain had sounded like childish attempts to discredit Picton, but when elicited by a lawyer in wig and gown it assumed a new and menacing significance. Picton's 'carrion-crows' were flocking in anticipation of a satisfying kill.

In order to keep feelings against Picton as aroused as possible Fullarton, who had brought Calderon home with him, had paraded her round his family and wide circle of friends as the blessed innocent who was the victim of Colonel Picton's tyranny. Robinson, in referring to this, adds a caustic footnote speculating upon the effect that the young woman must have made on the uncompromising decorum of the ladies of Scotland, and indeed she must have made a considerable impact—a promiscuous young coloured woman, brilliantly dressed, with a taste for rum and cigars and the self-confessed accomplice in a theft by one of her lovers from another. Perhaps in the heat engendered by the case it was possible for her less desirable characteristics to be masked by her martyrdom, even in the eyes of these formidable ladies. Even at the trial itself the effects continued, for although it was the height of winter the young woman was produced dressed from head to foot in demure white muslin.

Mr Garrow, who conducted the prosecution, seems to have been determined to obtain a conviction by any means—one of which had been to produce coloured pictures of a girl being tortured, for the edification of the jury, and then asking them not to let such things influence their minds. The real shock however came later when the prosecution produced a surprise witness. This was a protégé of Fullarton's, a Spanish lawyer from Trinidad named Vargas. He was another dubious character who admitted under cross-examination that he had been in England illegally in 1799, when he had acted as a go-between for Miranda and Napoleon. He gave evidence to the effect that Spanish law did not permit torture and produced what appears to be the only relevant Spanish legal manual available, three massive tomes with which he did not appear to be very familiar. Nevertheless he stuck to his story, and as the defence was given no opportunity to see a translation or obtain expert evidence of their own it was impossible to refute it.

Vargas' evidence was conclusive; the case was proved to the jury's satisfaction and Picton was found guilty. No sentence was passed, and in view of the fact that the offence was a capital one that was perhaps just as well.

Fullarton and his supporters professed themselves well satisfied at the verdict and Picton and his friends were correspondingly downcast. In the midst of this period of deep depression however he was greatly encouraged by a most generous offer from the inhabitants of Trinidad, who had raised the sum of £4000 to help defray the costs of his trial. He felt himself unable to accept this money but being also very reluctant to hurt the feelings of the contributors he was for some time in great doubt what to do with it. At about that time however Port-of-Spain, the principal town of the island, was devastated by a disastrous fire. Picton at once returned the money with a request that it might be used to relieve the victims of the disaster, a generous and tactful way out of his dilemma.

On 20 April 1806 application was made before Lord Ellenborough and three judges for a new trial: this application was based chiefly on the fact, which could now be amply proved, that Spanish law *was* in force in Trinidad at the relevant time and that the Governor had acted in strict accordance with it; and upon this submission a new trial was granted.

Before it could be heard however, the Privy Council, which had by then completed its investigations, issued a statement which cleared both Picton and Hood; this must have been gratifying to both officers, although it did not in any way diminish the barrage of unpleasant pamphlets from Fullarton's party, which reached its climax when Hood stood as prospective Member of Parliament for Westminster, in the form of a scurrilous poem castigating the unfortunate Whig members of the Privy Council.

Then, as often happens, public opinion changed. This probably occurred partly because Fullarton and his friends had overplayed their hand, but there is no doubt that feelings were also influenced by the appearance of a book written in defence of Picton by Lieutenant-Colonel E. A. Draper of the 3rd Guards, who had been on the staff in Trinidad at the crucial time. It was couched in dramatic language and wildly extravagant in tone—Fullarton was said to have 'uncloaked the stiletto and endeavoured to plunge it into the heart of one of our bravest and most meritorious officers', and so it went on for page after furious page. Sullivan and the Under-Secretary for the Colonies was also castigated and both he and Fullarton promptly sued Draper for libel.

A few months before the second trial Picton was presented at Court. Fullarton took this as a personal affront but by then he was powerless. His money was almost gone and his pamphleteering cronies, seeing that there was little more to be gained from the case, soon deserted him for more fruitful fields. His libel case against Draper did not go particularly well; a great deal of unwelcome dirt was dragged up concerning earlier allegations of his misuse of government money and horses while in command of the 23rd Dragoons and although nothing was proved it is difficult not to believe that there was at least some substance in the allegations. Fullarton was by this time behaving very oddly and at one stage there was a distinct possibility that he himself would be committed for contempt of court on the grounds that he had been tampering with witnesses. Then, early in 1808, he contracted pneumonia and died, and such were the circumstances that Miranda, the failed revolutionary who had kept in touch with him, strongly suspected suicide.

Just before the second trial was due to open the Duke of Queensberry, the notorious 'Old Q', approached Picton through a mutual friend, and having conveyed his conviction of his entire innocence offered, in the most generous and tactful way, a very large sum of money to defray the costs of the trials. Picton, who had never met the Duke, was deeply touched by this surprising offer but as his old uncle the general, whose favourite nephew he had always been, had already made a similar offer he was able to refuse (although of course with the most grateful thanks) the offer of the eccentric old nobleman. The matter therefore ended with mutual esteem but without a meeting between the two. 'Old Q' indeed hardly ever stirred out, for he was then well over eighty and although his mind was still very active he was suffering physically from the cumulative effect of some seventy years of systematic vice and debauchery, his exploits in this direction having long been famous.

The second trial opened on 11 June 1808 and Picton appears to have faced it with equanimity, partly because with Fullarton's death the barrage of abuse had ceased and the trial was therefore able to take place in a dignified atmosphere very different from the hysterical and hate-ridden performance of 1806, and partly, and perhaps chiefly, because on 25 April of that year he had been gazetted Major-General, a sure sign of the old King's continued favour.

The trial proceeded without any great fireworks; conclusive evidence was produced that Spanish law *did* permit torture at the material time and a great number of witnesses also gave a quantity of slightly irrelevant evidence as to the general excellence of Picton's administration. The jury, having heard all the evidence, then produced a rather remarkable special verdict which stated: 'That by the law of Spain torture existed in the Island of Trinidad at the time of its cession to Great Britain and that no malice existed in the mind of the defendant against Luise Calderon, *independent of the illegality of the act.*' There the matter was allowed to rest and no judgment was ever given. According to Howells, however,

> it was thought by the bar that had the opinion of the Court been delivered it would have been against General Picton, but that upon a consideration of the merits it would have been followed by a punishment so slight, and so little commensurate with the magnitude of the questions embraced by the case as to have reflected but little credit to the prosecution.

The proceedings had dragged on almost interminably, for although the first trial had started on 4 May 1804 the final verdict was not given until June 1810. The proceedings had not of course been continuous; Lord Ellenborough, who presided, was a busy man and had frequently adjourned the case because of urgent legal business elsewhere.

It was not until 1812 that the Court finally ordered Picton's recognisances to be respited.

Anyone reading the case must be struck by the remarkable verbosity of the proceedings. It is the business of lawyers to talk but even allowing for the loquacity of the early nineteenth century they still said a great deal—and repeated it fairly frequently. The report of the cases in Howells' *State Trials* runs to something over a third of a million words, which does not include a further 7000 for the special verdict or some 35,000 for the argument on it.

Although Picton was greatly relieved to be finally quit of the law the inconclusive ending to the second trial did not please him. He had not been acquitted, and although the public clamour against him had died down he was clearly destined to be left in the public mind as the governor who had permitted torture, for this, as the final phrase in the verdict clearly shows, was the real crux of the matter. The British people in those days were by no means squeamish, and accepted public hangings, floggings and brandings as necessary punishments for quite minor offences; but there lay the difference—these were punishments legally awarded *after* a proper trial, and it was therefore no good to prove that the girl was guilty and the torture legal. As far as the bulk of the people of England were concerned Picton was held morally responsible for what had occurred, and nothing would change their views.

There is another fact too which affected the issue. Public conscience in England had been stirred for some years by the horrors of the slave trade, which thanks to the efforts of Wilberforce was abolished in March 1807 in so far as the export of slaves from Africa was forbidden. Total prohibition throughout the Empire did not in fact come until 1833 but the seed had been well sown. V. S. Naipaul comments in his book *The Loss of Eldorado* that Picton was tried for being the governor of a slave colony, and he is a writer whose views merit attention.

Once the trial was finally over the characters dispersed fairly rapidly. Luise Calderon asked for passports to Trinidad and thereafter disappeared, while several others settled in England. Miranda, who was not actively or directly concerned with the trial, continued his unlucky attempts to further rebellion on the South American mainland until 1812, when he was captured while leading yet another wild and hopeless insurrection in Venezuela. He was later removed to Spain and died in prison in Cadiz in 1816.

One of the people who suffered from the affair was Colonel Draper. His first libel case, brought by Sullivan, went against him in spite of a sworn statement by Doctor Lynch and as a result he was sentenced to a fine of £100 and three months in the Marshalsea prison.

The second case, brought by Fullarton, has already been referred to briefly. After Fullarton's death his widow pressed on grimly with it until Lord Ellenborough finally and sensibly suspended the proceedings indefinitely. Draper was an interesting character. He had served with some distinction with his regiment in Flanders, Holland, the Mediterranean and Egypt, and a large number of senior officers, mostly of his own regiment but including the bold Sir Samuel Hood, gave unstinting testimony to his gallantry and general good character. Judging from his writings and actions in the Picton case it seems likely that Earl Grosvenor was closest to the mark when he described Draper as being 'of great rectitude, very eager, zealous and extreme in his personal zeal on all occasions in the cause of his friends'.

It is now unlikely that the whole truth will ever be known; the local support for Picton—the testimonials, the subscriptions, the swords— although generally referred to as coming from 'the inhabitants of Trinidad' came in fact from a relatively small number of the more influential members of the community who, it can be argued, may have had particular reasons for wishing to stay on the right side of the governor. Nothing was ever heard from the lower classes from whose ranks his victims, if victims there were, were alleged to have come; but would anyone have believed their evidence if any had been forthcoming? The general evidence as to their roguery and depravity is so great that almost any testimony from them would immediately be suspect.

It is a commonplace that absolute power tends to corrupt and that dictatorship (or virtual dictatorship), springing as it often does from violence, may frequently bring into the light the darker side of human nature; and in this respect, if no other, Fullarton's parallel with Zelucco may be a shrewd thrust—the more so in that it was later to some slight extent substantiated by a chance remark of Wellington who, having told Stanhope that he asked for Picton in the Peninsula chiefly on the strong recommendation of Miranda, went on to say that the latter had however warned him not to trust Picton 'for he has so much vanity that if you sent him to the West India islands he would attempt to become Prince of them'. This is poor evidence and it is only fair to say that the Duke added that he personally never saw anything in Picton's character to confirm the truth of what Miranda had said; nevertheless, Miranda's opinion is of some interest in the conditions of almost absolute power under which he had known Picton, although as the latter never again held a comparable position it is impossible either to prove or disprove it. On balance, however, it seems that the worst one can say of Picton is that he was a rough, hard man who used forceful methods to impose a very considerable degree of order on a lawless, turbulent and largely disaffected community.

CHAPTER 5

WALCHEREN

As soon as the trials were over, Picton, free at last from the years of anxiety and the tedious processes of the law, again began to consider the possibilities of military employment. He cannot at first have assessed his chances very highly, for he was fifty years of age and although a major-general he had seen virtually no active service nor, except for a very short period, had he ever commanded anything larger than a peacetime company.

Fortunately the commander-in-chief, the Duke of York had a discerning eye for honest service, however obscure the quarter in which it had been performed, so that presently Picton, to his great delight, was offered active employment in a situation suitable to his age and seniority.

He must have had some apprehensions regarding active re-employment, for, apart from some very brief periods in the West Indies, he had not served with troops since his far-off days with the 75th Regiment over a quarter of a century previously. He was a well-read officer, and one possessed of considerable self-confidence in his own ability; nevertheless, it is probable that he had some secret reservations regarding his ability to succeed in an army which had changed beyond all recognition in the period he had been absent from it.

In spite of its ultimate failure the British army had had little reason to be ashamed of its performance in the American War of Independence. It had done a great deal to modify its tactical doctrines to the needs of the theatre and its individual regiments had fought well; the chief causes of ultimate lack of success had been poor leadership, both military and political, and the final intervention of the French on the side of the rebellious colonists.

After the American War the army had again fallen into disrepute; recruiting was bad and this shortage of new blood had reduced its once fine regiments to mere cadres, while neglect combined with shortage of money and supplies of all kinds had caused even the framework to decay, with the result that when it was called upon to operate in Flanders in 1793 the whole system collapsed in confusion.

After this however things gradually improved, for both government and people began to see that the war against the French was one of survival, and as country after country in Europe was overwhelmed by the swarming, yelling, ragged French infantry it began to take on the aspect of a crusade. It was eventually realised that this was no mere dynastic war of the old type from which Great Britain, secure behind her fleet, could withdraw at will. Admiral Collingwood wrote: 'The question is not merely who shall be conqueror . . . but whether we shall any longer be a people . . . whether Britain is to be enrolled in the list of nations or disappear . . .' ; and once the country realised this hard truth it set out to see the thing through.

Fortunately trade flourished; there was ample raw material, the navy guarded the sea routes and the economy began to expand, so that both money and equipment could be made available. Recruiting improved in both quantity and quality, and the few scientific, forward-looking soldiers who had survived the long period of shameful neglect were at last able to put some of their theories into practice and start to train the army on modern lines; of these Moore was perhaps the greatest, but there were many others too, and together they gradually wrought great improvements in the British army. Generals began at last to realise that the leisurely days of short marches, set battles against a courteous enemy, and frequent dignified retirements to refit were over. War had become a matter of hard marching and hard fighting against a fierce, active and numerous enemy, quite untrammelled by any outmoded eighteenth-century teachings, and with this realisation began the stripping and stream-lining of the British army into a formidable instrument of war. The infantry gradually divested itself of gaiters, powder and pigtails, and by 1809 was wearing a comparatively simple and practical service dress of felt shako, short red jacket and grey trousers with ankle-boots. Its ranks had been reduced from three to two so as to afford every man in them free use of his musket (still the flintlock) and the fire of a battalion had already reached a height of deadliness never before seen on a battlefield.

The new light infantry were properly trained and knew their business, but as they were not in themselves strong enough to contend with the swarming French skirmishers whole battalions were being retrained in the light infantry role. Regiments of riflemen had also been raised and armed with the new Baker rifle. Inconspicuously clad and superlatively well trained and led, they could skirmish, hold a line of outposts, or attack a breach grenadier-fashion with the greatest confidence.

The lessons of the American War had been largely infantry ones and the training of the cavalry had perhaps lagged behind; nevertheless that arm was composed of good-quality men, superbly mounted and drilled, who when their turn came would give a good account of themselves. The artillery, always a corps with high professional standards, had also been improved, notably by the introduction of light horse artillery designed to act with cavalry to supply the fire-power which the latter lacked.

Behind all this there were engineers, medical services, a commissariat and a system of ordnance supply, and behind these again—less immediately obvious but having important long-term implications—were improvements in pay, conditions, recruiting, the gradual introduction of proper training for officers (particularly staff officers) and a host of other innovations.

None of these great changes blossomed overnight, and while they were in progress the British army had also seen a good deal of fighting which although often unsuccessful had been a valuable, if expensive, means of testing new techniques. The first serious operations were those undertaken by the Duke of York in Flanders, which revealed endless weaknesses and ended in disaster. The army fought well enough—or rather its old soldiers did, for the reinforcements sent to it were of appalling quality—and the cavalry in particular had some splendid days, but the system as a whole was rotten and quickly failed under the strain of operations. Leadership was poor and staff-work almost non-existent; the replenishment of food, clothing, and ammunition all failed and the medical services collapsed almost at once. Wellington, who commanded a battalion in the campaign, remarked later that it at least taught him the way not to do things, and that simple sentence probably sums up the value of the early, fumbling, operations against the French. Later on however it will be seen that the Duke of York retrieved his failure in the field by showing remarkable ability as commander-in-chief at the Horse Guards, in which capacity he contributed not a little to the later successes of the British army.

In 1797–8 a serious rebellion was put down in Ireland, and in 1799 General Stuart captured Minorca, while in 1800 an expedition made a further descent on the European mainland in Holland but was compelled to withdraw after some fierce fighting had proved both the courage and rawness of the British troops and the inherent weakness of their allies. In the next year another expedition made a well-planned and executed attack on the French in Egypt; almost inevitably it was led by Abercromby, and brief reference has been made in an earlier chapter to Picton's grief at the death of his old commander at the moment of triumph.

There was a short break during the Peace of Amiens, after which the bulk of the army was necessarily held in England to repel an expected French invasion. The strength and successes of the Royal Navy, however, rendered this a hazardous project and in 1805 Nelson's decisive victory at Trafalgar finally caused Napoleon to abandon the idea in favour of further adventures on the mainland of Europe.

This removal of the danger of invasion made some British soldiers available for operations elsewhere in the world; early in 1806 a force seized the Cape of Good Hope and later that year a slightly unofficial expedition landed in South America to raise the colonists there against their Spanish masters. Unfortunately, Admiral Sir Home Popham caused so much indignation by his arbitrary seizure of goods and treasure that the colonists finally rose against their 'liberators' and eventually forced a considerable number of them to surrender. This ignominious failure of a project so dear to Picton must have been a great disappointment to him, although he was not directly involved.

Meanwhile in the Mediterranean, General Sir John Stuart had landed a small force in Italy and had decisively beaten a somewhat stronger French force. The British troops engaged were of good quality and although the battle achieved little else it did demonstrate very clearly the new efficiency of the British infantry, particularly in the shattering effects of their musketry, which far exceeded anything the French had ever previously encountered.

In the summer of 1807 the British government, believing, as indeed they had every grounds for doing, that Napoleon was preparing to seize the Danish fleet, forestalled him by swift descent on Copenhagen. The Danes resisted gallantly but hopelessly and the town had to be shelled into surrender before their fleet could be safely removed.

It was a somewhat arbitary operation, and there were squeals of piracy from the French and elsewhere, but England was in no position to be too particular for she was waging war single-handed against the full might of Napoleon. Various continental nations had indeed in the past entered into alliances with her, partly through patriotism and partly through the temptation of large subsidies, but these had all been wooed, cowed or hammered into submission by the French.

Napoleon, being unable to cross the Channel and end the war in one short savage campaign, then attempted to strangle England's commerce—whence came her wealth and her ability to resist him—by closing all the ports in Europe against her, and this led indirectly to England's first large-scale intervention on the mainland of Europe.

England's oldest ally, Portugal, had for long resisted French attempts to close her ports and in 1807 Napoleon, tired of temporising, sent an army through Spain (with the full agreement of the Government of that country) and seized Lisbon; fortunately the Portuguese Regent, after much very understandable hesitation, was persuaded to sail for Brazil with his fleet, the seizure of which had been one of Napoleon's objects, just before the French arrived.

Napoleon, although he had gained control of Lisbon and hence virtually of Portugal without a shot being fired against him, was still not satisfied, and soon decided that Europe would be a better place (presumably for the French) if he had control of Spain as well.

A quarrel between the Spanish King and his son gave him his chance, for both sides, ironically enough, asked for his help and Napoleon, thus positively invited to intervene, did so decisively by seizing the whole country, removing both the King and his son, and placing his brother Joseph upon the Spanish throne. All this happened with such speed and efficiency that for the moment it looked as though the whole coup had succeeded without bloodshed and Napoleon, extremely pleased by his quick success, at once began to prepare plans for seizing Gibraltar and thus closing the Mediterranean to the British navy.

He was however quickly disillusioned; the bulk of the Spanish people had but little regard for their weak and corrupt government, controlled as it was by Godoy (whose Royal service had started in the King's Guards and finished in the Queen's bed), but they were a proud people and if they despised their old ruler their hatred for the new regime knew no bounds. Within weeks, almost within days, violent but quite unconnected revolts broke out all over the country. The French, once over the surprise, were not slow to react and in the towns at least their guns were soon able (although not before fierce resistance had been offered) to pound the inhabitants into some sort of sullen obedience. Their army however was not strong enough to exercise any effective control over the more remote provinces and here the revolts flourished. The Spanish army, which had been reduced to near-impotence by a long regime of neglect and corrupt government, was nevertheless still able to act as a nucleus for the great swarms of excited patriots who clamoured only for arms before being led against the French.

The collapse of the central government had led to the setting up all over the country of small independent juntas or governing bodies and a number of these at once turned to England for assistance; England, although still technically at war with Spain, quickly saw a splendid opportunity to harry the French and at once began to pour money, arms and equipment into the country. She also began to assemble an expeditionary force so as to be able to take an even more active part in the affairs of the Peninsula.

As it happened there were, for once, both troops and transports ready to hand, for a force of some 8000 men was actually assembled at Cork in preparation for some wild and ill-defined operation against South America under the command of that promising young general, Sir Arthur Wellesley.

The little army under Wellesley had some heartening successes but then the government, apprehensive of leaving too much to such a junior general (even though he was their protégé) superseded him just after the victory of Vimiero by a kindly nonentity of vast seniority, who after twenty-four hours was replaced in his turn by an even more senior example of the same species. The follow-up operations therefore languished and the French were permitted to evacuate their troops under the generous Convention of Cintra. Wellesley, fully convinced that nothing could be expected from the timid old gentleman over him, signed this in the honest belief that it was the best course. The government and the British public however were horrified and the senior officers concerned were recalled, with the result that the only officer to have had a satisfying run of success against the French found himself in disgrace.

Sir John Moore took over command and tried a desperate gambler's advance into Spain in the belief that the Spaniards were fighting furiously. He was soon driven back by superior forces under Napoleon himself and found himself obliged to run for Coruña in the north-west corner of Spain where the fleet and transport were waiting. Napoleon, having more urgent business elsewhere, handed over to Soult, who continued the pursuit. Moore however turned outside the town and fought a successful action which ensured a safe evacuation. He himself was killed in the battle but his army, mauled indeed but intact, sailed away to fight another day.

The British government, in spite of these disasters, decided to persevere in the Peninsula and in April 1809 Sir Arthur Wellesley, who was presumably considered to have done his penance for Cintra, returned to Lisbon (which the French had never attempted to re-occupy) with another army and orders to defend Portugal. He had assured the government of his ability to do this and his carefully considered plan, allied to his known military capacity, had induced the government to give him command again. A very considerable part of his plan for this task was to hold Portugal, which necessarily involved the complete reorganisation of the Portuguese army and this he entrusted to Major-General Beresford and a strong cadre of British officers. Thereafter Wellesley wasted no time; having collected some supplies and transport locally he struck northwards towards Oporto (which was occupied by a force under Soult), forced the crossing of the river Douro, and drove the French from the town and from Portugal.

In the meanwhile fresh operations were being planned nearer home; Moore's regiments from Coruña had been brought up to strength, re-equipped and redisciplined, and the government, having this force available, felt constrained to strike a blow somewhere in north-west Europe so as to create a diversion in favour of Austria who, having again declared war against Napoleon, needed all possible help.

A considerable force and fleet were therefore assembled under the overall command of Lord Chatham; this choice of commander was a strange and remarkable one, for Chatham, although an excellent administrator, had seen almost no service; as however the appointment was made on strictly political grounds the disability was apparently accepted without comment.

The operation was to be directed against the mouth of the Scheldt. Chatham's instructions were to seize Walcheren, then press on up the river, capturing, sinking or burning all the ships he could find, and then, finally, to destroy the great arsenals of Flushing, Antwerp and Terneuse. After achieving this, or as much as was possible, he was to bring the expedition back to England, leaving however a strong garrison in Walcheren, which it was intended should remain in British hands as a permanent threat to the French.

Picton was offered command of a brigade in this expedition, which he accepted gladly enough. It is clear that he would have preferred the Peninsula, which looked as though it was likely to prove the main theatre for some time, but commands there were not easy to get.

The long series of campaigns, all of which Picton had missed, had thrown up a considerable number of competent and experienced officers and these naturally had first claim. Chief of them was Wellesley, eleven years his junior, and if he had achieved most of his appointments by enormous patronage it was equally true that he had held them by even greater ability; there were lesser lights too, dashing young men well on their way to fame and the coveted red riband of the Bath, and it must have been clear to Picton that he could hardly be expected to join this select band without at least some preliminary trial.

Embarkation of troops, horses and stores was completed early in July and after some delays the expedition sailed. Just before it did so news arrived that the Austrians had been badly beaten and had asked for an armistice; it was however confidently hoped that the British intervention on the continent would encourage them to continue the fight and the expedition therefore proceeded as planned. The French, who seem to have had early warning of the project, were at first much alarmed but took advantage of the delays to reinforce their garrisons in the threatened areas.

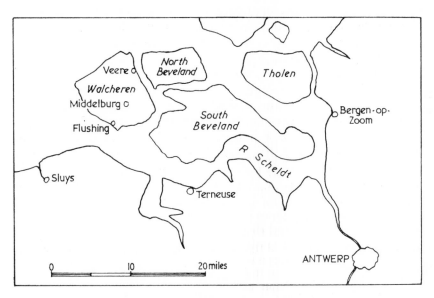

Walcheren

The operation was necessarily a combined one; it was planned that the navy would land troops to seize such forts and batteries as commanded the West Scheldt, so as to open a way for the ships to sail still further up the river and land the bulk of the army as close to Antwerp as possible.

The initial attack on Walcheren began on 30 July 1809, and that evening Picton landed with his brigade of General Mackenzie's division. His first task was to send, although in fact he took, one of his battalions, the 1st/36th, to Veere in order to support a surprise attack on that town by Colonel Pack; this attack was launched by night but failed to take the place, so the next morning Mackenzie came up with the rest of Picton's brigade and invested Veere, which surrendered a few hours afterwards without standing an assault.

The brigade then moved forward to take part in the assault on Flushing. This town was besieged in a very amateur way which demonstrated the almost complete lack of experience of both British commanders and their engineers in this type of operation. Fortunately, however, no assault was eventually necessary, for after fifteen days of steady pounding from land and sea with shell, roundshot and rocket the town surrendered.

Picton and his brigade were left on the island of Walcheren as part of the garrison and for them the campaign was practically over. They worked hard at restoring and improving the defence of the place in expectation of an eventual French attempt to retake it, but otherwise life settled into the dull routine of garrison duties. Fortunately there are available a number of letters written at this period by Picton to a close friend, a London solicitor named Lewis Flanagan, and in one of these he gives a lively account of life on the island. He wrote: 'I always sleep in boots and spurs upon a bundle of straw, to which I take more kindly than I had any idea of, considering the contrary habits of so many years', and at first sight it does indeed seem very hard that a major-general could not do better. Later in the same letter however he goes on to say: 'I am in a small Farm house. Myself, aide-de-camp and Brigade Major in one room. These gentleman have a bed each, I content myself with a bundle of straw', so that it is clear that this was a matter of choice. He was to make similar allusions in later letters, so that we are rather driven to conclude that it was to him a somewhat stylised way of indicating the general hardships of a campaign. It seems likely also that it represented a concrete indication that he was at last on active operations.

Apart from the sleeping arrangements however he does not seem to have fared badly:

I have a soup and good bouillé, an Irish stew and a curri, or something of that kind every day with Burgundy, Claret and Hock. We are three in a family and I generally have three and sometimes four officers of the Brigade at dinner; so you see in that respect I carry on the war tolerably well.

He was impressed by the richness and prosperity of the inhabitants and notes that 'Everything is beautiful except the human species' adding regretfully: 'The women are extremely plain. I have not yet seen a tolerable one since my arrival, and I can assure you that I have preserved my Chastity intact.'

There is little more to tell of the Walcheren expedition, except to say that almost everything went wrong. Chatham and his naval commander Admiral Strachan were soon not on speaking terms; the army, short of money, was compelled to requisition what it wanted and so turned the Dutch inhabitants firmly against the British; the French reinforced Antwerp and finally the health of the army deteriorated alarmingly. Walcheren, in spite of its prosperity and beauty, had always been a bad place for mosquitoes, and the partial flooding of the dykes by the French in order to hamper the British operations caused them to increase alarmingly, so that the troops sickened and died of malaria in great numbers. Rifleman Harris, who was present (and whose own health was permanently ruined there), later recollected that the victims could not eat or even—horrifying thought to a British soldier—drink their ration of spirits (which, incidentally, was half a pint of gin a day) but simply lay shivering uncontrollably and getting weaker and weaker. Thousands were ferried back to England where they were carried ashore, often to die, by rough but sympathetic militiamen. These appalling casualties through sickness soon made it obvious that the campaign would have to be abandoned and that even the plan for holding Walcheren permanently would have to be scrapped. Its defences were therefore demolished and the place evacuated, and by September 1809 the operations were finally and hopelessly over. Even in August Picton had been very pessimistic as to the outcome of the business; he had never really approved of the expedition and wrote bluntly to Flanagan:

The object (which was the capture of a few ships) was in every respect paultry [sic] and most unworthy of the national exertions made on the occasion. . . . It would have been more possible to have marched on Paris than to have seized Antwerp in the midst of all the Fortified places in Holland, Brabant, and Flanders . . . I rather think John Bull will not think he has had a good penny-worth for his penny. This island cannot be retained; it will be more than madness to attempt it.

These criticisms, coming from a soldier of Picton's seniority, cannot lightly be disregarded but nevertheless they seem to be a little severe. The operation was by no means badly conceived, and with a better commander and staff and more careful planning generally might have achieved a spectacular success, for it is certain that the French were extremely alarmed by even the faint chance of the loss of Antwerp. The real enemy was the malarial mosquito, which made service on Walcheren somewhat more dangerous than service in the West Indies, and the casualty figures tell a sad tale; according to Fortescue they were as follows:

		Officers	Other ranks
(a)	Embarked for service	1738	37,481
	Killed in action	7	99
	Died on service	40	2041
	Died since sent home	20	1859
(b)	Total returned home	1671	33,373
	Number of these currently sick (at 1 February 1810)	217	11,296

The campaign had therefore gone far to kill or incapacitate a considerable part of the British army; virtually everyone who served at Walcheren suffered recurrences of the fever, so much so indeed that later on, in Spain, Wellington was to request that no more 'Walcheren' battalions were to be sent out to him because of the alarming rate at which they sickened and died on active service.

Picton himself succumbed to the fever soon after the fall of Flushing and was evacuated home where he resorted first to Cheltenham and then to Bath in his efforts to throw it off; he never fully succeeded and it recurred at intervals for the rest of his life, as indeed it did to many of the other participants in the expedition. The causes of malaria were not then known; they were attributed to the mist rising from low, swampy ground, and the mosquitoes, which were in fact the real culprits, were regarded as a separate (though very irritating) discomfort. The use of quinine to effect a temporary cure was well known, but the seeds of the fever remained in the system and could not be eradicated. It was not until well into the twentieth century that any permanent cure became possible.

Picton went through a period of deep depression after Walcheren. The failure of the expedition, and perhaps in particular his failure to gain even a trifle of the military distinction which he so desired, left him very low, a condition much accentuated by the debilitating effects of malaria. His morale was adversely affected, and for some time he felt that his career was over. He was fifty-one, a sick soldier who at a time of great military activity had seen no action, and with the notoriety of the Calderon trials still in people's minds he could perhaps be forgiven for thinking that he was finished.

Then, at the end of 1809, in the depths of his despair and when all seemed lost, he was suddenly ordered to Spain to join the Army under Lord Wellington, the title under which Wellesley had been elevated to the peerage following his success at the battle of Talavera.

The circumstances under which this dramatic change of fortune occurred are by no means clear; it is obvious however from Wellington's frequent letters on the subject that he was chronically short of senior officers who measured up fully to his own uncompromisingly high standards of duty. Very many general officers were men of property, married men with considerable family and financial interests in England, and they took an eighteenth-century view of campaigning. Fighting was all very well in the summer months but they expected to spend much of their winters at home as a matter of right. They wished to shoot, to hunt, to manage their estates, to enjoy the company of their families, but understandable though this might be it was no good to Wellington; he wanted hard, dedicated professional soldiers who would subordinate their private interests to those of the war, and knowing of Picton's reputation, and presumably ambitions, he was probably only too glad to accept him when offered. His later assertion, that he asked for Picton on the recommendation of Miranda, has already been referred to in Chapter 4.

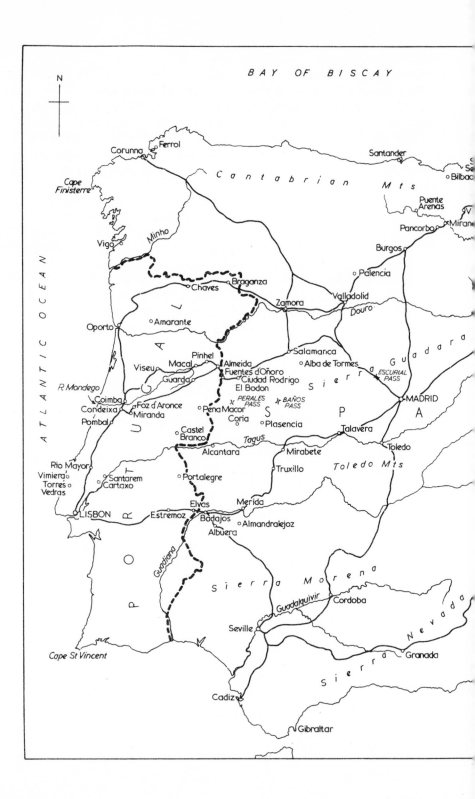

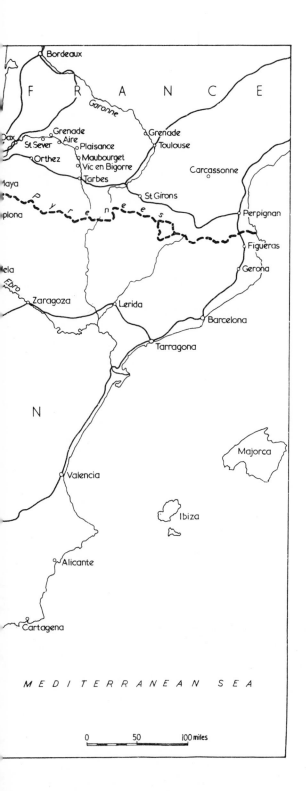

Spain and Portugal

CHAPTER 6

DIVISIONAL COMMANDER

In the Peninsula Wellesley, having driven Soult and his army from northern Portugal, then turned his attention to the army under Victor which was at Merida on the Tagus, and for the first time found it necessary to act in co-operation with the Spaniards. Initially all went well and the Spaniards, apparently setting themselves out to be helpful, made the most generous offers of supplies and transport for the use of the British army, although as it subsequently turned out they were quite unable to provide anything at all. Other things went wrong too—chiefly due to the obstinacy of the Spanish commander, the old General Cuesta, who by his initial refusal to fight, gave Victor the chance to withdraw. Cuesta then pursued him with great vigour until Victor, having received reinforcements, struck back at him suddenly and drove his army back in confusion upon the British. Wellesley, seeing no other alternative, took up a strong position at Talavera and, without much help from his shaken allies, defeated the French in a bloody and hard-fought battle. Thereafter however he was compelled to retreat; he had no food, was encumbered by large numbers of wounded, and had just discovered that another strong French army was moving down from the north to cut his communications with Portugal. He therefore withdrew his army to the Portuguese border where he put his troops into cantonments, whereupon the French, also desperately short of supplies, withdrew eastward to better foraging grounds.

The news from the rest of Europe was bad. Austria, in particular, had been badly beaten and had made peace, which meant that a considerable French army would become available for operations in the Peninsula. This obviously could not happen immediately: communications in Spain were bad and the French, unable to use the sea, were compelled to bring all their troops and stores over hundreds of miles of primitive roads infested with Spanish guerrillas. Their system of living off the land, moreover, although an excellent one in the fat farming countries of Western Europe, was difficult to operate in a poor and badly cultivated country like Spain, so that much time was wasted in assembling supplies of food and wagons to transport it.

Wellington therefore calculated, correctly as it turned out, that the French would be unable to launch a major offensive against Portugal before the spring of 1810 at the earliest and he made good use of the breathing space thus granted to him. His first care was to improve the discipline, training and administration, with particular attention to the organisation of a proper system of supplies, for he realised that, heavily outnumbered as he was, his only hope was to keep his army concentrated and beat the scattered French in detail. An efficient commissariat gradually took shape; all his stores and much of the food could be brought in quickly and cheaply by sea to his base at Lisbon, whence it was brought forward by a complex system of river-boat, country cart, and mule-train. He also relied very much on local purchase for a good deal of food, and particularly for bulky items like forage, and this system worked well as long as there was gold to pay for it; when the gold ran out however the supplies at once dried up, for the Spaniards and Portuguese were understandably reluctant to accept paper promises from an army which might still, they thought, be compelled to re-embark in the face of French superiority of force. Later on in the war the situation improved in this respect, but in 1810 everything was on a strictly cash basis. While all this was being organised the retraining of the Portuguese army proceeded rapidly under Beresford and as its units reached a satisfactory standard they were pushed forward to the frontier and incorporated into the British army. This however was not all, for at the same time Wellington, unbeknown to most of the army, was employing thousands of Portuguese labourers under British engineer supervision to convert the peninsula on which Lisbon stood into a vast fortress by means of a treble line of elaborate defensive works across it. His plan was to retire slowly before the French into these positions, which later became famous as the lines of Torres Vedras, laying waste the country behind him and there remain on the defensive until hunger compelled the French to retreat. The allied army, having its flanks and supply lines guarded by the Royal Navy, could afford to wait. This plan was a well-conceived one, bold and far-sighted, but its essence was secrecy and Wellington's chief worry was that his preliminary retreat might so depress the people of England as to force the British government to make peace with Napoleon. All this was however in the future, and in the meanwhile the British army on the Portuguese border waited for the gathering storm to break over it.

75

Wellington's apparent inaction also induced the French to extend their conquests and at the end of 1809 King Joseph and Soult, having defeated a Spanish army at Ocaña, then invaded Andalusia, thus further increasing the commitment of their already over-extended army. They overran the province with ease but failed to capture Cadiz, which was held by the Spanish army, later reinforced by some British troops.

Picton spent the last few weeks of 1809 in putting his various affairs in order and making preparations for the campaign. The Iberian Peninsula was then a wild enough place, sadly lacking in amenities and it was thus necessary to make full arrangements in England. This was particularly so for a general who was expected not only to live in considerable style himself, but also maintain a suitable ménage for his 'family' of aides-de-camp and staff officers, and for the entertainment of his fellow generals and the senior officers of his own division. All this involved considerable purchase of china crockery, cooking utensils and camp equipment of every kind; mules and pack-saddles there would be no difficulty about for they could be obtained locally relatively easily, but horses were better bought in England; in those days all commanders necessarily relied on horses for their mobility and, allowing for casualties, a general could hardly hope to start a campaign with less than six.

A very few days before he sailed Picton had his first and only meeting with the Duke of Queensberry; he was staying at his usual hotel in London at the time, when the Duke's card was brought in to him with a request that Picton might spare him a moment outside. The latter, mindful of the old man's generous offer of financial assistance during the Calderon trials, at once complied, and had a short conversation with 'Old Q', who was too infirm to leave his carriage. The Duke made but one request, with which Picton gladly offered to comply, namely that the general should write to him occasionally giving him some reliable news of operations in the Peninsula, an apparently harmless arrangement which was to cause Picton a good deal of trouble in the course of the next few months.

Early in 1810 Picton left London en route for Portsmouth; he was in a great hurry to sail, and drove on through the night in a hired post-chaise until the unfortunate postboy upset the vehicle into a deep, wet ditch, thus throwing the general, his servant and his baggage into a heap inside. They eventually extricated themselves through a window and then had a long wait of an hour and a half on a cold wet road until help arrived. All this hurry was of no avail as it turned out, for on arrival at Portsmouth the wind was foul and Picton was left fuming for several days before they finally sailed. In a letter written to Flanagan during his wait he displayed considerable pessimism over affairs in the Peninsula and having outlined the grave disadvantages went on to say that 'under these conditions it will be prudent to press for a timely evacuation, unless some great important object, sufficient to countervail the exposure [i.e., the risk of embarkation on an exposed coast] should be attainable, of which I have not the slightest conception.'

In February 1810 General Picton disembarked at Lisbon and at once made his way to Wellington's headquarters at Viseu. In spite of his haste he was able to observe the country through which he was passing very carefully and later described it as 'extensive tracts, of worse mountains that I ever saw in any part of Wales'. He was favourably impressed with the industry of the Portuguese peasants, of whom he noted: 'these people will get rich where Highlanders starve.'

He met his new commander at Viseu; no record exists of this interview, but it can safely be assumed that Wellington, having appointed him to command the 3rd Division, gave him a fairly detailed briefing as to the situation generally and his own personal likes and dislikes. It is unlikely that future plans were mentioned (for Wellington was not inclined to confide in his subordinates) but more than probable that he made it clear to Picton that he considered that the first duty of a divisional commander was to be obedient.

This interview over, Picton at once set off for Celorico to assume command of the 3rd Division. The divisional system, it should be said, was at that time a new one in the British army; the term division was of course a very old one but it had previously been used as a very general term to describe simply a part of the army. Previously the highest permanent formation had been the brigade, and it was not until 1809 that Wellington grouped his brigades into permanent numbered divisions in our modern sense of the term. The process was in fact by no means complete when Picton arrived, for as fresh reinforcements, both British and Portuguese, reached the army the number of divisions increased; new divisions were not however formed entirely from these new and untried units, but were made up by a careful mixture of fresh and seasoned troops.

Just before Picton arrived Craufurd's famous Light Brigade, which had previously formed part of the 3rd Division, had been withdrawn and built up into what was soon to become the even more famous Light Division, and its place had been taken by Lightburne's brigade from the 4th Division.

When Picton assumed command of the division it thus consisted of the following:

Colonel Mackinnon's Brigade of 1st/45th, 1st/74th and 1st/88th
Major-General Lightburne's Brigade of 2nd/5th, 2nd/58th and HQ and
   3 companies of the 5th/60th
Colonel Harvey's Brigade of 9th and 21st Portuguese Infantry

The Portuguese Brigade had only just been added and Picton was not particularly impressed. He indeed agreed in a letter home that 'they appear good, able men and perform their military movements with considerable precision', but goes on to say that 'they are so miserably officered that we can have little reliance in their co-operation. I have two thousand eight hundred attached to my Division and entres-nous I had much rather be without them.'

His military staff consisted of his Deputy Assistant Adjutant-General, Captain Hercules Pakenham of the 95th Regiment, his Deputy Assistant Quartermaster-General, Captain Thomas Anderton of the 7th Fusiliers, and Lieutenant John Tyler of the 45th Regiment as his ADC. He must have had other ADCs but he never mentioned them at this stage except for a remark in one early letter that 'my Aide-de-camp Sir O. Gordon has had several relapses of the Walcheren fever and is, in consequence, so reduced in health as to be under the necessity of returning to England for change of air'.

The new commander of the 3rd Division very soon made his presence felt, his first victims being the 88th Regiment, the Connaught Rangers. The 88th was a fine fighting regiment, undoubtedly one of the best in the army, and it was an admirably steady regiment on parade under the iron hand of its Scottish commanding officer, Lieutenant-Colonel Wallace, but its conduct off parade was appalling for then it drank, looted, robbed and burned with the same unrestrained enthusiasm that it showed in battle. The reasons for this are not difficult to understand; in the early nineteenth century, Ireland was truly 'a distressful country' whose people lived in dire poverty under what they considered, perhaps with a good deal of justice, to be the heavy and oppressive rule of a foreign race. Although understandably enough they had but little love for the British, the hopeless squalor and poverty of their lives drove them to enlist in large numbers into the British army, which offered them a standard of living far higher than anything they had previously experienced—bread, beef, rum, a roof and a bed, decent clothes and coppers in their pockets, all of which were luxuries to men brought up in smokey sod cabins on a diet of potatoes. Besides, there was always the hope of plunder on active service. When under proper discipline their natural wild courage and hardiness made them excellent soldiers; their outlook was however to great extent mercenary and, once free of restraint, their extreme lawlessness led them into every sort of villainy, often for no more than a few coppers or a bottle of wine. Fortunately for the military student of the period an officer of the 88th, Lieutenant William Grattan, later wrote a most interesting account of the day-to-day life of the regiment and gives us a full description of the division's first glimpse of Picton. After admitting that there was a strong dislike of the general in the army, due of course to the Calderon affair, he goes on to say:

Punctual to the appointed time General Picton reached the ground accompanied by his staff; every eye was turned towards him, and, as first impressions are generally very strong and lasting his demeanour and appearance were closely observed. He looked to be a man of between fifty and sixty, and I never saw a more perfect specimen of a splendid looking soldier. In vain did those who had set him down in their own minds as a cruel tyrant seek to find out such a delineation on his features. No such marks were distinguishable; on the contrary there was a manly open frankness in his appearance that gave a flat contradiction to the slander, and in truth Picton was *NOT* a tyrant, nor did he ever act as such during the many years that he commanded the 3rd Division. But if his countenance did not depict him as cruel there was a caustic severity about it, and a certain curl of the lip that marked him as one who rather despised than counted applause. The 'stern countenance, robust frame, caustic speech and austere demeanour' told in legible characters that he was not one likely to say a thing and not do as he said. In a word his appearance denoted him as a man of strong mind and strong frame.

Grattan next tells us that the division then performed several evolutions in a very superior manner which he noted 'seemed to surprise the General'. It is a little difficult to see how Grattan, a subaltern with his regiment, was able to see this surprise and it may be a trifle of embroidery, or, and perhaps more likely, the sort of rumour with which a division might congratulate itself. There may however be some truth in it, for Picton had had but few direct dealings with soldiers for many years, so that the remarkable improvements in the modern army, particularly the troops in Spain, may well have surprised him.

So far all had gone well in this first meeting between the general and his new division, but unfortunately in the middle of the parade two marauders of the 88th Regiment, who had stolen a goat while marching up from Lisbon with a draft, arrived in the charge of a detachment of Portuguese militia and Picton at once ordered a drum-head court martial in front of the whole division. This was assembled and the two men were tried, found guilty, and publicly flogged.

When this was over the new general addressed the assembled troops with some severity and in language which Grattan describes as 'not of that bearing which an officer of his rank should use'. This indeed is more than likely, for it is clear from many sources, from Wellington downwards, that Picton was much given to foul language. He castigated particularly the 88th Regiment, calling them 'the Connaught footpads' and making some offensive remarks on their country and religion, and with this outburst the parade ended. Picton's motives for this inauspicious first meeting with his new division are perhaps fairly clear from what has already been seen of his character; he could well have complimented the troops on their drill and appearance, pardoned the two looters, and ridden off parade conscious that he had thereby gone far towards dispelling the prejudices which he knew must exist against him. This however was not his way; he clearly intended to start as he meant to go on, and thus perhaps welcomed the chance of a little early severity. He knew that the discipline of the Army as a whole was still imperfect and it is very certain that Wellington had impressed upon him very strongly the necessity for checking sharply all offences against the people of the country, for the latter knew well enough, moral con-siderations apart, that without their active goodwill he might quickly be forced to evacuate the Peninsula completely.

This particular episode did not end there, for as soon as the parade was over Wallace of the 88th at once made an official complaint to his brigade commander, who as promptly passed it on to Picton. Nothing happened for some time but eventually Picton sent for Wallace and after a private interview, invited him to dine; and at dinner Picton, in the presence of a number of the senior officers of his division, acknow-ledged that he was satisfied that every attention had been paid to the conduct and appearance of the 88th and that he had been pleased with its conduct since he had assumed command of the 3rd Division. This officially ended the matter and Wallace expressed himself as well satisfied with Picton's conduct, which he described as 'very gentleman-like and handsome'. The episode however left a good deal of feeling in the 88th Regiment which lasted until the end of the war.

General Picton may have felt that the impression made by his conduct at his first meeting with the troops he was to command was satisfactory, for it is a curious fact that when the 94th Regiment joined his division from Cadiz towards the end of 1810 he also treated them to a sample of his invective as soon as they arrived, finishing with the words 'You are a disgrace to your moral country Scotland'. Donaldson, a ranker in the 94th who recorded the scene, then went on to say very much what Grattan had said, and affirmed that Picton was 'not the character which we, by prejudice, were led to think him. Convinced of the baneful effects of allowing his men to plunder, he set his face firmly against it, but in other respects he was indulgent; and although no man could blame with more severity when occasion required, he was no niggard of his praise when it was deserved.' This assessment of his character is particularly interesting because it comes from a soldier in the ranks, and one moreover by no means always inclined to lavish praise on officers.

By the spring of 1810 Napoleon had assembled some 300,000 men in Spain; a great many of these were of course engaged in occupation duties, anti-guerrilla operations and various subsidiary campaigns against the Spaniards, but three corps, numbering in all some 65,000 men, had been designated the Army of Portugal, placed under the command of Masséna, and given the task of driving the British out of the Peninsula.

Picton, like the bulk of the officers in the army, was extremely pessimistic over the outcome of the campaign; in a letter of 20 March to his friend Colonel Pleydel he went so far as to say: 'I am of the opinion that it will be something very nearly allied to madness to attempt seriously the Defence of this country'; and a few weeks later he told Flanagan: 'This country, in every political and civil consideration is, without contestation, one of the most miserable in the world, and the arrival of the French cannot fail to ameliorate the situation of the inhabitants in general.' It was an opinion that he was soon forced to change.

In this same letter to Flanagan he also referred for the first time to the eye trouble which was to worry him so much in the future, by saying (in apology for not having answered a letter sooner):

I was so ill of a fever, which terminated in a severe inflammation of the eyes, that I was totally incapable of reading it for nearly three weeks, and it is not without considerable difficulty that I now make use of my eyes to read and write, which I am directed to do very sparingly, for fear of bringing about a relapse in that delicate organ.

Much of the country along the Portuguese frontier is extremely rugged and in those days only offered two practicable routes for an army entering the country from Spain. The first of these was in the south along the road through Badajos but this route had the disadvantage, from the French point of view, of making it necessary to cross the Tagus in order to get at Lisbon; this relatively unlikely line of approach was guarded by General Hill with his 2nd Division and a considerable force of Portuguese.

The second, and much more likely route, was the northern one through Ciudad Rodrigo, Celorico and Coimbra, and it was to cover this route that Wellington concentrated the bulk of his army. A few other minor paths, little more than goat-tracks, were guarded by Portuguese militia.

The Army of Portugal advanced slowly. Like all French armies it lived off the country and the bleak Spanish plain offered but little in the way of either wagons or food, so that it had spent several weeks of intensive searching before it had been ready to move at all; nor were affairs improved by the obvious distaste of its commander for the task he had been set. André Masséna was a very fine soldier who on the outbreak of the Revolution had risen rapidly from the ranks of a cavalry regiment, but although still quite a young man (he was born in the same year as Picton) years of arduous campaigning—allied it must be said to a most dissipated way of life—had aged him far beyond his years.

Eventually however all was ready and the invasion started, the French, as Wellington had anticipated, taking the northern route. Their first obstacle was the Spanish fortress of Ciudad Rodrigo, to which they laid siege on 15 June 1810; it was a strong place but held only by Spaniards in whom Wellington placed little reliance; rather to his surprise however the garrison made a most gallant resistance, so much so indeed that it became almost an embarrassment to him, for as the days and weeks went by his own army began to murmur openly at the disgrace of leaving their unfortunate allies to fight it out alone. Wellington however remained unmoved, for he knew well enough that if he ventured down into the plain with his small army to relieve the fortress, he would be beaten, and perhaps destroyed.

He knew also that time was on his side; the French were advancing into country which the British were converting into a desert, and the longer they took to move the greater were their chances of starving. Besides this, every day gained by the allies helped to perfect the training of the Portuguese, improve the supply system, and further increase the great lines in front of Lisbon. Few people however knew what was in Wellington's mind, or even knew of the lines; as far as the army at large was concerned the campaign would consist of a retreat to Lisbon as a preliminary to an embarkation and the disgraceful betrayal of its Spanish and Portuguese allies. Too many people remembered Moore's campaign to be very optimistic about the current operations.

Picton seems to have been one of the relatively few officers who saw the sense of Wellington's inactivity during the French siege of Ciudad Rodrigo, for on 7 September he remarked shrewdly in a letter to Flanagan that 'If we attempt to relieve the place the French will drive us out of Portugal, while, if they get possession of it they will lose time which is more important to them than Ciudad Rodrigo; but they have got to find this out.' It is however also clear from Picton's correspondence at the time that he saw little chance of the British army being able to stay in the Peninsula, although as time went by he began to change his opinion. On 10 September for example he confided to Colonel Pleydel that in his opinion it was Wellington's plan to draw the French well into Portugal and fight them there, where 'a decisive defeat would be followed by the entire destruction of their Army; for the whole peasantry of the country are furnished with Arms and Ammunition and are inveterate in their hatred of them.'

This pernicious habit of writing speculative and often pessimistic letters home was a widespread one in the army and understandably made Wellington furious, for the cumulative effect of these missives on public opinion was considerable and he was still afraid that the government would be too weak to withstand the pressure on them to end the war at any cost. Picton, to give him his due, at least always expressed his complete faith in Wellington as possessing the 'talents, decision and personal qualities necessary for his situation'; and this in itself was a considerable thing, for a great many officers in the army thought Wellington unfit for his position and did not scruple to write home to that effect to their friends.

Ciudad Rodrigo finally surrendered on 10 July 1810 and Masséna at once pushed Ney's corps across the frontier towards the corresponding Portuguese fortress of Almeida; and now occurred the affair which was to bring Picton and Craufurd into open collision and create so much antagonism between them.

Craufurd, who was a master of outpost work, was at that time holding a line of advanced positions on the east side of the river Coa in the vicinity of Almeida. Wellington's object in placing him there had been to encourage the garrison of Almeida and also to keep out probing French cavalry patrols and all this had been achieved; it is however very certain that Wellington never had the slightest intention that Craufurd should engage in a pitched battle with the Coa, running in a deep chasm and spanned by a single bridge, behind him. All Wellington's letters of the period to Craufurd emphasise this point in various ways but in spite of everything the Light Division, some 4000 strong, was still holding its positions on 24 July when Ney, advancing with six times its numbers, at once attacked it. Craufurd then rather lost his head but his subordinate commanders, fine officers in command of fine men, succeeded against all expectations in holding off the French and making good their retreat over the one available bridge. Once over they took up strong positions and then it was the turn of the French to suffer, for Ney, furious that the Light Division had escaped him, at once attacked the bridge with successive heavy columns of infantry which were quickly and bloodily repulsed by musketry.

Two separate and equally fierce controversies raged after this battle; the first (which did not involve Picton) was concerned entirely with Craufurd's reasons for fighting in the first place; of this William Napier says in his history that 'Craufurd resolved to fight in defiance of reason and the reiterated orders of his General', while George Napier—in every respect a kinder man—simply comments that his divisional commander 'let his vanity get the better of his judgement'. Craufurd's biographer produces a mass of conflicting and inconclusive evidence on the subject while Craufurd himself, in the strange manner of the day, wrote a long letter to *The Times* about it. This letter, which was published in the issue for 21 November 1810, admits, for practical purposes, that Craufurd was surprised, at which point it may be as well to leave that particular controversy and turn to the second, which affected Picton very closely.

When Craufurd first took up his outpost line in March 1810 Picton wrote to Craufurd to ask for notice of his movements so that he could plan support. So far then his responsibility is clear, nor does there appear to be any evidence that he was ever relieved of it by Wellington, but it is a remarkable fact that in spite of this the 3rd Division never stirred during the battle. It was this surprising omission which caused all the later bad feeling between the two divisional commanders but, although much was subsequently said and written about the affair, Picton's motives for refusing assistance to the hard-pressed Craufurd are still by no means clear.

Napier says that 'during the fight General Picton came up from Pinhel. Craufurd desired the support of the 3rd Division; it was refused; and excited by some previous disputes the generals separated after a short altercation.' After censuring Picton for this he adds:

> Picton and Craufurd were not however formed by nature to act cordially together. The stern countenance, robust frame, saturnine complexion, caustic speech and austere demeanour of the first promised little sympathy with the short thick figure, dark flashing eyes, quick movements and fiery tempers of the second; nor did they often meet without a quarrel.

Although these facts are not seriously in dispute, it is very difficult to accept Napier's clear implication that the refusal was occasioned by nothing more than personal dislike.

Robinson, as might be expected, goes to considerable lengths to justify Picton's conduct, but the result is by no means convincing. His first line of argument is that Picton and Craufurd never in fact met on the day in question, and in support of this contention he quotes an officer 'holding a high and distinguished name in the service' who had the 'good fortune to hold an appointment on the staff of Sir Thomas Picton', as denying that Picton ever left his headquarters on that day. This officer can only have been Lieutenant-General the Honourable Sir Hercules Pakenham, who was Picton's DAAG at the time, and with every respect to this officer it is probable that, after a quarter of a century, his memory of that particular day was at fault. Napier certainly produces two excellent witnesses in the persons of Colonel William Campbell and Lieutenant-Colonel Shaw-Kennedy, and on the basis of their very clear evidence it seems absolutely certain that a meeting *did* in fact occur. Colonel Shaw-Kennedy also produces some incidental, but very interesting, details of a previous quarrel between the two generals.

Robinson's next argument is the possible existence of some secret instruction from Wellington to Picton cancelling the earlier order for the latter to support Craufurd, but this is really quite impossible to credit. It thus seems clear that the order stood, and that the meeting did take place, which if anything, makes Picton's conduct even more difficult to understand.

Robinson read the obvious meaning into Napier's account of the affair, that it was due to personal animosity, although Napier himself later denied in a letter to him that he had in fact meant to impute such a motive to Picton. It is of course very clear that there was bad blood between the two generals, but even so it can hardly be credited that Picton would have cold-bloodedly risked the destruction of the Light Division out of mere personal animosity to its commander. The next possibility is that there was no time for the 3rd Division to reach the Coa, but this is unlikely; it is not known when the meeting took place, but it is fairly obvious that if Picton had had any intention of supporting Craufurd he would have set his division in motion as soon as ever the firing from that direction made it obvious that a serious engagement was in progress. The third possibility is that Picton used his discretion, and after going forward to assess the situation for himself, decided against intervening. This is at first sight a slightly more attractive possibility; in those days of poor communications generals had often to modify, or actually disobey orders in the light of changed circumstances of which the original giver of the order could have no knowledge. This theory however fails for the same reason as the second one advanced, namely that the 3rd Division never moved a step forward.

On balance the most probable answer seems to be that Picton never had any intention of supporting Craufurd east of the Coa. Apart from any actual personal dislike, it also appears that Picton disapproved of the other general's known tendency to provoke engagements without authority—his remark to his DAAG that 'that damned fighting fellow Craufurd will some day get us into a scrape' makes that clear enough. It is also known from his letters of the period, that he had correctly divined Wellington's plans for drawing the French deep into Portugal before offering any serious resistance. Lastly, it is obvious that in spite of his inexperience he had considerable confidence in his own military judgement, as witness his letter of advice to the Prime Minister soon after his return from Trinidad; and taking all these things into account it does seem probable that he believed that it would be better to risk sacrificing the Light Division rather than make a forward movement which must have led to a general action and probably disastrous defeat.

Moral obligations apart, Picton would have been tactically correct, for anyone who has examined the ground, or even had recourse to a good map, will realise the appalling risks involved. The Light Division, it is true, extricated itself but it is unlikely that two unco-ordinated divisions would have succeeded in making good their retreat across a single narrow bridge.

Robinson notes that Craufurd never complained subsequently of Picton's lack of co-operation, but this is probably due to the fact that Craufurd, conscious of his own disobedience, was glad enough, at least as far as Wellington was concerned, to let the matter drop.

Wellington for his part, chronically short of senior officers as he was, may also have preferred to forget the whole affair rather than conduct an inquiry which at worst might have involved the dismissal of both the generals concerned and at best, as Fortescue shrewdly suggests, might have ended with a 'Craufurd party' and a 'Picton party' in an already disgruntled and clique-ridden army.

The British casualties in this useless affair were considerable, being 333 killed, wounded and missing. Amongst the wounded were William Napier (whose personal recollections of the battle were perhaps later to contribute to his condemnation of the generals concerned) and Harry Smith. The latter (who eventually also became a general) notes in his autobiography that after the battle the wounded were treated '*en prince*' by Picton, which indicates that any prejudice he may have had against the Light Brigade was not extended to the individual soldiers comprising it.

The French did not at once follow up the partial British withdrawal after the Coa battle although Masséna made a series of feints which to some extent succeeded in confusing Wellington, particularly since information from Spanish sources, on which the latter relied greatly, had dropped off considerably after what the Spaniards considered as his betrayal of Ciudad Rodrigo.

Eventually, on 15 August, the French laid siege to Almeida, which Wellington hoped might cause them considerable delay. The fortress, although small, was very strong and being built on rocky ground it was difficult for the besiegers to dig trenches by which to approach it. The siege therefore opened slowly and for ten or twelve days made little progress until a lucky French shell fired a train of powder which had leaked from a barrel being carried into the magazine, the resultant explosion of which wrecked most of the town and killed and wounded a large number of gunners.

Colonel Cox, the English governor, was a resolute man and did his best to deceive Masséna when that general sent in a summons to surrender immediately after the explosion, but his Portuguese officers, seeing no prospect of continuing any effective resistance, forced him to capitulate.

The French thus gained in thirteen days a fortress which might well have held them up for almost as many weeks, and Wellington, anticipating a general advance on the part of the French, made preparations for an immediate retreat. The French, however, still delayed, chiefly because of the great difficulty they had in finding supplies, and it was not until 15 September 1810 that they finally began the great advance intended to drive the British into the sea.

Picton, writing to Flanagan on 1 August, reports the army as being 'ready to continue our retreat towards the positions between the Tagus and Torres Vedras, where we calculate to make a successful stand for some time, so as to carry our reputation unimpaired on board the Transports . . .' and it is clear from this letter that the existence of the lines of Torres Vedras was just beginning to be rumoured about. It is however equally clear that the thought uppermost in the minds of the army was still an evacuation—an evacuation, it is true, rendered more honourable to national feeling in that it was to be preceded by a suitable period of defensive fighting behind elaborate works, but still the abandonment of allies. Only Wellington remained confident, for only he knew the full situation. Very sensibly, in all the circumstances, he kept his knowledge to himself.

CHAPTER 7

BUSSACO

By 17 September 1810 British cavalry patrols had ascertained that Masséna, misled by bad maps, was advancing along the appalling road through Viseu, north of the Mondego. Wellington, well content, then began his withdrawal along the more southerly road to Coimbra, pulling in his outlying detachments as he did so.

The French, although not in contact with the British except for very occasional patrol clashes, found plenty of obstacles in their way; their men, straggling as usual in search of food, fell easy victims to the merciless Portuguese guerrillas, and their artillery train, which had dropped behind because of the weakness of its underfed horses and the bad state of the roads, was very nearly captured by a detachment of Portuguese militia under the British Colonel Trant.

By 21 September Wellington had most of his army within a few miles of the great ridge of Bussaco which he thought offered 'a most excellent position' for one of his famous defensive battles. He was however apprehensive on two counts; the first was whether Hill, who was marching at all speed north-west to join him, would be in time, and the second was that the French would find the quite passable road which led round the northern end of the feature and thus turn his left flank. By 22 September it was however clear that the ever-dependable Hill *would* arrive in time and with this doubt resolved, Wellington sent Trant and his militia off to guard his northern flank and prepared to fight Masséna. On 24 September the French reached Mortagoa and Wellington drew back most of his army leaving Craufurd at the foot of the Bussaco feature. The next day Reynier's corps advanced, whereupon Craufurd, repeating his error of the Coa, at once offered battle; fortunately Wellington was at hand and succeeded in extricating the Light Division, which he then sent to the summit of the hill to take its place in the line which he was preparing for the battle which now seemed inevitable.

The position which he had chosen was a remarkably strong one on a long, healthy ridge which ran north and south some nine miles across the main line of advance of the French. Its summit was broken and rocky but wide enough to draw up a line of troops well back from the crest. The southern end of the feature was protected by the gorge of the Mondego river but the northern end could be turned fairly easily; apart from this, the main disadvantage of the position was that it was too long for the fifty thousand troops available, many of whom were raw Portuguese. Even this disadvantage was largely compensated for by the excellent observation then available. This has now changed, for the ridge is covered with pine forests, and although magnificent distant vistas can still be obtained it is impossible, even from the few remaining viewpoints, to see much more than the tops of trees with the red roofs of a few villages showing amongst them. In 1810, however, the rocky slopes were bare except for gorse and scrub so that a few well-placed observers on the crest could cover the whole area. As it was hardly possible for a column of tired, hungry, and heavily laden infantry to have made the ascent from the valley in much under two hours Wellington thus had ample time to shuttle reserves along the reverse slope to meet any threat.

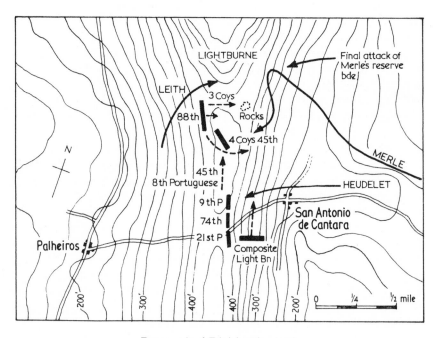

Bussaco (3rd Divisional sector)

The part of the position entrusted to Picton and his division was about the centre of the feature at a point where the track from San Antonio passed over it on its way to Palheiros. On his left was Spencer's 1st Division and on his right Leith's 5th Division, although the length of the feature made it inevitable that there should be long gaps between the 3rd Division and its neighbours. Further north near the convent was Craufurd's Light Division, the extreme left flank being guarded by the 4th Division under Cole; the southern end of the feature was held by Hill with the 2nd Division. The artillery, which in those days had an extreme range of about a thousand yards with roundshot, was necessarily dispersed by batteries and half-batteries to cover the whole front, while the cavalry, whose value on a rocky hilltop was of course very limited, were withdrawn behind the left centre of the position where they were well placed to parry the northern outflanking movement which Wellington feared.

The British expected to be attacked on 26 September but the French spent most of the day in reconnaissance and in closing up their straggling army; all their actions were overlooked by the British, for although Wellington in his usual way had posted his army well out of sight on the western, or reverse, slope of the feature, a great many individual officers were impelled by curiosity to make their way to the crest of the hill to see what was happening. There was plenty to look at—young Moyle Sherer, of the 34th Regiment in Hill's Division, related:

My Regiment had no sooner piled Arms than I walked to the verge of the mountain on which we lay, in the hope that I might discover something of the enemy. Little however was I prepared for the magnificent scene which burst on my astonished sight. Far as the eye could stretch the glittering steel, and clouds of dust raised by cavalry and artillery, proclaimed the march of a countless Army; while, immediately below me at the foot of the precipitous heights on which I stood their picquets were already posted; thousands of them were already halted in their bivouacs, and column too after column, arriving in quick succession, reposed on the ground allotted to them and swelled the black and enormous masses . . . This then was a French Army; here lay, before me, the men who had once, for nearly two years, kept the whole coast of England in alarm; who had conquered Italy, over-run Austria, shouted victory on the plains of Austerlitz and humbled in one day, the power, pride and the martial renown of Prussia on the field of Jena. Tomorrow, me thought, I may, for the first time, hear the din of battle, behold the work of slaughter, share the honours of a hard-fought field, or be numbered amongst the slain.

The French reconnaissances of the 26th do not seem to have been very thorough, for Masséna was far behind the leading elements of this army, the reason being (according to Marbot, one of his staff officers) the fatigue of his mistress whom he had rather unwisely brought with him to soften the rigours of the campaign. Ney carried out a reconnaissance on the morning of the 26th and gave it as his opinion that if he were in chief command he would attack at once; Reynier and Junot, the other corps commanders, both agreed with this, so that when Masséna finally came up he was faced with a unanimously optimistic appreciation of the situation. This he accepted, and after a perfunctory inspection of the position turned and rode back to Mortagoa.

Marbot tells us that on the way back he and some of the other members of the staff contrived under cover of darkness to get so close to their general that he was able to overhear, 'by accident', their views on the position which, it is needless to say, differed widely from those of their seniors. The same officer also claims that he and a brother staff officer were actually guided to the northern road that evening by a Portuguese, but that Masséna declined to believe them and persisted in his plans for a frontal attack at daylight on the 27th; in fairness to the French commander-in-chief however it must be admitted that the bold Marbot was not above tampering with fact in order to make his own role seem more important.

The British army, on its side, took things rather more seriously; on the evening of 26 September Wellington had detached Picton's left-hand brigade (Lightburne's) a good deal further north towards the 1st Division, and at the same time ordered up some Portuguese of the 5th Division to replace them. Picton however, very wisely, was not prepared to put the same faith in untried Portuguese that he would have done in Lightburne's British battalions and he therefore re-organised his remaining troops to meet these changed circumstances. By last light on 26 September the disposition of the remainder of his Division was as follows: the Palheiros road was covered by the 74th Regiment, the 9th and 21st Portuguese Regiments, and a composite light battalion. This latter was an *ad hoc* unit, formed in the manner of the time by adding the light companies of the brigade to the three companies of the 60th, the whole being under command of Lieutenant-Colonel Williams of the latter regiment. The 88th had been posted a mile or more to the left to cover a re-entrant which afforded a comparatively easy and covered approach to the summit, while the 45th Regiment, together with the two battalions of the 8th Portuguese, were in reserve.

By now it was quite dark and Picton, his new dispositions made, dismounted from his horse and having removed his cocked hat and replaced it with a coloured nightcap (for it was chilly on the hilltop) wrapped himself in his cloak and lay down among his soldiers to sleep for what remained of the night.

The battle which took place next day was a complicated one and certain aspects of it, particularly the timings of the various French attacks, are still by no means clear. This of course was true of any battle in those days; there was no convenient signal logs or war diaries for later reference; messages were scrawled without duplicates and rarely timed or dated; few officers had watches and fewer still the time or inclination to refer to them in the heat of battle, so that later reconstruction is difficult. Even commanders could not give a complete picture, for they could only be in one place at a time; for the rest they had to rely on the reports of their staff officers and subordinate commanders who again were only able to see what occurred on their own little piece of the front. Wellington himself described the situation admirably when he said that 'the history of a battle is not unlike the history of a ball. Some individuals may remember all the little events of which the great result is the battle won or lost; but no individual can recollect the order in which, or the exact moment which, they occurred, which makes all the difference to their value and importance.' The situation at Bussaco in this respect was further complicated by the great extent of the position, which made it inevitable that there should be wide gaps between divisions and even brigades. The jagged, undulating summit of the ridge made observation to a flank difficult at best, but once the firing had started the rolling clouds of smoke soon made it impossible to see anything, and the whole battle developed into a series of isolated actions fought by brigades or battalions, out of sight of their comrades and, often, of their commanders. In order to compose a coherent account of the battle it is therefore necessary to place these isolated incidents in chronological order, which can only be done by the careful examination of the main, and often conflicting, individual accounts. When all else fails, it becomes necessary to fall back on intelligent conjecture or, as the late Colonel Alfred Burne so happily called it, 'inherent military probability'.

It is particularly important to be able to establish the sequence of events at Bussaco as accurately as possible because there was subsequently a good deal of controversy over the part played by the 3rd Division. This controversy, the causes of which will become apparent later, did however have one good effect; it induced Picton to sit down not long after the battle and write his version of it for Wellington's benefit.

This account can almost certainly be taken to be broadly correct; it is clear from other sources that he certainly had no cause to be ashamed of the conduct of the 3rd Division, so that the worst that can be said of it is that he gave himself a good write-up, a not uncommon fault in commanders at any time. It must however be borne in mind that Picton suffered from exactly the same disability as every other commander, namely that he could only vouch for what happened under his own eye. In order to describe events which happened at the other end of his line, or while he was galloping from flank to flank through the smoke, he had perforce to rely on other witnesses. It is for this reason therefore that while the following account of the battle is based (like that of Fortescue), on Picton's own narrative it diverges from it whenever it appears from other sources that he was either mistaken or misinformed as to events.

Both sides were astir early on the morning of 27 September; the British, who had slept in their battle positions, had few preparations to make; they rose, rolled their blankets and cleaned and loaded their muskets carefully so that the first volley should be as effective as possible. There was no cooking, but the few prudent souls who had saved something from their rations were able to eat some biscuit and cold beef and refresh themselves with a mouthful of rum, after which they fell in and remained quiet. A few officers went forward to watch the French but the bulk of the army, being drawn back, could see nothing but the crestline to their front, lit by the first welcome rays of the sun which fortunately were just beginning to disperse the night's mist.

Masséna's plan was based on faulty information; he had no idea that Hill had joined Wellington, and the reports of his corps commanders (together with his very own imperfect examination of the British position on the previous day) had given him a false idea of both the size and the dispositions of the British forces. He believed them to be no more than twenty thousand strong (for, perhaps understandably, he dismissed the Portuguese as being of little account) and as a natural corollary to this gross underestimate he supposed the British line to be much shorter than it really was. His plan therefore, which was based on the belief that the ground held by Picton's division was the right of the British line, was a very simple one which might well have succeeded had the premises on which it was based been correct.

94

One corps was to assault and turn the supposed right of the British position while a second was to menace the supposed centre below the convent to prevent reinforcements being sent to the right. As soon as the corps on the right had begun to roll up the British line to the north, the second corps would strike in at the centre, and the battle would be over. Masséna had never fought the British but his extensive experience against most of the other armies of Europe had given him the perhaps justified belief that no line of battle could withstand the hammer-blows of a series of French columns so much superior (for he must have calculated that he had two or three times the numbers of the British) in strength to their adversaries.

The attack on the British right was entrusted to General Reynier, and by half-past five in the morning his divisions were on the move. Merle's division, consisting of eleven battalions, struck straight up the hill, parallel to and just north of the Palheiros track. It was led by the 36th line and preceded by swarms of skirmishers, and it seems certain that the regiments were formed into columns of double-companies which would have put them into solid rectangles of men with a frontage of fifty or sixty and a depth of between twenty-seven and thirty-six depending on the number of battalions in each regiment.

Although they started off in échelon from the right the whole presently veered northwards and so formed one huge, clumsy column; the hillside however was very steep—so steep according to Anderton of the 24th that the day before his old Colonel had been carried up in a blanket by four sergeants because no horse could climb it—and the French soon began to straggle. They were heavily laden and many of them were underfed so that the column, perhaps never very exactly formed, soon became little more than a swarm of men.

Reynier's second division, under Heudelet, also started up the hill along the line of the track (but a little later than Merle) while further north Ney's corps simultaneously began its ascent against the troops near the convent. The whole attack was purely an infantry one; for obvious reasons it was impracticable to employ cavalry and the height of the hill made it almost impossible for the French to make any effective use of their artillery. A few guns, presumably howitzers heavily over-charged, did succeed in landing a shell or two on the ridge but their effect on the British was negligible.

By this time the mist had cleared and the toiling French columns were in full view from the crest; Colonel Mackinnon, who had been up to visit Wallace, was thus soon able to see that Merle's division,

still veering somewhat to the north, would reach the summit somewhere in the area of the 88th. He at once galloped off and reported
this fact to Picton, who despatched four companies of his reserve
British battalion, the 45th, under Major Gwynne of that regiment,
to reinforce Wallace. There was of course time to do this, because of
the length of time it must have taken the French to make the ascent.

As it turned out, Merle's skirmishers reached the crest even further
north than the 88th, and were met and stopped by the heavy fire of
Lightburne's skirmishers and two guns. A few fell on both sides
(including it seems one or two of the 88th) but presently the French
drew back down the hill and changed direction, this time to their
left, in a second effort to reach the summit.

Further south Heudelet's division was still marching steadily
upwards towards the dip in the skyline over which ran the Palheiros
track; they were under the heavy and accurate fire of two batteries of
Portuguese six-pounders (which at first fired roundshot but later, as
the range lessened, changed to canister), and they suffered many
casualties; they pressed on resolutely however until presently they
met the 74th Regiment standing in line with a Portuguese battalion
aligned on each flank.

The old story of the column versus the line was then repeated; at a
hundred yards or less the line fired its first volley and upwards of
fifteen hundred musket balls smashed into the head of the column
and brought it to a halt. Before the smoke had cleared the British and
Portuguese had reloaded; the latter then wheeled slightly inwards so
as to bring a converging fire to bear on the column and a second
terrible volley followed the first. At the same time, Colonel Williams
led his battalion of light companies against the left flank of the French,
at which the column finally retreated, although reluctantly and to no
great distance, leaving piles of dead and wounded behind it.

At the beginning of the battle Picton had stationed himself at the
head of the Palheiros track, which he rightly considered to be his chief
responsibility, and was therefore able to see the whole of this action.
It is not difficult to imagine him sitting there impassively on his cob,
with only the steady tap-tap-tap of his stick on the animal's mane
(a habit he had in times of stress) to show that he was perhaps a little
apprehensive. If he was however he had some reason to be:
it was his first real battle; the great mass of the French columns
looked extremely formidable; and neither he nor any one else in the
allied army knew whether the Portuguese would fight or run. It was
however soon apparent that Heudelet's division was beaten, and once
he was certain of this Picton, having given hasty orders for the

remainder of the 45th Regiment and a battalion of the 8th Portuguese to follow him at their best speed, galloped north to where heavy firing told him that Wallace also was engaged with the enemy.

The 88th had been formed in line well back from the crest, with the original reinforcement of four companies of the 45th some distance to their right. Soon after Merle's skirmishers had disappeared, Wallace sent Captain Dunne of his grenadier company forward to a conspicuous cluster of rocks on the crest to report on the movements of the French, and that officer very soon hastened back to report that not only were the rocks in the possession of the French but that a column was passing below them with the obvious intention of attacking the 45th.

Wallace, a most capable officer, at once detached his grenadier company and his 1st and 5th battalion companies to deal with the French in the rocks, while he himself led the remainder of his battalion off to the assistance of the 45th, who had just opened fire on the French column as it appeared over the crest. In doing so, according to Grattan, the 88th suffered some casualties from the fire of a battalion of the 8th Portuguese which was firing from behind them at the French, although it should be said that no one else mentions this particular battalion as having been there.

The 88th formed on the right of the 45th and fired one volley. Then, led by Wallace and Gwynne, the whole force, which can hardly have numbered more than eight hundred bayonnets, hurled itself upon the French. The latter, exhausted and disorganised, broke almost at once and ran back down the hill to avoid the murderous bayonets, at which moment Wellington, who usually contrived to be present at the decisive point, arrived from the north with two guns, the fire of which completed their rout.

Picton arrived too late for this part of the battle, which had rolled away down the hill before he got there, but when he reached Wallace's original ground he found the French still firmly ensconced in the rocks with two companies of British infantry retiring before them. Later he said that they were the light companies of the 74th and 88th but this is rather difficult to credit, and it seems at least probable that they were in fact the remnants of the three companies of the 88th which Wallace had left behind to clear the feature. The 74th wore white facings, the 88th yellow, and allowing for fading and dirt it would not have been difficult for Picton, with his poor eyesight, to have mistaken their identity in the smoke and confusion. Whoever they were, they were rallied by Major Smith of the 45th who led them forward again in a frontal attack against the rocks while Picton, placing himself at the head of Birmingham's battalion of the 8th Portuguese which his DAQMG had just brought up, attacked the position from the flank. The fire was heavy and for a moment the new Portuguese hesitated before it; and it was then that Picton, snatching off his hat to wave them on, revealed to the delighted soldiery that he was still wearing his nightcap. This broke the tension, and with a roar that was half a laugh and half a cheer the attack plunged forward and quickly cleared the French from their position.

While all this was going on General Leith was riding northwards along the rough track behind the crest of the position, followed by his leading brigade. Wellington had empowered him to do this if there were no enemy to his front, and the arrival of a very agitated staff officer from the 2nd Division, who reported that the French had broken Picton's line, convinced him that he was urgently required. When his ADC reported to Picton, who had now returned to his original station near the Palheiros road, he was told however that all was well there, but that some assistance might be required further north in the long gap between the 88th and Lightburne's brigade. This gap had worried Picton ever since the battle started, and rightly so, for even then the reserve brigade of Merle's division was scrambling up the hillside towards it at a point where it was held only by the 45th Regiment (less its four companies with Wallace) and three very young Portuguese battalions. The latter were driven back in confusion and the 45th, although never for a moment broken, were compelled to withdraw before enormously superior numbers, leaving the French in possession of the crest. At this critical juncture Leith arrived on the scene and at once counter-attacked with the 9th Regiment, supported by the 38th. The French were in one huge and disorganised mass with General Foy urging his exhausted horse amongst them in an attempt to get them deployed; he was however too late, for the 9th fired one devastating volley and at once charged, upon which the whole confused mob turned and tumbled back down the hill, all order gone. Foy himself was wounded and this is perhaps not surprising when it is considered that he was the only mounted officer to reach the summit. His own horse was killed far down the slope but he borrowed one from his aide-de-camp (presumably leaving him to make the climb on foot). This was probably his undoing, for a single mounted officer would have offered a conspicuous mark to the British muskets.

Further north, near the convent, Ney had also started his attack against Craufurd under the mistaken impression that Merle had reached his objective, and he immediately met with fierce resistance.

The riflemen of the 95th and the Portuguese Cacadores caused heavy casualties amongst the officers at the head of the column, while two batteries poured roundshot into its flank and the shrapnel shells of Ross's Chestnut Troop, bursting over it with beautiful accuracy, showered down their content of musket balls on to the heads of the sorely harassed French infantry. The columns still came on however with remarkable determination until presently its head reached a false crest behind which Craufurd was waiting with the 43rd and 52nd Regiments of his division. Craufurd at once charged and the French, scourged by bayonets and bullets, fled; Ney's second division, which had attacked a little further south was then recalled, and the battle was over.

Masséna, having achieved nothing except the partial destruction of three of his divisions, then sent out cavalry patrols to the north, and these soon found the road to Sardao which Marbot claims to have discovered (and reported to Masséna) before the battle. Trant should have been at Sardao with his militia and Wellington had calculated, rather optimistically perhaps, that his presence there would prevent a French turning movement to the north and so compel Masséna to attack the Bussaco position again. A panicky Portuguese general had however diverted Trant elsewhere for some obscure reason, with the result that the French were able to pass round the northern end of the Bussaco feature unhindered, whereupon Wellington at once resumed his retreat through Coimbra to the lines of Torres Vedras. This was apparently a disappointment to the British general. It is often said that the British government was tottering and that Wellington, fearing the Whigs, felt it his duty to provide a 'safe' victory in order to bolster it, but this is probably not so. In his despatch of 3 November 1810 to the Earl of Liverpool he wrote: 'If the expedition into Portugal had been founded on military principle only it would have ended at Bussaco; and I do not hesitate to acknowledge that I expected that Masséna would retire from thence, or at all events would not advance beyond the Mondego', which indicates that he had had real hopes of stopping the French permanently at Bussaco. This, had he been successful, would have saved a good deal of Portugal from the consequences of the 'scorched earth' policy which he subsequently had to employ in order to deprive the French of supplies. Even so he must have been reasonably satisfied with the results of the battle; his British troops had behaved well, the Portuguese had been successfully 'blooded' and the French had lost almost a thousand dead and about three thousand wounded.

Not long after the battle Picton wrote a number of letters to friends in which he described the action as he had seen it; this naturally placed much emphasis on the part played by his division, Ney's attack on the Light Division being either not mentioned or dismissed lightly as 'a mere feint'. In view of his previous promise it is not surprising that one of these letters should have been to the Duke of Queensberry; that nobleman, delighted to have authentic news of the battle, at once regaled his many friends with its contents and one of these, thinking innocently that such an interesting letter deserved a wider circulation, contrived to make a copy of it which he sent to the *Courier*. The *Courier* published it, the newspapers concerned reached Spain, and the fat was in the fire. Craufurd and his division were understandably furious and said so in unmistakable terms, and the matter reached such a state that on 10 November 1810 Picton felt constrained to write a letter to Wellington; it started:

> In consequence of an extraordinary report, which has been circulated with a good deal of assiduity, it becomes necessary that I should make a written detailed report to your Lordship of the circumstances which preceded and attended the action which took place upon the heights of Bussaco on the morning of the 27th September, inasmuch as they relate to myself and the troops I had the honour of commanding on that occasion . . .

The letter went on to describe the battle as Picton saw it. He was however privately furious over the publication of his letter, for he realised well enough that even a private communication from a senior general might be regarded almost in the light of a despatch when published in the newspapers.

Picton, who had obviously written a good many letters soon after the battle, was at first by no means sure how the leakage had occurred, for in a letter to Flanagan written on 12 December he admits that 'I . . . don't even now recall whether the letter was addressed to you or Marryat . . .' It is however certain that the letter had in fact been written to Queensberry.

Years after Picton's death a further controversy arose over the battle, this time, it is almost needless to say, between the historian Napier and the biographer Robinson; Napier's version of Bussaco as published in his great history is both incomplete and inaccurate; he lumps all the various encounters on the front of the 3rd Division into one great attack on its right and says that although a part of this attack was repulsed by the 88th and 45th Regiments, the main French effort broke Picton's line and was only finally driven back by a counter-attack delivered by Leith and one of his brigades.

The reasons for this inaccuracy are not quite clear; even now, with all the sources available, it is remarkably difficult to sort out the sequence and timing of the series of disconnected attacks which make up the battle; companies, battalions, and columns of British, Portuguese and French loom up out of the mist and smoke, play their part, and disappear again; and it may be that Napier, having neither the time nor the inclination to put the pieces together, was content with his 'potted' (and incorrect) version. It seems however equally probable that Napier, having decided that Picton's line had been broken, took no more trouble to investigate but simply turned his conjecture into firm history by the simple method of writing it down and having it published. He was by no means an impartial historian and had few scruples about manipulating his narrative so as to blacken the character of people he did not like. There were, it should be said, a considerable number of these (for Napier was a bigoted and savagely intolerant man) and amongst them, and very close to the top of the list, must be placed General Picton. Napier, himself a Light Division man and a participator in many of its battles, would have hardly forgiven Picton for his inaction on the Coa or forgotten his remarks regarding the part played by the Light Division at Bussaco, and was probably glad enough to seize upon any chance of belittling him. These peculiarities of Napier (which were much aggravated by the almost constant agony he received from an old spinal wound) were well known in the army and it is often said that many officers who felt themselves unfairly treated in his pages preferred to suffer in silence rather than risk the vitriolic blasts which were his usual rejoinder to any criticism.

Robinson had no such prejudices; he was no military expert but he was able by careful reading and comparison of the authorities then available to detect the errors in Napier's account, and these he pointed out firmly in his biography of Picton, adding that the wide discrepancy between Napier's account and the one contained in Picton's letter to Wellington was tantamount to saying that the latter account had deliberately been falsified by Picton. He made great (and perhaps justifiable) play with the fact that the 88th and companies of the 45th had undoubtedly been far off to Picton's *left*, flatly denied Napier's assertion that a battalion of the 8th Portuguese had ever been broken, and (perhaps rendered somewhat over-confident by his detection of the original error) virtually denied that any serious attack by Leith's Brigade had ever taken place. As far as the 9th Regiment and its commanding officer, Colonel Cameron, were concerned he went so far as to say that 'doubtless this

Officer would have led, and his Regiment would have made, as brave
and well conducted an attack upon the enemy as that described by
Colonel Napier—only it was not there. . . .'

Napier, as was to be expected, reacted briskly to this; his reply however was not quite as fierce as usual, from which it is perhaps
permissible to infer that he may have suspected that there was more
than a grain of truth in certain of Robinson's assertions. He maintained however that his account was substantially correct and
produced letters from a number of officers who had taken part in the
battle which proved, if nothing else, the remarkable confusion
regarding the sequence of events. He did however make one shrewd
point over Picton's letters for, having stated that 'it would be hard
indeed if a man's veracity was to be called into question because his
letters, written in the hurry of service, gave inaccurate details of a
battle' he goes on to comment that Robinson himself had already
admitted that another of Picton's letters was 'so inaccurate as to
give general offence to the Army'. There it may be as well to let the
controversy die and return once more to the movements of the
British army, which was steadily continuing its retreat to Coimbra.

CHAPTER 8

TORRES VEDRAS

Masséna, having lost the chance of cutting the British off from Lisbon, continued his pursuit very cautiously. He was of course already finding himself in a difficult situation, for he had abandoned his communications and was living on the country, he had very few wagons, and he was greatly encumbered with wounded whom he dared not leave behind him in such a hostile country as Portugal.

The British were therefore also able to retreat slowly and in good order, laying waste the country as they did so; this latter measure caused great distress to the local inhabitants but was clearly necessary in order to deny supplies to the French. The people had been warned earlier to destroy what they could not carry and withdraw to Lisbon, but it was a difficult order to enforce and a large part of the inhabitants had therefore remained in their towns and villages, still hoping that Masséna's army would be halted before it reached them. The continued withdrawal of the British therefore threw them into a panic and large numbers of refugees took the road to Lisbon in great fear and disorder; some buried their few valuables and hurried off south-westwards encumbered with bundles, while others piled their goods and old people on to mules or, more commonly, the slow creaking ox-carts of the country and made the best of their way to the safety of the lines. There were old people, invalids, children, ladies of fashion and nuns, all tramping miserably along the muddy roads in cold, cheerless rain, intermingled with the marching British who, hard and rough as they were, were filled with pity at the tragic spectacle. They could however do little to relieve the sufferings of these refugees for they themselves were hungry and their wagons overloaded. Sometimes indeed they were compelled to add to the misery of the unfortunate people by forcing them off the roads in order to let the guns and wagons go by.

Augustus Schaumann, a Hanoverian commissary in the British service and an acute observer of the military scene wrote that:

The retreat of the Anglo-Portuguese Army from Coimbra to the fortified lines, over a march of thirty leguas, presented a sad spectacle. The roads were littered with smashed cases and boxes, broken wagons and carts, dead horses and exhausted men. Every division was accompanied by a body of refugees as great as itself, and rich and poor alike, either walking, or mounted on horses or donkeys were to be seen, all higgledy-piggledy—men and women, young and old, mothers leading children or carrying them on their backs, nuns who had left their convents, and, quite strange to the world, either wandered about helplessly, beside themselves with fear, looking timidly for their relations, or else, grown bold, linked arms with the soldiers and carried the latter's knapsacks. Monks, priests and invalids—everybody was taking flight. The nearer the procession came to Lisbon the greater was the number of animals belonging to the refugees that fell dead either from fatigue or hunger, and very soon ladies were to be seen wading in torn silk shoes or barefoot through the mud. Despair was written on all faces. It was a heartrending sight. This wretched vanguard of the divisions was followed by a herd of bullocks destined for slaughter, among which these refugees who were unable to proceed were constantly becoming involved. Behind these came the mules laden with bread, corn and rum; then followed the baggage, transported partly on mules and partly on donkeys, together with tired, sick or wounded soldiers, either in carts or on foot. Then came the guard with the provost-marshal and the prisoners, the divisional artillery, and finally the divisions themselves, many of which numbered 10,000 men. The tail of the procession was made up by exhausted, weeping and wailing refugees.

The British withdrew from Coimbra on 30 September amid scenes of destruction; houses, mills, granaries, and sometimes whole villages, were left in flames and the disorder was much increased by the followers of the army and the bad characters always to be found in its ranks who, encouraged and excited by the atmosphere of lawless destruction, at once took the opportunity to indulge in an absolute orgy of looting. Wellington dealt vigorously with this outbreak and a number of British, German and Portuguese offenders were summarily hanged and their bodies left there as a warning to their fellows; these measures, drastic as they were, were only partially successful and the trouble continued in some measure until the army was once more stationary (within the lines), when order could again be restored. Well to the fore amongst the offenders were the Irish of Picton's Division, and in view of his known strong views in the matter of looting and his own propensity for sharp punishments it is certain that the severity with which he dealt with offenders did little to improve his already strained relations with his command.

Taking all the circumstances into account it is difficult to blame the soldiers unduly; young Kincaid of the Rifles remembered that:

> . . . the commissariat were destroying quantities of stores which they were unable to carry off. They handed out shoes and skirts to anyone who would take them, and the streets were literally running ankle deep with rum, in which the soldiers were dipping their cups and helping themselves as they marched along.

With this sort of thing going on all round them they can perhaps be pardoned for wishing to make the best of such unusual circumstances. Most of them, and particularly the many Irish among them, had been brought up in dire poverty, and can hardly be blamed for thinking such destruction a waste and doing their best to profit from it.

On 1 October the French army entered Coimbra and in the true spirit of the Revolution sacked it with great thoroughness. This was indirectly of some assistance to Wellington, for in spite of every precaution a considerable store of food and other useful supplies had been left in the town and these, had they been properly requisitioned and issued, would have been of great value to the French. As it was, great quantities were either wantonly destroyed or wasted, to say nothing of the fact that the delay caused by the sack gave the British even more time to make their arrangements for the occupation of the lines.

Masséna was surprised and considerably worried by the fact that the British had not turned to fight again after the clear-cut success at Bussaco. He still knew nothing of the positions which had been prepared across the Lisbon peninsula, and had in fact been assured that the road to the city lay through flat, not easily defended country; it thus seems certain that he took this to be a repetition of Moore's retreat to Coruña and assumed that Wellington, having satisfied military honour on the ridge at Bussaco, was anxious only to scramble back to the sea and safety, leaving Portugal in his hands. He may also have believed that Wellington's reluctance to face him was due to the fact that the morale of the British had deteriorated to such an extent as to make a battle too dangerous a risk to accept. This was of course not so—the army was perfectly sound and the looting was the work of only a few of its worst criminals—but Masséna, seeing the scenes of chaos and the red-coated bodies swinging from the wayside trees, cannot altogether be blamed for supposing that Wellington's army had gone the same way as that of Moore.

Firm therefore in the belief that unless he speeded up his pursuit the British would escape him, the French general decided to make Coimbra his base and leave there his numerous wounded and sick and much of his heavy baggage. In order to have the maximum force available for the decisive battle which he believed to be inevitable if only he could move his army sufficiently fast, he decided to leave only a very small garrison in the place, for he calculated that he could destroy the British and get a division or two back from Lisbon before the Portuguese guerrillas could assemble in sufficient numbers to attack it. On 4 October therefore the whole French army marched out of Coimbra, leaving it guarded by no more than 150 armed sailors; and on 7 October Trant and his wild militia captured the place.

There is, understandably, some doubt as to what happened thereafter; Napier says that 'During the first confusion the militia ill-used some prisoners and . . . French writers have in consequence accused Trant of disgracing his uniform by encouraging such ferocity. But it was he who repressed the ferocity; only ten lives were lost. . . .' He goes on to refer to a letter of thanks from some French officers to Trant, which is published as an appendix to his great *History* and quoted as proof of his humanity.

The French were not convinced; Marbot says furiously that over 1000 Frenchmen were massacred, and he may well perhaps be right, for with all due respect to Napier and Trant (whom Wellington later described to Stanhope as 'a very good officer' but 'as drunken a dog as ever lived') it is difficult to believe that the Portuguese militia, full of implacable hatred for the French invaders and very sketchily disciplined, could have been prevented from cutting a good many throats. It was simply that sort of war and men who had seen their homes burnt and their families slaughtered were unlikely to have any strange ideas regarding honour or the laws of war.

By 10 October 1810 the whole of the infantry (with the exception of Craufurd and his division) were inside the Lines and the withdrawal was over. Craufurd, as usual, was doing what he thought best, but his absence caused some consternation in the army and there was a report that the whole Light Division had been cut off. Eventually however he achieved his place within the fortifications, the cavalry (which had behaved splendidly throughout the retreat) followed him, and the whole army settled itself into its new positions and waited to see what Masséna would do. On 12 and 13 October there was some skirmishing between the French advanced guard and the British outposts but on the next day Masséna arrived and was horrified by the strength and extent of the British positions. He was a very experienced soldier and he soon realised that he was facing not mere works thrown up to cover an embarkation but a fortress. General Junot, commanding the French advanced guard, recommended an immediate attack but his commander-in-chief, with Bussaco still fresh in his mind, was not to be tempted into anything foolish. His army therefore took no further offensive action but entrenched itself in front of the lines and started its grim battle—against starvation.

The lines of Torres Vedras were a remarkable achievement; Wellington had planned them more than a year before and since then thousands of Portuguese labourers had worked on them under the supervision of British engineer officers until the country in front of Lisbon, already naturally strong, had been converted into a defensive position of immense strength. Rivers had been dammed to form inundations, whole hillsides scarped into precipices, and valleys blocked with vast stone walls and abattis of cut trees, while every hilltop was crowned by a powerful earthwork bristling with guns. The first line followed the Zizandre river eastward to Torres Vedras, then ran south to Perro Negro, and then eastwards again to Alhandra on the Tagus. The second line was roughly parallel to the first and some five or six miles behind it, while a third (and much more constricted) line had been built in the actual vicinity of Lisbon to cover any possible embarkation; both flanks of the lines were of course strongly guarded by the ships of the Royal Navy.

Once into the lines Picton's view of the situation became very much brighter, so much so indeed that in a letter to Flanagan he admitted jubilantly that 'all our opinions respecting the probable consequences of the Invasion of the country have proved erroneous', a remarkable tribute both to Wellington's foresight and the secrecy with which he kept his plans regarding the lines. On 3 November, in another letter, this time to his friend Colonel Pleydel, he explained with sober optimism that 'Masséna's situation every day becomes more and more critical, and his difficulty in obtaining subsistence for his Army must be daily increasing. If a considerable Army is not despatched in time to his assistance, little less than a miracle can save him from ruin.'

He did then go on to say that he did not like the British positions, which he felt to be 'too extensive to be strong', but this criticism was not wholly justified. The allied army, it is true, *was* holding a very long front but it was well fortified and supplied with lateral roads which, although of indifferent construction, made it possible to concentrate troops rapidly at any threatened point. The country on the French side of the lines was moreover so broken and difficult that the French were practically tied to the few available roads, which made it even easier for Wellington to foil any threatened attack. As the situation became more stable the whole front was largely taken over by the Portuguese militia, leaving the main allied army concentrated on or near the most likely points of attacks, and this virtually eliminated the risk of a sudden penetration of the British defences by some sudden well-concealed concentration by the French.

As soon as it had become apparent to Wellington that Masséna had no real intention of making a serious attack on the lines the situation inside them improved considerably. The troops were still harassed with early rising, stand-tos, and frequent alarms which often involved their remaining under arms for longer periods, but at least they were adequately fed and usually under some sort of cover. The situation as regards the Portuguese, particularly the refugees, was however less satisfactory. The Portuguese government was by no means efficient (and in any case its resources were small) while the main British effort was necessarily directed at keeping the army supplied and ready to move. The refugees therefore died in large numbers from the effects of exposure and malnutrition in spite of all efforts to help them; the British army made very considerable voluntary contributions of both money and food, so that in February 1811 we find Picton writing that: 'The inhabitants are kept from starving by the contributions of the officers (British) of the different Divisions of the Army. This division daily feeds above three hundred; but for this resource the greater part must have perished.' Wellington himself was also most perturbed about the situation, for on 27 Oct 1810 he felt it necessary to write a long letter on the subject to Lord Liverpool. In this letter, which is printed in his despatches, he pointed out that:

> Upon former occasions, the wealthy inhabitants of Great Britain, and of London in particular, have stepped forward to assist and relieve the distress of foreign nations, whether suffering under calamities inflicted by Providence or by a cruel and powerful enemy. This nation [the Portuguese] has received the benefit of the charitable dispositions of his Majesty's subjects, and there never was a case in which their assistance was required in a greater degree, whether the sufferings of the people, or their fidelity to the cause they have espoused, and their attachment to his Majesty's subjects, be considered. . . . I would therefore beg leave to recommend the unfortunate portion of the inhabitants who have suffered from the enemy's invasion, to your Lordship's protection; and I request you to consider the mode of recommending them to the benevolent disposition of his Majesty's subjects, at the moment which I hope may be not far distant that the enemy may be under the necessity of evacuating the country.

If the situation in the lines was bad, things outside had reverted to sheer primitive savagery; a good many Portuguese, having hidden their food, had remained in their houses naively confident that they could outwit the French. Never was confidence more misplaced; the French were hungry, and if food was available they proposed to have it. Their methods were simple, direct, and effective, for they hanged or tortured the heads of families until they, or others, divulged the whereabouts of the hiding-places of their food which the French at once appropriated, leaving the unfortunate Portuguese to starve. As time went by they necessarily became more and more severe as supplies were reduced, until eventually they regarded the very fact that a Portuguese was alive at all as an admission that he had food hidden somewhere; eventually the situation became such that they were killing or torturing the locals out of sheer irritation or frustration. The few surviving inhabitants then took to the hills and became guerrillas, leaving the country to revert to an untilled wilderness inhabited by wolves, foxes, and vultures.

As time went by, the French were almost fully occupied in foraging over a wide area, which made them very vulnerable to sudden swoops by guerrillas, who, naturally fierce and spurred on by the horrid example of the French, showed their victims no mercy. They boiled their prisoners alive, sawed them in half with rope, nailed them upside down over fires and emasculated them; only when they were in a great hurry did they kill them quickly by cutting their throats, which was by far the kindest fate that any Frenchman could hope for.

The situation within the lines was in many ways similar to that in a beleaguered fortress. Unlike a normal fortress, however, the Lisbon peninsula afforded some room for sport so that officers were sometimes able to hunt, shoot, or fish, while the more enlightened among them also arranged games, dancing, and amateur theatricals for their men.

A considerable number of senior officers looked upon the lines as the equivalent to the old winter quarters and demanded home leave after the leisurely fashion of the eighteenth century. This infuriated Wellington, who became so unapproachable on the subject that eventually very few officers had the courage even to submit applications: instead they did their best to slip away to the flesh-pots of Lisbon for a night or two, an indulgence which even their commander-in-chief appeared to consider reasonable. It was at this time that he made his celebrated comment that forty-eight hours was as long as any reasonable man could wish to stay in bed with the same woman.

There were also a few large social occasions; at Mafra, for example, Wellington invested Beresford with his Knighthood of the Bath, the event being rounded off with a large banquet. Young Anderson of the 24th Regiment, who managed to get an invitation, tells us that after it was over many British officers (who presumably had dined too well) lost their way and blundered into the French lines, but were all kindly returned next morning.

In mid-November 1810 Masséna withdrew his army to Santarem; his desperate soldiers had literally eaten up the countryside in front of the lines so that this move was forced on him in order to widen his feeding-grounds. Wellington followed him up cautiously (for the French were still dangerous) and his men, rough as they were, were horrified on their march by the state to which the country had been reduced. Everywhere there were murdered Portuguese and Frenchmen dead of disease or starvation, while the few ghastly survivors begged mutely for bits of biscuit from the passing columns. At Santarem, Masséna entrenched his army strongly in a naturally formidable position and Wellington at once followed his example; he knew that the French could not stay where they were for long, that lacking supplies they would soon be compelled to eat their way back into Spain and he was more than content to allow this to happen. By the end of November therefore the army was snugly under cover waiting for its work to be done for it by the twin effects of hunger and winter on the French.

Little is known of Picton's mode of living during this period; general officers commanding divisions were then expected to live in some state, run a good mess for themselves and their staff, and be prepared to entertain numerous visitors, and the establishment necessary to maintain this sort of standard would not be a small one. Firstly, there would be the personal servants, at least one to each officer, and possibly three or four; some officers took private English servants to the Peninsula with them, and it is possible that Picton followed this custom, for it will be remembered that he had a servant with him when his chaise overturned en route to Portsmouth. Then there were grooms, for the half-dozen or so officers of the headquarters staff would have twenty or more horses between them, all requiring attention.

A cook, perhaps with an assistant or two, was essential; captured Frenchmen, or Italians in the French service, were the fashionable thing, and it is certain that Tyler the ADC, a noted gourmet, would have taken good care to have the best available; Tyler supervised the catering and, as Picton said of him a little later in a letter home, he was 'as fat and good-humoured as ever, and amongst the Portuguese of the division he universally goes by the name of Adjuntanta Gordo or the fat ADC: but as long as he is well fed he does not care a farthing for the gibes and jokes . . .' We can be sure that this enormous officer took care to produce the best food available.

Wellington, however, had other views, for when briefing a newcomer on the culinary achievements of his divisional commanders he gave it as his opinion that 'Cole gives the best dinners in the Army, Hill the next best, mine are no great things, and Beresford's and Picton's are very bad indeed'. Bell, who quotes this comment in his book *Wellington's Officers*, goes on however to remark that others thought Beresford's dinners magnificent, so that the same may apply to those of Picton.

It can in any case be agreed that Wellington was not a competent judge. His own indifference to food was well known—he preferred cold meat and toast and is said on one occasion to have eaten a bad egg without noticing—and a man of these spartan tastes could hardly claim to be able to give an authoritative opinion on such an important subject.

There would be an assortment of soldiers too, batmen, orderly dragoons and the like, with a proportion of NCOs. Carts and wagons were very much frowned on by Wellington, so that the transport was all on a mule basis and a large number would have been required, together with their attendant muleteers. Inevitably there would also be a host of others on the fringe of the establishment, deserters from the French army, which numbered in its ranks men of most of the races of Europe, as guides, interpreters and general handymen, and hosts of Portuguese, rendered homeless by the war, and only too glad to attach themselves to the entourage of such a great man as a divisional commander. They were a motley crowd, dressed in the cast-off rags of uniform of four armies, but loyal and faithful and useful as foragers or as herdsmen for the inevitable flock of goats which provided milk for the general's tea.

Lastly, there were the women: a few lawful wives of attached soldiers, with a much greater proportion of local girls who, having lost their families and homes, had attached themselves to the troops or muleteers as the only alternative to starvation.

Divisional headquarters would if possible be situated in some large farm or other house with plenty of room and adequate stabling, and most people at divisional HQ level lived very comfortably. It is true that in a letter of this time to his friend Marryat, Picton said that he had no more than a bundle of straw for a bed, but it is already clear from similar references during the Walcheren expedition that this was more a matter of choice than necessity. Not much is known of his social life at this time, except for a few scattered references which do no more than note his presence at various dinner tables, but there is little doubt that the notoriety of the Trinidad affair had given him a peculiar reputation which rather set him apart from many of his fellow generals, and that he himself was uncomfortably conscious of this.

His relationship with his personal staff seems to have been excellent, although at about that time one of these caused a great stir by going home without leave or, in plain words, deserting. This was his DAQG, Captain Thomas Oliver Anderton of the 7th Fusiliers (who had been responsible for bringing up the 8th Portuguese at Bussaco) and his behaviour has never been explained. His previous career had been unexceptionable: after leaving the Royal Military College at Marlow he had first been posted to the 4th Division as DAQG but Cole, its commander, had disliked him (although for no clearer reason than that he was 'too much the fine gentleman') and he had therefore been transferred to the 3rd Division in a similar appointment in March 1810. He then served under Picton, apparently in complete harmony for nearly a year until, after repeated applications for home leave had been turned down, he resigned from the Quartermaster-General's department and took himself to England. This naturally caused much fury, and the Horse Guards were at first anxious to bring him to trial by court-martial; but in deference to his father, who was well known in the City (and who may possibly have appealed direct to the Duke of York), he was finally allowed to sell out in the usual way. He later became a lawyer and a Queen's Counsel and was a bencher of Lincoln's Inn. His reasons for desertion were never revealed but in view of his age (he was twenty-four at the time) it is very possible that a woman was involved. He was quickly replaced by Captain Tryon of the 3rd Regiment (Buffs). Picton never gave his version of the affair; as far as one can ascertain he had never complained of Anderton and there is no reason to suppose that he was at all responsible for that officer's peculiar conduct. The affair nevertheless gave rise to much gossip and it is possible that there were renewed murmurs of tyranny.

In December 1810, Picton lost a friend, although he cannot fairly be described as a close one, in the person of the extraordinary old Duke of Queensberry whose death brought to an end a career of dissipation almost without parallel; born in 1724 he had been a hardened roué at the age of fifteen and his career for the next seventy years had been an astounding one even in a period not famed for morality. The usually forbearing *Dictionary of National Biography* says of him that 'in later years he became a patron of the opera and ballet, although it is said that his interest was chiefly in the young women with whom he thus came in contact rather than the Arts themselves'.

Whatever the Duke's character, however, his generous offer of help at the time of the Calderon trials had impressed Picton deeply. It is true that it was due to the old man's indiscretion that Picton's letter after Bussaco had been published in the press, but 'Old Q' made handsome amends for this by leaving him £5000.

From scattered references it is clear that Picton was still very worried at this period by the bad state of his eyes, which were becoming weaker and more cloudy as far as close work, reading or writing was concerned. Fortunately, to use his own words, he could 'still discover objects at a distance as well and as particularly as ever' so that his military capacity was not affected; he was nevertheless under-standably worried at the prospect of any further deterioration which might have affected his military career very badly.

Masséna and his starving army still maintained their position grimly, and Wellington began to worry seriously about the effect of the long deadlock on public opinion at home. The government was not strong and was moreover expecting to be dimissed, for old King George III had gone mad again, a Regency was imminent, and the Prince of Wales was then confidently expected to establish his Whigs in power. This would probably have meant peace at any price, and Wellington was justifiably horrified at the prospect of leaving the Portuguese in the lurch after having advocated, indeed it may be said, demanded, so many sacrifices from them.

Napoleon was well informed of the political situation and it was for this reason that he ordered Masséna to hold on. As long as he did so it could not be said with confidence that the British were gaining any advantage over the French, whereas once the latter retreated with Wellington in hot pursuit the ascendancy of the British would then be so obvious to the people of England that even the Whigs might hesitate to end the war in the teeth of public opinion.

In order to strengthen Masséna, Napoleon had ordered Soult to move northwards to support him with a part of his army. Soult, however, was reluctant to do so, for Andalusia was rich and peaceful and he did not want to leave it; it is true that part of his army was engaged in the siege of Cadiz, but that town was so strong that operations had reached a state of deadlock and thus hardly interfered with Soult's enjoyment of his semi-independant position as ruler of Andalucia. Even Soult however dared not openly disobey Napoleon, so after delaying as long as possible he set off northwards at the end of December 1810 with 4000 cavalry, 14,000 infantry and 54 guns, with the intention of creating a diversion in Extremadura. On 22 January 1811 he captured the weak Spanish fort of Olivenza and on 19 February he defeated the Spanish army covering Badajos and at once laid siege to that fortress. Although only held by Spaniards it was strong and well-provisioned and Wellington was reasonably confident that it could hold out almost indefinitely.

All Napoleon's plans in the Peninsula were then suddenly brought to nothing by no less a person than the Prince of Wales; the Regency Bill had become law on 5 February 1811 and the Whigs were busy planning a government when they were told arbitrarily that the new Regent proposed to retain the old government in power. His reasons for this are not very clear although they probably stemmed from the fact that he was by no means in sympathy with the Whig outlook but had professed friendship for them in order to annoy his Tory father with whom, in true Hanoverian fashion, he was on the worst of terms.

Whatever the reasons for this change of heart, once it became known Masséna decided, very rightly, that his situation was hopeless and that Soult's intervention was unlikely to have much effect; on 5 March 1811 therefore, much to Wellington's undisguised relief, he started his long and painful withdrawal to the Spanish frontier.

CHAPTER 9

THE FRENCH RETREAT

Masséna began his retreat with great skill and for a day or two Wellington was puzzled as to his intentions. He followed up, but cautiously for the French still outnumbered him.

In spite of his good start, the French general was soon in difficulties, which were due in part to the hunger and disorganisation in his army but also largely to the insubordination of his generals, who did as they thought best, often moving their troops without reference to him and disregarding in other ways his excellent master-plan for the conduct of the retreat. On 9 March Wellington arrived at Pombal upon which Ney, in spite of strict orders to hold the place, started to withdraw. Early next morning the Light Division took advantage of this to drive in his rearguard and seize the bridge, and for a short while it looked as though the French were in serious trouble. Ney, always at his best in a crisis, then thrust them back with a brisk counter-attack, set fire to the town and made good his escape under cover of the smoke, thus extricating himself neatly from a potentially dangerous position.

More British troops, including Picton and his division, then arrived on the scene, and Wellington resumed his pursuit. He came up with the French again at Redinha, where Ney had taken up a very strong position with both flanks covered by woods and rivers, and at once attacked him. The Light and 3rd Divisions struck at the right and left flanks respectively while Pack kept them occupied in the centre.

Wellington's tactics were sound in concept but failed in execution, due mainly to the fact that Pack's attack was not pressed seriously enough. The conduct of a holding action is always difficult, since the operation must be convincing while not involving the attackers too deeply. In this case Ney soon decided that Pack's advance was no more than a feint, and concentrated on holding off the threat to his flanks by sharp local counter-attacks. Under cover of these he again got his rearguard back to the bridge (the existence of which, according to Picton, was not known to the British).

The French behaved so well and showed such confidence that Wellington decided to suspend the attack until more troops arrived, with the result that Ney had plenty of time to complete his movement. When the British finally resumed their attack, Ney's rearguard fired one tremendous salvo from all its muskets and guns and retired behind the smokescreen so formed. The British at once pressed on to the bridge, but Ney had this well covered by the fire of a number of guns from the high ground behind it, and once again was able to retreat practically unmolested. Three miles further back he stood again and Wellington at once made new dispositions to attack him, sending Picton and his division off on yet another wide outflanking movement round the French left; the country however was difficult, progress was slow, and night fell before the movement was complete, upon which Ney withdrew under cover of darkness towards Masséna at Condeixa.

At this stage of the operations, Masséna's plan was to hold a strong covering position at Condeixa while he forced a crossing of the river Mondego behind him; he then proposed to establish himself in a permanent defensive position behind that river, with good foraging grounds in his rear. His reasons for this were sound enough; the country south of the Mondego was virtually a desert, and he calculated that even the excellent British supply system, which in spite of seapower necessarily depended to a considerable extent on local purchase, would be unequal to the task of keeping the British fed. Furthermore, not yet knowing that Soult had returned to Andalucia after capturing Badajos, he had hopes that that general would seriously hamper the British by operating on their rear.

Masséna's generals had other views on the matter; they were all thoroughly tired of campaigning in Portugal, and wished to get back to Spain, and they therefore did all they could to hamper his plans. This was not difficult; the Mondego was in fact only lightly held by Portuguese militia with a few guns, but it was not hard to build this up into a formidable opposition; in the meanwhile, reconnaissance patrols sent out to find fords were slow in doing so, while the French engineers took an inordinate time to gather material for a bridge. All this wasted days; and Masséna, with the British close on his heels, could not afford to waste even hours for he dared not be caught with his back to a major water obstacle. After some delays he was finally induced to abandon his plan by the report (untrue but effective) of a considerable British seaborne landing somewhere on his western flank, and thereafter decided to retire eastwards into Spain via Ciudad Rodrigo, which was of course exactly what his generals had hoped.

On 13 March Wellington came up to Condeixa (which was held by Ney) and during his reconnaissance saw the French baggage moving eastward, from which he was able to divine Masséna's new line of retreat. He therefore at once despatched Picton with his division in a wide outflanking movement eastwards with a view to cutting off the French retreat, but Ney observed this in time and having set fire to Condeixa at once retired. Unfortunately he sent no notification of his intentions to Masséna (at least if he did it failed to arrive), with the result that the French commander-in-chief was very nearly cut off and taken by a British cavalry patrol; fortunately for Masséna his escort and staff showed a bold front and he was able to extricate himself from a very dangerous position, but he was naturally furious about this and said roundly, and apparently with some justification, that he believed it to be a deliberate attempt by Ney to get him captured. True or not, the very possibility throws an interesting light on feelings in the French army at the time.

Ney's sudden withdrawal also left exposed the division of Montbrun (who was trying to persuade the Portuguese commander in Coimbra to surrender) and caused him to retreat in considerable haste.

On 13 March Wellington received the unwelcome news that Badajos had surrendered to the French three days earlier in circumstances which sounded very like treachery, and he therefore determined to detach Beresford southwards with a force in order to menace Soult.

The decision, although a sound one, cannot have been easy to make, since it left him in the extraordinary position of pursuing the French with an army much inferior in numbers. He must of course have calculated that although the French rearguards were boldly handled the army as a whole was not in a position to fight a major action. The French, once cut off from their line of retreat, must have dispersed and perished in the mountains and Masséna was too good a soldier to risk this contingency.

Within a day or two Wellington was also much cheered by the receipt of good news from distant Andalucia, where the Anglo-Spanish garrison of Cadiz, taking advantage of Soult's absence with a considerable part of the besieging army, had landed further along the coast and fought a successful battle against a strong French detachment under Victor.

The Spanish general concerned behaved very badly and left the British to fight alone, and for a while the situation was desperate; but eventually the small British force under Graham succeeded in defeating the French decisively at Barossa on 5 March. When Soult heard this he at once set off southwards towards Cadiz, taking care to leave a strong garrison in Badajos. His departure removed a very considerable threat to Wellington's right and rear and when the news reached him he was able to continue his pursuit with more confidence than might otherwise have been the case.

On the night of 13 March the British, marching hard, were close behind the French when the two armies bivouaced. On the morning of the 14th there was a heavy fog from which came much noise of French movement and Erskine, temporarily in command of the Light Division, at once pushed forward on the rash assumption that it presaged a French retreat. The fog then lifted suddenly and the Light Division found itself seriously committed but fortunately Wellington, as usual, was well forward and at once despatched Picton on yet another of his 'right hooks', which quickly caused the French to retire. Wellington has been criticised for the apparent caution of these outflanking tactics, although it is hard to see why. The country was difficult and there was little point in butting head-on against a well-handled rearguard if manoeuvre would do the trick. The French were kept moving while their men fell out by hundreds. More collapsed through exhaustion than would have been killed in a major action, and Wellington was satisfied.

While these movements were in progress, Masséna discovered that a second and much wider outflanking movement launched earlier by Wellington was making good progress and as a result of this information decided that he must hasten his retreat. He therefore ordered the destruction of much baggage, many wagons, and all his unserviceable draught animals, and thus unencumbered marched off eastwards again on the night of 14 March; his plan was to cross the Ceira and hold a strong position at Foz d'Aronce with a rearguard, thus giving his main body a chance to disengage cleanly. This plan, like many others, was a perfectly sound one, but like many others it was spoilt in its execution by the negligence of a subordinate general, in this case the gallant but impetuous Ney, who although he arrived at the river Ceira in plenty of time decided for some perverse reason to bivouac on the near side of it. His reasons for this are not known; he had only two divisions and a few cavalry with him, yet in spite of his dangerously exposed position he took almost no precautions against surprise.

The British advance troops, consisting of the Light and 3rd Divisions, arrived late on the evening of 15 March and the two generals, Erskine and Picton, decided after consultation not to attack.

This was fully in accordance with Wellington's general policy, which until then had been to hold in front and outflank, but when that general came up the weakness of Ney's position was so apparent that he at once ordered the two divisions forward.

The Light Division struck at the French right while Picton attacked their left, supported by the 1st Division which had just come up, and there was a brisk fight. The French centre then collapsed rather suddenly and there was a general, panicky scramble for the bridge in which many French soldiers were drowned and the eagle of a regiment left in the river. For the moment it looked as though the whole force might be destroyed, but then Ney, recovering himself, collected a few troops and counter-attacking with his accustomed dash and gallantry held back the British attack long enough for his troops to get back across the bridge in comparatively good order. The bridge was then blown and Ney got away cleanly under cover of darkness. When it became apparent, during the early French panic at the bridge, that a number of baggage animals would fall into the hands of the British the French hamstrung several hundred and left them, to the great fury of the British who seem to have been more incensed by this than by any previous (and often much worse) atrocities committed on the retreat. Every diarist who was present mentions it, and all say how hardly it would have gone with the French had the British caught up with them.

In a letter to Colonel Pleydell dated 24/29 March Picton wrote that the French position was 'immediately attacked', thus implying that it was done on his initiative, but this was not in fact so. Wellington said later in his dispatch: 'When I came up I immediately made arrangements . . .' so that his version seems a good deal more likely. It is clear that his divisional commanders had digested the idea that what he required from them was not initiative but obedience.

On 16 March the British remained halted, partly to allow the engineers to repair the bridge at Foz d'Aronce, and partly allow their supplies to catch up with them. The rapid pursuit had strained the commissariat and rations were getting short; the Portuguese system in particular collapsed almost completely, and a number of them actually died of starvation on the march. Masséna planned yet another stand on the Alva but was again frustrated by the insubordination of one of the generals. This time it was Reynier, who had been ordered to close in to cover Ney's left flank but who for some reason chose, in a manner reminiscent of Craufurd, to remain in a position of isolation. The morning of 18 March was foggy, but the weather cleared suddenly, revealing to Reynier that the British were advancing upon him, whereupon he withdrew in great haste, thus jeopardising the whole French position and compelling Masséna to continue his retreat. Wellington however did not on this occasion follow with his whole army (which was still very short of supplies) but sent on the cavalry and the Light, 3rd and 6th Divisions to continue the pursuit. The disparity of force was thus so great that the British could do little more than keep the French moving and pick up a number of sick or exhausted stragglers.

On 21 March Masséna, conscious of the slackening pressure, ordered his army to halt for a few days near Almeida and there announced to his astonished generals that his plan was to move to the area of Coria and Plasencia with a view to reinvading Portugal along the valley of the Tagus. He proposed to leave his sick and wounded in Almeida and draw supplies for his new venture from that fortress, although it was by no means well stocked. His motives for this were clear enough: if he continued his retreat behind the frontier fortresses it would be an open admission of defeat, whereas a thrust southwards would have at least the appearance of a renewal of the threat to Lisbon. The decision was however a bad one; his troops were disorganised and exhausted and had neither food nor ammunition nor boots, and his horses were dying in large numbers; but the main trouble came from the generals who were almost in a state of open mutiny. D'Erlon, whose corps was not strictly a part of Masséna's army, did not bother to argue but simply marched off with his troops towards Ciudad Rodrigo, while Ney protested in such strong terms that he was relieved of his command and sent back to France.

In spite of this opposition Masséna continued obstinately with his preparations and on 24 March marched off southwards. Inevitably his rash operation was destined to fail, for food was hardly to be found and the rugged country was too much for the weary French and their starving horses. After a couple of days of hardship Masséna thus bowed to the inevitable and turned again to his original line of retreat.

Wellington, having halted, had momentarily lost touch with the French, particularly after Masséna's sudden turn southwards towards Coria, but on 27 March he regained contact near Guarda and at once prepared to attack, sending Picton and his division off on a wide left-flanking movement over country so rough that Picton was compelled to leave his artillery behind and take a Portuguese mountain battery instead. The 3rd Division made excellent time and by 9 am on 29 March came up with the French rearguard at Guarda; there it established itself within 400 yards of General Loison, and although the latter had 15,000 infantry with him he suffered them to remain there unmolested for two hours until the remainder of the British came up, when the French moved off hastily.

Masséna's weary army then continued its retreat as far as the Coa, where it took up a strong position behind the river and awaited the arrival of the British. Wellington issued his order for the attack on the night of 2 April, his plan being to keep two of Masséna's divisions engaged next day with two of his, while his remaining four fell upon Reynier's corps and destroyed it. The latter was apprehensive of this very moment and had been given discretionary orders to retire if he thought fit, but for some reason decided against doing so.

The morning of 3 April was unfortunately foggy and when the Light Division marched off under Erskine one of its brigades was left behind in the confusion; it subsequently came up under Colonel Beckwith, an excellent officer, and, fording the Coa under fire, began to climb the hill on the other side. At this moment the fog lifted and Beckwith found himself committed to a battle with a vastly superior French force. Having in fact no option he pressed forward boldly, but must have been destroyed had not the second brigade of the Light Division come up to his help. Even then the situation was desperate, but fortunately the 3rd Division was soon across the river and scrambling up the slope on Beckwith's left.

Picton, seeing that the situation was urgent, wasted no time by halting but simply brought his division from column into line on the move, and placing himself in the centre led it briskly forward against the French. Donaldson, tramping along in the ranks of the 94th Regiment, watched admiringly as 'General Picton rode up in front of us with his stick over his shoulder exposed to the heavy fire of the enemy, as composedly as if he had been in perfect safety'. The attack was completely successful but fortunately for the French a heavy storm then came on, under cover of which they were able to withdraw. On the night of 3 April Masséna again retreated and the next day the British followed, but apart from some minor skirmishing there was no more fighting; on 11 April the French reached Salamanca and the British, faced by the frontier fortresses of Almeida and Ciudad Rodrigo, which they were unable to pass, broke off the pursuit.

During most of the retreat the French appear to have been completely out of control, and perpetrated the most horrible offences against the unfortunate inhabitants of the towns and villages along their line of retreat. The places themselves were usually burned, and although this can perhaps be justified militarily for its delaying effect on the British advance, nothing can excuse their brutality towards the

Portuguese. Young John Kincaid of the Rifles, then a comparative newcomer to the Peninsula, said of Pyrnes:

> This little town and the few wretched inhabitants who had been induced to remain, under the faithless promises of the French generals, showed fearful signs of a late visit from a barbarous and merciless foe. Young women were lying in their houses brutally violated—the streets were strewn with broken furniture, inter-mixed with the putrid carcases of murdered peasants, mules, and donkeys, and every description of filth that filled the air with pestilent nausea.

The Portuguese took their revenge where they could. The French had to leave behind them great numbers of soldiers who were unable, because of wounds, disease or starvation, to keep up with their units, and these the furious peasants murdered with every refinement of torture. This may have been reprehensible, but in view of the earlier excesses of the French it was hardly surprising that they should have taken their revenge where they could.

Wellington had much cause to be pleased with the operations, for he had driven Masséna from Portugal, his men had fought and marched well, and his supply system, although by no means perfect, had proved adequate to the considerable demands made on it. The army, it is true, was still raw and the staff-work imperfect, nor were the divisional and brigade commanders always as good as they might have been. This was to some extent due to the fact that some of the better ones were at home on 'urgent private affairs' but chiefly perhaps to Wellington's insistence on implicit obedience to the letter of his instructions, which tended to make his subordinate commanders chary of using too much initiative. A good example of this was of course the initial stage of the engagement at Foz d'Aronce where the two leading divisions refrained from attacking Ney. Erskine's hesitation is understandable, for he was a thoroughly bad divisional commander and the Light Division disliked him heartily, but Picton, who had a good eye for ground, must have realised the extreme weakness of the French position.

Apart from this minor episode, however, Picton did well during the advance: in spite of his relative inexperience he seems to have been able to get the best out of his troops under bad conditions and his frequent employment on wide outflanking movements indicated that Wellington was prepared to trust him out of his sight. Much of his success was due to the marching ability of his divisions: Grattan, not slow to praise the 88th, says that they could outmarch almost any battalion in the army, especially when conditions were bad, for 'this plain reason, that scarcely one wore many pairs of shoes prior to his enlistment, and as to the rations (the most part of them at all events) a dozen times had been in all probability the outside of their acquaintance with such delicacies'. Having thus praised his own regiment however he goes on to pay a handsome tribute to 'that first-rate battle Regiment, the 45th, a parcel of Nottingham weavers, whose sedentary habits lead you to suppose that they could not be prime marchers; but the contrary was the fact and they marched to the full as well as my own Corps'. It is very probable that the rest of the division were also up to this standard of excellence.

Wellington next decided to blockade Almeida, for although a convoy of supplies had been allowed to slip into Ciudad Rodrigo it was well known that the former fortress was desperately short of rations. Having made the necessary dispositions he rode off southwards to visit Beresford who was operating, although without conspicuous success, against the French in the vicinity of Badajos. He was by no means happy about leaving the bulk of his army under Spencer, for he had but little regard for that general's ability, but he reckoned that it was safe to do so on the assumption that it would take months for Masséna's battered army to reorganise and refit and be ready for further offensive action. He had reasonable grounds for this assumption, for Masséna had lost, in one way or another, about a third of his men and a great number of horses and guns. He was also short of money, clothes, food, boots, wagons and ammunition, in fact of every warlike store, and his men were ill, disorganised, and showing tendencies to mutiny; nor, as we have seen, were his generals disposed to help him. In spite of these handicaps however he worked a near-miracle for in three weeks he had not only re-organised and re-equipped his army but had also assembled a considerable convoy of rations which he proposed to throw into Almeida, even in the teeth of the British.

Wellington, urged on by worried letters from Spencer, rode back hastily to the main army and on arrival there on 28 April realised from the information available that the French had apparently made a rapid recovery and were again preparing to try their luck, probably in an attempt to relieve, or at least to revictual, Almeida. He was quite prepared to risk a general action; his army, due to the considerable detachment he had had to make in the direction of Badajos, was inferior in numbers to the French, and composed moreover partly of Portuguese whose value in a pitched battle was still uncertain in spite of their success at Bussaco. Nevertheless he reckoned, rightly as it turned out, that these disadvantages would be more than compensated for by the fact that the French could not conceivably have recovered fully from their long ordeal in Portugal. Masséna might have reorganised them, re-equipped them, even fed them after a fashion, but the British commander-in-chief was convinced that their morale must still be low.

On 2 May 1811 Masséna advanced towards Almeida with his army, which consisted of some 42,000 infantry, 4–5000 cavalry and 38 guns, and which was followed by a considerable convoy of wagons carrying supplies for the fortress.

Wellington at once moved out to meet him and quickly placed his army in a defensive position which he had reconnoitred previously; he was not disposed to take the offensive for he was numerically much inferior to the French, having but 34,000 infantry (of whom about two-thirds were British or German and the remainder Portuguese) and less than 2000 cavalry. He was however superior in artillery, having 48 guns.

The position which Wellington had selected was a good one; it faced east behind the line of a stream, the Dos Casas, which ran parallel to and some six miles east of the Coa. His right rested on the village of Fuentes d'Onoro which was strongly built and well suited for defence and which was moreover concealed from long-range enemy reconnaissance by the fact that it lay in a hollow, while his left rested on Fort Conception, some seven miles north of Fuentes and about six miles east of Almeida. The position was rather too extensive for the force which Wellington had available, but the bed of the Dos Casas was so steep and rocky along much of the front that he rightly calculated that it would be practically impassable to the French. The length of the position was of course forced on the British general because of the necessity for him both to screen Almeida *and* cover his line of communication with Portugal. Apart from its extent its chief disadvantage was that the Coa, with its single bridge at Castello Bom, might prove a fatal barrier if the British were by some mischance compelled to retreat.

The bulk of the army was posted near Fuentes d'Onoro; the village itself was held by the twenty-eight light companies of the 1st and 3rd Divisions under the command of Colonel Williams of the 60th, while behind it stood the two divisions themselves, the 1st on the right and the 3rd on the left. Behind these again stood the reserve, consisting of the Light Division (behind Picton) and the 7th (behind Spencer). Further to the north was Campbell with his 6th Division, and the 5th Division which held the left of the position, the cavalry being in reserve under Wellington's own hand behind Fuentes d'Onoro.

On the afternoon of 3 May, Masséna, having decided that the village was the key to the position, launched a series of heavy attacks on it from the east; these however made practically no progress and at nightfall the village was still firmly in British hands, although unfortunately the gallant Williams had been seriously wounded.

On 4 May Masséna took no offensive action but spent much of the day in making a detailed reconnaissance which revealed to him the fact that the British right could be turned, for the only troops much south of Fuentes were a band of Spanish guerrillas at Nave de Haver. He therefore decided that the next day he would pin down

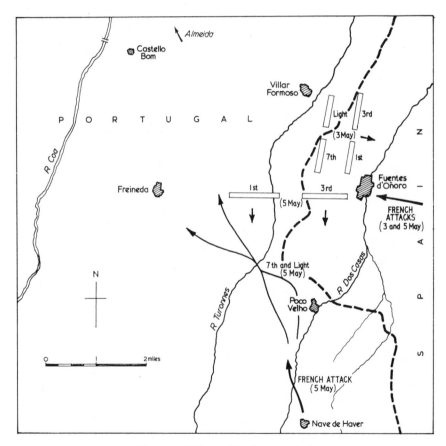

Fuentes d'Onoro (southern sector)

the British by making a series of feints against them with a part of his army while passing the bulk of it round their right flank with a view to launching his main attack from the south. By these means he hoped not only to roll up the British line but also to cut them off from their only practicable line of retreat, the bridge at Castello Bom. Wellington however was uneasy about this flank, and having deduced from the reports of the French movements the direction from which their next attack might be expected, he sent off General Houston's 7th Division to some high ground at Poco Velho, about two miles south of Fuentes, in order to meet it.

By the morning of 5 May it had become very apparent from the reports of patrols and the statements made by prisoners taken a few hours earlier that the bulk of the French army was to be employed in the attack from the south, so Wellington at once sent off his cavalry and the Light Division to reinforce Houston; at the same time Spencer and Picton changed front to the south, Picton's division still being on the left with its left resting at Fuentes d'Onoro. A rocky outcrop offered a good natural defensive position and as the ground to the south was relatively open the new line was a strong one.

The immediate requirement was to extricate the 7th and Light Divisions. There was heavy and confused fighting for some time but fortunately the French attacks were uncoordinated, and the withdrawal was able to continue. Houston veered off to the north-east and was soon clear of the enemy, whose whole weight fell upon the Light Division and the cavalry. The open country where the action took place was ideally suited to the employment of cavalry and the British horsemen, though greatly outnumbered, proved a match for their French counterparts. It was here that the celebrated horse artilleryman, Captain Norman Ramsay, saved two guns by galloping them through the centre of the swarming French cavalry.

Presently the Light Division reached the security of the new British line, which was so strong that Masséna hesitated to attack it. Instead he again turned his attention to the unfortunate village of Fuentes d'Onoro, which presently was heavily attacked by Ferey's corps from the east. This attack was well supported by artillery, and pressed with such gallantry by the French that after a savage and costly fight they succeeded in driving the British out of the place and on to the high ground just behind it. The situation then became desperate, for with the fall of the village Wellington was faced with an immediate and difficult retreat unless he could retake it. In order to do this he ordered a counter-attack, and presently the 88th Regiment of Picton's division came doubling towards the village in columns of sections, led by

Wallace, their commanding officer, Mackinnon, their brigadier, and Major-General Edward Pakenham, the Adjutant-General, elder brother of Picton's AAG. Grattan, who on that day commanded the leading company, said that his battalion was cheered all along its way down the line; unusually however they made no reply nor sound of any kind until they came in sight of the French when Grattan, turning to look back at his men, was given a cheer 'that a lapse of many years has not made me forget'. The 88th then attacked the village so savagely that the French holding it broke and ran after suffering heavy casualties; one party of about a hundred and fifty ran by mistake into a cul-de-sac where the pursuing 88th fell upon them with the bayonet and killed every last man of them, and with this bloody finale the battle ended.

It had been a close thing, a good deal closer than Wellington cared for. Later he was to comment that 'if Boney had been there we should have been beaten'; and this may be true. Masséna claimed a victory on the grounds that he had driven in several miles of Wellington's right but his claim lacks conviction. He fought to supply Almeida and was forced to retire without doing so, and this seems conclusive. After the battle he used the convoy of provisions to feed his hungry army, which he then withdrew with all despatch to the neighbourhood of Ciudad Rodrigo, having first sent messengers into Almeida ordering its governor to blow up the place and fight his way back with his garrison if he could. On the night of 10 April this was done, and to Wellington's great fury (for there was much neglect on the part of several senior officers) the governor and a large part of his garrison actually succeeded, against all expectations, in blowing up the place and rejoining Masséna.

About this time Napoleon removed Masséna from the chief command of the army and replaced him by Marmont, who at once withdrew the army to Salamanca, thus finally ending the campaign. On receipt of this information Wellington left the army to Spencer and, ordering the 3rd and 8th Divisions to follow him at their best speed, rode off southwards towards Beresford, who was by no means happy in his situation near Badajos. The reason for his unease was that Soult was again, though reluctantly, on his way north to succour Badajos, so that by 16 May 1811 Beresford had raised the siege of that place and was in a defensive position near the village of Albuera and behind the stream of that name. The position he chose has been much criticised, although it was not perhaps as bad as commonly made out. Most maps of the field tend to exaggerate features which on the ground are barely perceptible, so that even Napier's famous bloodstained hill where the principal action took place is in fact no more than a gentle ridge.

The main fault of the position was that it was masked in front by an extensive wood and Beresford's main fault in occupying it was that he put his Spaniards on the exposed right flank. Although brave enough, they were notoriously unable to manoeuvre quickly, so that when the inevitable attack came in against their right flank they were quite unable to change front in time and were driven back in great confusion and with heavy casualties; it is however only fair to say that in spite of their disorganisation many of them fought well.

The rolling up of the whole line was only prevented by the arrival of British troops who behaved with unparalleled courage and eventually drove off the French, although not without terrible casualties. For some time after the battle Beresford was by no means sure whether he had won a great victory or suffered a defeat; but on 18 May Soult finally retreated and by thus acknowledging his inability to relieve Badajos gave the victory to Beresford. It is an odd comment on Anglo-Spanish relationships that the only local memorial of the battle is an imposing monument to General Castanos, commanding the Spanish troops under Beresford. It stands in the village square and its florid inscription appears to make no reference to the presence of British troops at the battle.

Wellington arrived soon after the fighting was over, and although he was far from pleased by the way in which Beresford had fought the battle and the great number of casualties, he wasted no time in recriminations for he saw that in spite of everything Soult's retreat had given him an opportunity, if he were quick, to seize Badajos. The 3rd and 7th Divisions, marching by Castelo Branco, Nisa and Portalegre, arrived at Camp Maior on 24 May 1811 and a few days later Badajos was again under siege. Wellington's only hope of success lay in capturing the place quickly, for although Soult had withdrawn it was clear that as soon as he had picked up some reinforcements and replenished his supplies from the ample resources of Andalusia he would come plunging north again in an attempt to drive the British away from the threatened fortress. Marmont too, although for the moment busy reorganising Salamanca, might be expected to take a hand in the game at any moment.

Wellington resolved to attack Fort San Cristobal (on the north bank of the Guadiana) and the castle of Badajos simultaneously with the 7th and 3rd Divisions respectively, and on 27 May Picton crossed the river with his division and commenced operations against the castle. From the start neither project prospered; Wellington, always fearing a sudden evacuation of the Peninsula, had never dared land his cumbersome siege train, and was therefore compelled to improvise a scratch collection of heavy artillery from the guns in Elvas. Many of these were ancient and some at least bore the cypher of Phillip II, who reigned from 1556 to 1598; they were made of soft brass in unusual calibres, so shot had to be culled for each gun individually by picking over the great piles in the magazines. There was also a serious shortage of trained engineers and of engineer's stores, but in spite of all these disadvantages the siege was duly opened.

The construction of approach trenches was difficult in front of San Cristobal, where the ground was rocky and soil scarce, but on the south side there was no such problem and the 3rd Division were able to make good progress with their digging. Fire was opened on 3 June, and although many of the ancient cannon either melted or exploded, or otherwise disabled themselves, some progress was made and a breach finally opened in Cristobal. This was assaulted by a party of the 7th Division on the night of 6 June but without success, for the breach had been blocked by the French and the ladders they carried were too short for an attempt at escalade elsewhere; the stormers were therefore compelled to retire, having lost half their numbers to no purpose. A second attack on 9 June had no better success, so that the operations on this side are chiefly remarkable for the gallantry of Ensign Dyas of the 51st, who led the forlorn hope in each case and, almost miraculously, survived both assaults.

So far the guns of the besiegers had had little effect on the solid masonry of the castle, but on 10 June some good British siege guns arrived from Lisbon and soon pounded a practicable breach; unfortunately however there was no parallel closer to it than four hundred yards and no time left to dig one, for Marmont was at last on his way south. Wellington therefore abandoned the whole project and withdrew.

There were several reasons for the failure of the operation; Napier says, truly, that 'there is no operation in War more certain than a modern siege if the rules of the art are strictly followed'—but in this case they were not. The work was pushed against time without adequate resources of men, guns or stores and its failure was fairly certain from the first; Picton, whose extensive experience of the Courts had perhaps given him a taste for legal jargon, subsequently commented caustically that Badajos was 'sued in forma pauperis' and the statement is probably a fair one.

On the other hand, it would be unfair to criticise Wellington for making the attempt since he was on the spot and therefore in a position to weigh the chances. The French were in disarray and he presumably thought that the place might fall to a *coup-de-main*, and had it done so it would have saved a good deal of British blood a few months later. It is also probable that his only previous experience of sieges, in India, had caused him to underrate the power of resistance of a relatively modern fortress defended by good troops.

The 3rd Division had little opportunity to distinguish themselves in their part of the siege, their activities being confined to trench work. This the soldiers hated, for it was hard, uncomfortable and extremely dangerous without offering any prospect of a real clash with the enemy. Grattan dismissed the operations with a characteristic anecdote or two and was more concerned to note, with a gourmet's pleasure, that the Guadiana was well stocked with good mullet.

Picton was depressed at the results of the siege and with the operations generally; in a letter to Flanagan on 22 June he complained that:

> Until the last few days I have never had my clothes off since July last year. I have begun to find that this sort of life is too trying for a constitution of 54 . . . I am neither ambitious of a Red Ribbon or of any other Distinction, and therefore can easily make up my mind to the insipid walks of private life.

A few days later, on 2 July, he wrote in similar vein to his old friend Marryat, telling him that the British were in no state to attempt offensive operations and that the Portuguese regular forces were weak and their militia useless. He also commented, shrewdly enough, that the guerrillas who harassed the French were 'equally formidable to the Spanish inhabitants who dread them to the full as much as they do the enemy', and went on to say that 'the great mass of inhabitants of the neighbouring provinces have submitted to the French Yoke and are not disposed to make any further struggle'. He ended gloomily by saying that he did not think the contest could last long.

It was probable that this depression was due almost entirely to bad health. Long years in the tropics, followed by bouts of malaria at Walcheren, must have had their effect on his constitution and, as he rightly surmised, fifty-four was a considerable age at which to be undergoing a rigorous campaign in a country which at times and in places could be notably unhealthy.

CHAPTER 10

CIUDAD RODRIGO

By the end of May 1811 Marmont had reorganised his army in and around Salamanca and felt ready to resume active operations. On 1 June therefore he set off southwards in fulfilment of a promise made to Soult to co-operate with that general against Wellington. He stopped on his way to revictual Ciudad Rodrigo, a proceeding which, in the absence of Wellington at Badajos, filled Spencer with terror, and on 18 June Marmont and Soult met at Merida and set about preparing a joint plan to deal with the British, whom they believed to be still in the vicinity of Badajos.

Wellington, who had by then been joined by Spencer with the bulk of the army by a shorter route than that taken by the French, had however learnt early of the French plans from a captured despatch and being outnumbered had decided only to give battle under the most advantageous conditions. He therefore withdrew to a strong position with his left on the fortified town of Oguella and his right on Elvas, the 3rd Division being near Campo Maior in the centre of the position.

On 23 June the two French marshals made a reconnaissance of Wellington's position but did not much like what they saw and refrained from attacking it; in the meanwhile time was, as usual, against them, for their supplies began to run out; and on 24 June Soult, seriously worried by news of the successful activities of the guerrillas in his beloved Andalusia, broke up the combination by announcing that he must return there at once. Marmont was furious at what he considered to be a betrayal and the two quarrelled bitterly in the manner of French marshals; Soult finally had his way although he condescended to leave 15,000 of his troops behind to help Marmont and marched south with the remainder on 28 June, leaving Marmont to do the best he could.

Wellington soon learnt of Soult's departure but was not at first sure how many troops had gone with him, so that both armies remained for some time facing each other, a state which the exasperated Picton, still seeking glory, described as 'undergoing all the disagreeable and inactive routine of garrison duty, although with an enemy's force more than one fourth larger than our own immediately in our front'. The deadlock was inevitably broken by the French, who on 15 July were driven by shortage of supplies to seek better foraging grounds in the valley of the Tagus, upon which Wellington withdrew the bulk of his army into cantonments along the Portuguese border in the area of Castelo Branco and Estremoz, the 3rd Division being at the former.

The stay there was not of long duration, for Wellington very soon decided to lay siege to Ciudad Rodrigo and in order to achieve this he at last had his battering train disembarked from its ships at Lisbon, where it had lain for so long, and brought forward to him. This operation was necessarily a long one, however, so while the heavy guns were being brought forward painfully over the rough roads he placed the fortress under blockade. By 2 August the Light and 3rd Division, plus a brigade of cavalry, had effectively cut off Ciudad Rodrigo from all communication with the French.

Picton, in a letter of 12 August to his friend Marryat, surmised that 'the insuperable difficulty (from the distance and the nature of the roads) to the transporting forward of the heavy ordnance and stores for a siege, will effectively prevent our attacking Ciudad Rodrigo', and fully expected to push forward to Salamanca. This letter shows very clearly the secrecy with which Wellington conducted his operations and how little he took his generals into his confidence, but in view of their letter-writing propensities this was perhaps wise on his part. Picton then went on to emphasise the necessity for ready cash to prosecute the war, commenting that 'as long as we have money in abundance, supplies of all kinds find us out; but as soon as the means fail us, we are obliged to go the Lord knows where in search of them. Dollars here are the only sinews of War.' As he was writing to a Member of Parliament he may perhaps have hoped that his ideas might be repeated into the right ears at home.

At about the same time he opened his heart to Flanagan, who seems to have been the most intimate of his correspondents, about the unfairness of things generally, and complained bitterly that

> By way of economy we are made to perform the duties of Lieutenant-Generals with all the expense of an increased staff, upon Major-Generals emoluments, and the rising sun concentrates all his rays upon those who have never done an hours service except about St James's. I shall very shortly request permission to retire from his staff and let those who have all the loaves and fishes do the business.

While waiting for the heavy siege guns to arrive from Lisbon the British, most of whom were spread along a line between Fuentes d'Onoro and Fuente Guinaldo, busied themselves with preparations for a siege and when this news reached the ears of Marmont he decided that it would be necessary for him to revictual Ciudad Rodrigo as quickly as possible. He was at first too weak to act against Wellington on his own, but presently General Dorsenne, who had offered his assistance, arrived at Salamanca from the north with some 25,000 men, bringing the total disposable strength of the French to over 60,000. The British were thus considerably outnumbered and the situation was further aggravated by the exceptionally large numbers of sick in the army, due partly to the poor state of the recent reinforcements (many of whom had been at Walcheren) and partly to the recent stay in the unhealthy Guadiana valley. Wellington, who had very accurate information as to the numbers of the enemy, therefore decided not to fight a battle if he could avoid one but to wear down the French (and make them consume their hardly gathered reserves of rations) by skilful manoeuvre, for even if he achieved nothing else the mere fact of keeping a large French force concentrated gave the guerrillas a chance to make headway in those parts of the country thus relieved of their occupation forces.

On 24 September Marmont entered Ciudad Rodrigo with his army and a convoy, but Wellington, in spite of the obvious apprehensions of his generals, made no effort to concentrate his scattered troops, probably believing that Marmont would be content to revictual the fortress and withdraw. This however was not to be the case, for the French marshal, suspecting that the British were widely dispersed, decided on a reconnaisance in force; on the next day, therefore, two strong bodies of French moved out of Ciudad Rodrigo in order to investigate the true position of the British, one going to the west and the other to the south. The first one, which consisted of fourteen squadrons of cavalry, reached Carpio unopposed but pressing forward thence towards Marialva was roughly handled by the British and driven back in disorder. The second one, under Dorsenne himself and consisting of four brigades of cavalry with horses artillery and a force of infantry, was however more fortunate and came near, as will be seen, to achieving a considerable success.

Picton's division, like the rest of the army, was widely scattered, its chief object being to cover the two roads leading from Ciudad Rodrigo to Fuente Guinaldo. Wallace, commanding a brigade in the absence of Mackinnon, was at Pastores on the eastern road with the 74th Regiment and some companies of the 60th under Colonel Williams (recovered from his wound) and behind him at El Bodon was Picton himself with the remainder of the brigade, the 45th and 88th Regiments. The advanced post on the western road was held by the 2nd/5th, with Colville and the remainder of his brigade (the 77th, 83rd and 94th Regiments) some two miles further back.

Wellington was for some time in doubt as to which road Dorsenne proposed to use but presently it became clear that he was on the western one, upon which Wellington reinforced the 2nd/5th, on whom the first blow would fall, with two Portuguese batteries and five squadrons of cavalry, and also ordered up the 77th from Colville. This little force (less the 77th, who were of course still marching hard towards the scene of action) at once took up a position at the top of a long, boulder-strewn slope, admirably designed to disorganise the French cavalry and exhaust their ill-fed horses; on the right were the Portuguese guns with the 5th; in the centre were two squadrons of German hussars; and on the left (and slightly in rear) were the other three squadrons, two of them being of the 11th Light Dragoons and the third German.

Dorsenne's mounted troops were in full view and approaching rapidly but no infantry were visible; Fortesque says that this was because Marmont, fearing a trap, would at first only employ cavalry; but Grattan, perhaps with more reason, says that the French cavalry simply got excited and, advancing much too quickly, left their infantry far behind. Whatever the cause the French were committed to fight with horses and guns only. They came on with great gallantry in the face of heavy and accurate fire from the Portuguese artillery, but being met by the British and German cavalry with equal determination were at first driven back. Presently numbers told, and while the British cavalry were fully occupied on the left and centre a further force of French charged the guns and took them; a few of the Portuguese were sabred round them, but the bulk of them, very sensibly, retired with their limbers and teams behind the 5th Regiment.

The French did not pursue them but contented themselves with milling their exhausted horses aimlessly around the silent battery, cheering wildly. This sight proved too much for Major Ridge, the commanding officer of the 5th, who, keenly aware of the disgrace of losing guns, at once determined to retake them and promptly advanced. The French were taken completely by surprise by this move, for which indeed there were few precedents; a few opened an ineffective fire with carbines and pistols, and a few more (perhaps the sensible ones) retired as fast as they could persuade their mounts to move, but the bulk of them merely sat on their jaded horses, not quite knowing what was likely to happen. They were not left long in doubt; twenty yards from them the 5th halted, raised their muskets, and discharged one devastating volley which cut down half the horsemen where they stood, whereupon the survivors at last galloped off, pursued by the British with the bayonet. The Portuguese then ran back to their guns, which had not even been spiked, and reopened fire, the 77th arrived on the scene, and the situation was thus handsomely restored.

Presently a more formidable enemy made its appearance in the shape of a division of French infantry, while at the same time the cavalry, abandoning costly frontal attacks, began to edge round the British flank; a retirement was thus clearly necessary and the 5th and 77th therefore moved off southwards in a single square, while the Portuguese artillery and the remnants of the British and German cavalry galloped off for shelter behind a square formed by the 21st Portuguese whom Wellington had brought forward from Fuente Guinaldo.

The French horsemen concentrated all their strength against the unsupported British infantry, and it looked for the moment as though nothing on earth could save the solitary square of redcoats. The French cavalry closed in exultantly until presently, with trumpets sounding, they bore down simultaneously upon three sides of the square. The British halted, the muskets came up steadily, and there was a long, breathtaking pause. Then the volley rolled out and the scene disappeared in a wreath of grey smoke which presently cleared to reveal the square not only intact but surrounded by a barrier of dead or dying horses and men which effectively prevented any repetition of the attempt. The French, severely shaken, retired to a safe distance and the square marched coolly off again. Napier was quite overcome with admiration at this remarkable display and, after commenting how vain it was 'to match the sword with the musket, to send the charging horsemen against the steadfast veteran', went on:

> The multitudinous squadrons rending the skies with their shouts closed on the glowing squares like the falling edges of a burning crater and were as instantly rejected, scorched, and scattered abroad; the rolling peals of musketry echoed through the hills, bayonets glittered at the edge of the smoke, and with firm and even step the British Regiments came forth unscathed as the holy men from the Assyrian's furnace.

A good illustration of romantic hyperbole.

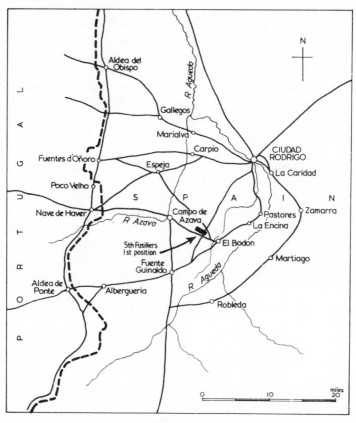

El Bodon

Further south Colville had also started to retreat with his battalions, and he too was attacked heavily but unsuccessfully by the French horsemen; presently he was able to join up with the 5th and 77th Regiments and the whole then continued their dangerous way south while the enemy cavalry, baulked in their attacks on the steady infantry, swarmed over the plain and concentrated instead, on capturing the British baggage. At one stage even Wellington and his staff were assailed by a party of them, and had to draw their sabres and fight their way through them.

While this was going on Picton had with great difficulty extricated the remainder of Wallace's brigade from El Bodon, for the village was full of enclosures and surrounded by vineyards, which hampered movement considerably. At one stage in the confusion the 88th were left behind in a maze of stone walls and seemed likely to be cut off, but the Irishmen succeeded in breaking through these barriers and were presently able to form in quarter-column and march off after their comrades. The men were as usual in tearing spirits and spoiling for a fight, and as they marched they jokingly assured their officers that if the French would but charge every one of them should have a horse to ride for the rest of the campaign. The French however had realised the futility of charging the red squares.

At this stage of the battle the whole of the 3rd Division (less the 74th and the companies of the 60th which had been cut off in Pastores) was retiring steadily across the plain under the irritating but fortunately ineffective fire of the French horse artillery. Picton, careless of the prowling French horsemen, rode backwards and forwards from one brigade to the other, restraining the impetuous, encouraging the nervous, and advising everyone, with many tremendous oaths, to maintain correct dressing and distance in their columns so that they could form square quickly if necessary. Donaldson reported with a certain sober satisfaction that the nervous and unpopular captain in temporary command of the 94th was told sharply by Picton: 'Never mind the French, mind your Regiment; if the fellows come here we will give them a warm reception.'

He rode the last mile or so beside the 88th, and Grattan related that when they were very close to Fuente Guinaldo

> Mountbrun, impatient lest we should escape from his grasp, ordered his troopers to bring their right shoulders and incline towards our column; the movement was not exactly bringing his squadrons into line but the next best thing to it, and at this time they were within half-pistol shot of us. Picton took off his hat, and holding it over his eyes as a shade from the sun looked sternly and anxiously at the French. The clatter of the horses and the clanking of the scabbards was so great when the right half squadron moved up that many thought it was the fore-runner of a general charge; some mounted officer called out 'Had we better not form square?'—'No' replied Picton, 'it is but a ruse to frighten us, but *it won't do*'.

He was quite right, for at that moment a strong force of British cavalry rode up, at which the French withdrew.

Incredibly enough the casualties in the 3rd Division did not exceed sixty altogether; at first it had been thought that the troops left in Pastores would inevitably be killed or captured, but with great judgement they crossed the Agueda and by a long march south-west eventually rejoined the main army having, for good measure, captured a small French cavalry patrol en route.

The day's operations presented several remarkable features, not least of which was Wellington's apparently reckless refusal to concentrate even a part of his army in the face of Marmont's threat, but once the fighting had started the affair is chiefly notable for the consistently excellent conduct on the British side. The cavalry fought superbly against heavy odds, and Ridge's sudden audacious dash at the French horsemen was a fine achievement, while the subsequent long, unsupported march of the squares across an open plain swarming with French cavalry and artillery provided a remarkable example of steadiness and discipline. It was essentially the sort of affair at which Picton excelled—a close battle, almost medieval in character, in which his quick eye, confident bearing, steady courage, and loud voice were all displayed to their best advantage.

By the evening of the 25th, Wellington had taken up a strong position at Fuente Guinaldo with such troops as he had but he was still very thin on the ground. Craufurd was, as usual, late in coming up with his division; he had almost been cut off during the day's operations but had withdrawn in time and then, disliking the prospect of a night march, had waited until dawn on the 26th before resuming his march back to the army. Wellington was furious, although his anger seems to have made little, if any, impression on the erring but unrepentant commander of the Light Division.

Marmont spent the whole of the 26th in bringing up his army to face the British and both sides anticipated a battle; as it happened, both commanders had the same idea, namely to retreat, and during the hours of darkness of the 26th/27th the two armies turned their backs on each other and stole away. Marmont's rearguard discovered the British withdrawal, and Marmont then made a considerable attempt to change his own retreat into a pursuit, but, as he was only able to despatch two infrantry divisions and a few cavalry after the British, they were not seriously pressed. There was a somewhat inconclusive action at Aldea-de-Ponte on 27 September, but by next day, Wellington had retreated as far as he intended and was in a remarkably strong position across a bend in the Coa with his right on Quadrazaes and his left on Rendo. The river thus protected both flanks admirably, while the stretch behind him, being everywhere fordable, did not bar his further retreat should it become necessary.

There was, however, no question of any further retreat, for Marmont, having examined the British position, disliked what he saw and at once drew back; he was also so short of rations that he was compelled to allow his army to consume a good part of those intended for Ciudad Rodrigo and this fact further influenced him in his decision to break off operations. The net value of his campaign was therefore slight; he had left a few extra provisions in Ciudad Rodrigo, he had destroyed a good many British siege stores, had driven a part of Wellington's army back for some miles, and captured some baggage. He might however have achieved a much greater success against the scattered British, and the fact that he did not do so is largely due to the gallant conduct of Picton and his men.

By the beginning of October 1811 Marmont's army was back in the area of Talavera, widely scattered as usual in its unceasing search for food, while Dorsenne had returned to the valley of the Douro, so that Wellington was able to canton his army south and west of Ciudad Rodrigo without much risk and resume his interrupted preparations for a siege. The 3rd Division was in the general area of Aldea-de-Ponte, its headquarters being at Albergueria, and it seems that Picton enjoyed the comparative rest of cantonments. He was quartered in the curate's house and had to pass through the curate's bedroom to reach his own with its usual 'straw bed and a couple of blankets'. 'In point of living', he told Flanagan in a letter of 5 November, 'we are not quite so badly off. I have a flock of excellent sheep which afford mutton fully equal to the best in Wales or Scotland. We have also abundance of good beef and pork.' He added sadly, however, 'we get no kind of bottle wine under five shillings a bottle, and even that is generally very indifferent'.

Having less to do than usual he was also able to devote some time to the interests of his staff and made considerable efforts to get Tyler a captaincy. He also noted without further comment the arrival of another ADC, a lieutenant Taylor, and one may wonder whether the similarity of names led to any confusion.

Whilst at Albergueria Picton learnt that his old uncle the general had died on 14 October at the age of 87, and although not a demonstrative man he was noticeably, and understandably, upset by this news. He had been the old man's favourite nephew, had learnt much of his early business under him in the far-off days in Gibraltar, and it had been he who had provided funds for the legal expenses of the Calderon trials; after the first shock however the sadness was perhaps softened by the news that the old soldier had left him his entire estate.

Other financial benefits accrued in the same period, for he was finally appointed local lieutenant-general with effect from 6 September 1811, while his service was also rewarded by the colonelcy of the 77th Regiment which, with the 5th, had behaved well at El

Bodon. These marks of favour may perhaps have caused him to modify the rather harsh views on patronage which he had expressed so forcibly to Flanagan a little earlier.

Towards the end of 1811 Napoleon (who had an irritating habit of trying to run the Spanish war from Paris) ordered Marmont to detach a considerable part of his army to the assistance of Suchet, who was making good progress against the guerrillas in eastern Spain, and also withdrew several veteran French regiments for his coming campaign in Russia. When Wellington heard of this he decided that if he moved quickly he might be able to seize Ciudad Rodrigo and thus secure one of the two principal routes into Portugal, and in spite of the cold weather he at once commenced operations against that fortress with the 1st, 3rd, 4th and Light Divisions, Picton's being at Martiago and Zamarra.

Ciudad Rodrigo was a strong fortress standing on high ground on the north bank of the Agueda. It was well fortified and well supplied with artillery (since in addition to its normal armament it held the siege train of the army in Portugal) but its garrison was rather too small for the extent of the works; nor, for reasons already known, was it well stocked with food. Its chief disadvantage however was that it was over looked from the north by a considerable piece of high ground, known as the Great Teson, at a range of little more than 500 yards. This high ground was crowned by a strong outwork and this work in its turn was supported by the fire of two other strongpoints, both converted convents, one, that of San Francisco, being some 400 yards to the east and the other, Santa Cruz, about 700 yards south-west.

On 8 January Wellington reconnoitred the place carefully and soon came to the conclusion that the proper approach to it was from the north; his reasons for this were sound and can be best made clear by a brief account of the normal methods of conducting a siege.

The besiegers, having decided their best point of attack, would then establish themselves as close to it as they could by digging for themselves, secretly and at night, a long cover trench, which, being usually parallel or nearly so to the face selected for attack, was always referred to as the 'first parallel'. While this was being done a covered communication trench was also dug back to some convenient piece of dead ground where an engineer and artillery pack could be formed under cover. The besiegers then sapped forward and dug a second (and if necessary a third and even fourth) parallel, the object being to provide a covered forming-up place for the assault troops as close to

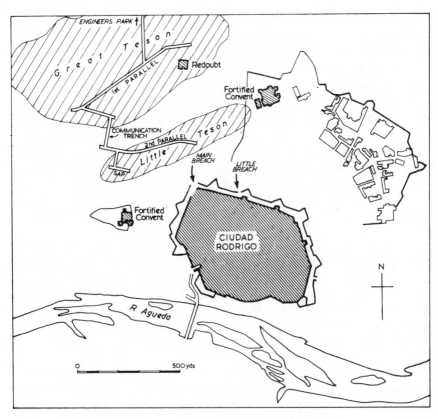

Ciudad Rodrigo

the point of attack as possible. At the same time parts of a suitable parallel would be converted into batteries whence the siege guns could batter a breach in the fortress wall. The engineers would then construct a small sap right up to the near face of the ditch (known as the counterscarp) and there sink a mine charged with powder. When the part of the wall selected for attack collapsed it usually partially filled the ditch with rubble thus offering a rough but practicable ascent to the breach, and just before the assault the counterscarp would also be blown in to provide a similar sort of descent into the ditch. The assault was then launched. It was also usually desirable to arrange for some diversionary attacks elsewhere with a view to dispersing the garrison. No fortress ever had enough men to defend the entire perimeter at the same time, so that if the commander could be kept in doubt as to the true point of attack there was always the chance that it might be only weakly defended at the crucial moment.

At first Wellington decided to establish his first parallel on the Great

Teson and then sap forward to the Lesser Teson, a similar but slightly lower feature 100 yards or more closer to the wall. Here he would establish his batteries, since the range, a bare 400 yards, was well within the capacity of his siege guns, while the height of the feature offered the gunners excellent observation. The dead ground on the north side of the Great Teson was also admirably suited for an engineer park. Before any of this work could be put in hand, however, it was of course first necessary to master the redoubt, and on the night of 8 January 1812 ten companies of the Light Division under Colonel Colborne made a surprise attack on it and entered it by escalade (by climbing its walls on scaling ladders) in twenty minutes. A strong working party then at once dug furiously on the parallel and by dawn all were well under cover.

Thereafter operations went fairly well; trench work was always unpopular with the British soldier, but as each of the four divisions spent one day in the trenches in turn the men at least got some rest. The ground was rocky and frozen hard, which also made progress slow, but Santa Cruz was taken on 13 January and, in spite of a brisk sortie by the defenders, the second parallel, about 250 yards from the point selected for breaching, was well established by the night of 15 January.

Wellington then began to worry about the amount of time he had left, for the French were reported to be on the move towards their threatened fortress, and after consultation with the engineers, none of them very experienced, he decided to make two breaches as quickly as possible with batteries on the Great Teson and assault them out of hand without constructing any closer parallels or batteries or even mining the counterscarp. By 18 January two practicable breaches had been made, on which heavy and continuous fire was directed that night so as to prevent the French from blocking them; and on the 19th Wellington ordered that the assault should be made that evening. Picton's division was selected to attack the larger of the two, known as the great breach, while the Light Division was to assault the smaller one. The plan, as far as the 3rd Division was concerned, was as follows: the 5th and 94th Regiments of Campbell's brigade were to clear any enemy posts from the ditch and the counter-guard (the revetted earth rampart protecting the base of the masonry wall) with the 77th in reserve, while simultaneously a forlorn hope under Lieutenant Mackie of the 88th was to assault the breach, followed first by a storming party of the light companies of Mackinnon's brigade and then by the remainder of his troops. The assault on the breach was to be preceded by a party of unarmed soldiers carrying hay-bags to throw into the ditch so that the stormers could leap in safely, for it must be remembered that as the counterscarp had not been blown the drop in the ditch was considerable. Similarly detailed orders were issued to the Light Division for its attack on the lesser breach.

Just before the assault was due Picton rode round to the different battalions of his division on his hog-maned cob and had a few words with each; his address to the 88th in particular was as short as it could be, for all he said was 'it is not my intention to expend any powder this evening. We'll do this business with the cold iron'—a statement which Grattan says evoked a roar of cheering from the excited Irishmen.

The attack started well; the 5th and 94th crept out silently and, sliding into the ditch on either side of the great breach by means of ropes tied to pickaxes, soon cleared both it and the counterguard, after which they converged on the breach. Here, to their great astonishment, they found that they had done their work so quickly that the stormers had not arrived, whereupon Colonel Campbell of the 94th, anxious that there should be no unecessary delay, at once launched his battalion into the breach, closely followed by the 5th. The stormers then arrived and with a great cheer the whole mass went scrambling up the uneven slope of rubble to the gap in the wall. This attack was met by a heavy and concentrated fire from the enemy defending the breach, but was pressed on resolutely, thus causing the French to withdraw. Unfortunately, a French magazine then exploded accidentally, killing many of the attackers (including General Mackinnon) and for a second the attack wavered, at which the defenders counter-attacked resolutely. The British quickly recovered, and again drove the French back, although they suffered appalling casualties from two well-served guns firing grape at point-blank range until three gallant Irishmen of the 88th flung themselves forward and slew the gunners with their bayonets; the attack was then finally successful.

The assault on the lesser breach was similarly successful and although it started rather late for some reason the Light Division, who it should be said suffered relatively few casualties, were into the town before the 3rd, although with the loss of their commander, Craufurd. Robinson, anxious as usual to praise the 3rd Division, says that the attack on the great breach drew off many of the defenders of the lesser breach and so materially assisted the Light Division and this may well be so although Grattan, himself a strong 3rd Division man, says very definitely that once the Light Division had carried their

143

breach 'they made all the dispositions necessary to ensure their own conquest, as also to render every assistance in their power to the 3rd Division'. Picton, as after Bussaco, gave the credit to his own division and in a letter to Marryat on 27 January said that 'the Third Division had by far the most difficult attack on the main breach where the enemy were most prepared . . . The Light Division *shortly afterwards* seconded in the attack allotted to them.' His letter to Colonel Pleydell two days later is not quite so definite but says (in relation to his own attack) that 'about this time the Light Division, which was rather late in the attack, succeeded in getting possession of the breach they were ordered to attack'. On balance it thus seems probable that the success of the two divisions was practically simultaneous. One most interesting feature of the assault is Grattan's description of the joy with which the men of the 3rd Division saw that they were to fight side by side with the Light Division for 'we were long acquainted, and like horses accustomed to the same harness we pulled well together'—a remark which shows that the two divisions were by no means disposed to behave to each other as their commanders did, but were clearly on excellent terms.

The troops of both divisions, once into the town, passed completely from under the control of their officers and gave themselves up to an orgy of drink, loot, rape and arson; there was perhaps some slight precedent for this, for certainly a number of regimental officers looked upon it as a sort of reward to their men for good service, but quite definitely there was no official approval. Wellington was furious but, for the moment, helpless, for it seems probable that he was surprised by the reaction of the troops and had taken no previous steps to prevent it; this (if so) is strange, for he had seen fortresses stormed in India and might have been expected to know what would happen. Picton at least was in no doubt as to what to do, for when he reached the main square, which was full of riotously drunken soldiers all firing their muskets blindly into the air, he at once took positive steps to deal with the situation: Kincaid, who was present, noted admirably how his voice 'with the power of twenty trumpets, began to proclaim damnation to everybody', while a number of officers, seizing the barrels of broken muskets, finally restored a semblance of order by the simple means of clubbing every soldier they could reach who attempted to load his musket. This was of course the sort of situation which Picton could handle, and one can easily imagine his tall powerful figure laying about him with the stick he habitually carried, and cursing furiously the while. It must have taken his mind back to the incipient mutiny in the 75th nearly forty years before.

By dint of great exertions on the part of Picton and the other officers, order was more or less restored by noon on 20 January, but the Irish were still full of themselves, for when Picton rode past the 88th he was greeted with shouts of 'We gave you a cheer last night; it's your turn now', whereupon he smiled, took off his hat and roared 'Here then you drunken set of brave rascals, hurrah! We'll soon be in Badajos.'

Later that day he gave more concrete approval of the conduct of his division; while visiting his troops before the attack he had promised the storming party of the light companies of Mackinnon's brigade a guinea apiece if they were the first to carry the breach; as it happened, the 94th and 5th had got there first, but on 20 January he generously announced in divisional orders that the money they would have had—about 300 guineas—would be divided among the British regiments to drink the health of the 3rd Division.

His letters of the period still made constant reference to the state of his eyes, which were so bad that he could only read with great difficulty. They were particularly affected by bright sunlight (it will be remembered how at El Bodon he shaded his eyes with his hat in order to observe the French although they were only a half-pistol shot, a very few yards, away), and it is for this reason that from the spring of 1812 onwards he wore a broad-brimmed beaver hat with his blue frockcoat instead of the more orthodox cocked hat. Over the years tradition, always ready to improve on the truth, converted this head-gear into a top hat, but this is improbable. The beaver hat was popular with shooting men, amongst which Picton numbered himself, and it seems logical that he should have considered it suitable for service wear.

This departure from regulation might have been regarded with disfavour by some commanders-in-chief, but Wellington was of all men the least insistent on uniformity in dress, with the result that many officers wore the most remarkable and unsuitable garments without any comment from their superiors. Some generals, it is true, were stricter than others and did what they could to enforce some degree of uniformity but Picton was not amongst them; his attitude to the whole thing was summed up by his single terse comment 'I don't care how they dress so long as they mind their fighting', and this attitude of course soon affected the whole division. Indeed one writer asserts that Picton and his personal retinue were known, from their disregard for the niceties of dress, as 'The Bear and the ragged staff'!

CHAPTER 11

BADAJOS

Marmont was horrified by the unexpectedly quick fall of Ciudad Rodrigo, for in 1811 it had taken the French twenty-five days to master it against a scratch garrison of untrained Spaniards and he had expected, reasonably enough, that a French garrison might have held out for a great deal longer than the twelve days it took Wellington to recapture it.

As soon as he had got over his first astonishment he ordered a concentration; but this was easier said than done, for the weather was very bad and the French, as usual, short of food. Nevertheless by great efforts he eventually assembled a reasonably strong force and scraped together a few siege guns (for his own had been captured in Cuidad Rodrigo) in the hope that he might get an opportunity to retake the place. His chances were in fact slight, for the usual shortage of food soon caused him to disperse his army before it starved.

Napoleon was at first extremely angry over the whole affair and issued a series of furious, and contradictory, orders on the subject, but his fury did not last. At the time he was fully involved with his projected invasion of Russia, for which he continued to draw veteran regiments from the Peninsula, to the dismay of his generals there, and was not inclined to have his attention distracted by affairs in Spain. Soult was particularly perturbed, for being a clear-sighted man he reckoned that Wellington's next objective would certainly be Badajos and he had but few troops to spare to counter any threat to that fortress.

Wellington, as soon as he was convinced that the French were completely immobilised through lack of food, did exactly as Soult feared and on 16 February 1812 set his army in motion southwards towards Badajos. He left his siege train at Ciudad Rodrigo (for the roads to Badajos were atrocious and his draught bullocks weak) and organised a second one composed partly of some new guns just arrived at Lisbon and partly of some borrowed from the Royal Navy.

These latter, as it turned out, were not well suited to siege work, for the Navy in those days preferred to fight ship to ship where speed and gun drill were everything and long-range accuracy unimportant. Wellington must nevertheless have reckoned that they were good enough, for he pressed southwards, and by 16 March Badajos was invested.

The fortress was a strong one; it stood on the south bank of the Guadiana and its eastern face was protected by a stream, the Rivillas, which ran into the main river close to the north-east angle of the works. It was also surrounded by strong outworks; on the north bank of the river there was a fortified bridgehead and a few hundred yards east of it a powerful redoubt, Fort San Cristobal, scene of an earlier British failure. On the east bank of the Rivillas were two more works, the lunettes of San Roque and Fort Picurina, while the southern face of the place was guarded by Fort Pardeleras, whence a system of mines ran west and north to the river. The garrison of Badajos consisted of 4–5000 good troops adequately supplied with food and munitions and under the command of Colonel Phillipon, a brave and enterprising officer.

The British broke ground on the night of 17 March and by first light on the 18th had constructed their first parallel (facing the east side of the fortress) and also a long communication trench running back eastwards towards the engineer park. Fortunately the night was a rough one and the enemy did not detect their presence until the next morning, by which time they were well under cover. The French of course then opened a heavy harassing fire from howitzers and mortars and caused a good many casualties in the trenches, but in spite of this good progress was made until 19 March, when the French made a spirited sortie. On that particular day the working parties were from the 3rd Division, and Grattan, who was in the forward trenches with them, observed so much suspicious activity in Fort Picurina and on the main ramparts that he eventually concentrated his men and ordered them to put on their equipment and load their muskets, with the happy result that when the French did come out they were sharply repulsed and driven back into the town. Soon afterwards Picton galloped up and, dismounting, ran into the trenches where to his great relief he found that all was well. Grattan said that he was lavish in his praise of the men of the working party, and also spoke to him 'in flattering terms'. Being however a true Connaught Ranger (and thus no lover of his general) he added bitterly 'for him', and went on to complain: 'There was an austerity in his demeanour which, even while he gave praise—a thing he seldom did to the

Connaught Rangers at least!—kept a fast hold on him, and the caustic sententiousness with which he spoke rather chilled than animated.' Captain Cuthbert, one of Picton's ADCs, also rode up behind his general but unwisely remained on his horse close behind the battery; here he offered a tempting mark to the French gunners and was almost at once struck on the hip by a roundshot which killed him and his horse instantly, mangling both of them dreadfully. His death was a great loss, not only to Picton but to the whole 3rd Division, for he had been a popular officer with none of the cold and distant hauteur then so often affected by staff officers, and his pleasant easy manner had done more than a little to counteract Picton's austerity.

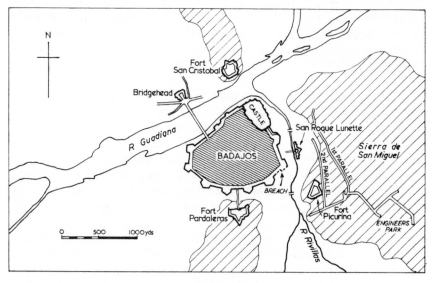

Badajos

Soon after this affair rain fell heavily and continuously and not only interfered seriously with the work but also made conditions in the trenches intolerable, so much so indeed that it was difficult to make the exasperated soldiers do anything at all. Luckily the weather had cleared by 24 March and batteries were then quickly constructed against the outworks of San Roque and Fort Picurina, and fire opened. By the night of 25 March Picurina had apparently been battered into ruins and General Kempt, who had succeeded to the command of Colville's brigade, was ordered to attack it. The rear opening of an outwork, known as the gorge, was usually only lightly protected by a ditch and a palisade, so that if captured it could be fired into easily from the main defences and thus rendered untenable, and Kempt therefore decided to pass troops round either flank of the work so as to threaten its relatively unprotected rear, while attacking it simultaneously from the front. The work was however in a much stronger state than its battered appearance suggested and for some time the issue was in doubt, but finally the attackers succeeded in fighting their way in. Many of the defenders were killed where they stood and a number of others were drowned while attempting to escape across the flooded Rivillas; the British lost just over half their numbers killed or wounded in this short but savage little affair.

This success enabled the besiegers to push forward, and although the fire from the east face of the fortress made Picurina itself untenable they quickly succeeded in constructing several batteries on either side of it, so that presently they were able to open fire against the south-east corner of Badajos.

Wellington then became worried by the movements of Marmont, who had scraped up a few wagons and supplies and was manoeuvring against Ciudad Rodrigo as a distraction to the British commander. He was in fact hardly likely to be strong enough to take the place; but as it was held only by Spaniards, Wellington, doubtless remembering their shameful surrender of Badajos in the previous year, was understandably anxious to bring his present siege to a swift and successful conclusion so as to free his army for more mobile operations.

British guns were carefully laid on the breaches at last light so as to be able to sweep them with grapeshot at intervals during the night, and so disable, or at least discourage, the enemy workmen. The gunners concerned appear to have neglected their duty on occasion, for at the end of March Picton found it necessary to administer a very sharp reprimand in divisional orders.

In spite of all the French efforts, three breaches were eventually made, and as soon as they had been reconnoitred by the engineers and pronounced practicable, Wellington ordered the assault to take place on the night of 6 April 1812. His plan was simple to the point of crudeness, an accusation which was subsequently levelled against it. The main attack on the breaches was to be carried out by the 4th and Light Divisions, while the 3rd Division was given the task of attempting the castle of Badajos (which stood at the northern end of the eastern face of the fortress) by escalade. This attempt was originally designed as a feint to draw defenders from the breaches, but Picton pressed for, and was eventually given, permission to launch a real attack. The 5th Division was to make a wide circuit to the south and then try to force an entry at the west end of the place, while the trench guards were to assault San Roque.

The whole operation presented a number of serious obstacles; the Rivillas, which had been dammed, would be difficult to cross, while the ditch, in which Wellington had planned to form his troops for the final attack, had been flooded. The breaches themselves were also formidable; access to them was difficult and they were all blocked with *chevaux de frise*—logs studded with sword blades—and defended by the most resolute of troops of the garrison, each armed with several muskets and well supplied with bombs, shells and heavy rocks to shower down on the heads of the unfortunate assaulting columns.

The evening of the assault was damp, and a heavy mist concealed the movements of the British. The scene on their side was oddly unwarlike, for the bands played and the soldiers strolled from one to the other and stood in groups of five or six listening to the music. A good many no doubt had a friendly drink together and a few at least sat down and wrote home, while the married men spent what might be their last few hours on earth with their wives and families.

By 9.30 pm the assault columns were formed and stood waiting grimly for the signal to advance. The men looked more like tramps than soldiers, for their faded red coats and patched trousers were filthy after days in the wet trenches and most of them had a ragged fringe of beard which added an extra fierceness to their brown faces. All were eager to begin and Grattan noted that their feelings had risen to a frightful height and that all they wanted after their long weeks of discomfort was to capture the place and sack it, a pastime for which their somewhat amateur first attempts in Ciudad Rodrigo had given them a decided taste. It is moreover very certain that a number of officers saw no harm in this, indeed looked upon a good night of drink, rape, murder, arson and loot as a very necessary incentive to the men for the fearful assault they had first to undertake. The fact that Badajos was a Spanish town and its civilian inhabitants therefore allies was merely unfortunate, although it is perhaps fair to say here that they were strongly suspected (and with some justification) of being Francophile.

A few minutes before 10.0 pm the trench guards stormed San Roque and the assaulting divisions then moved off a little earlier than had been intended. Picton, who had been slightly injured earlier in the day by a fall from his horse, was thus delayed and in his absence

General Kempt led the divisions forward in a solid column headed by the 45th Regiment. Picton, hurrying forward from the rear, reached the head of the column just as it approached the flooded Rivillas, and in the noise and confusion the firing from San Roque led him to believe that the column was moving in the wrong direction. He therefore at once laid violent hands on Lieutenant McCarthy of the 50th, his acting engineer and guide, whom he suspected of leading him astray, and drawing his sabre called him a blind fool and threatened to cut him down. Allowing for a certain natural anxiety, this was remarkably intemperate conduct even for Picton and it is perhaps permissible to speculate that he may have dined a little too well; but, whatever the cause, a sudden shower of fireballs from the castle lit up the scene and Picton, realising that the unfortunate McCarthy was in fact right, at once led his men forward into the flooded stream; it was here, probably, that Kempt was wounded and carried to the rear. The passage across the water was narrow and impeded on the enemy's side by a palisade. There was some hold-up in crossing, during which the division suffered not a few casualties both from the French shot and from drowning. Presently however McCarthy, possibly spurred on by the horrid prospect of Picton's further wrath, managed to get forward with a few men and tear a gap in the palisade, through which the whole division then streamed.

At this moment Picton was wounded in the groin; by his own later account the projectile, possibly already partly spent, was stopped by a bundle of papers in his breeches pocket and did not penetrate, but it rendered him *hors de combat* for the moment.

When this occurred the ladder party, temporarily without direction, reared their ladders not against the castle wall (which was a little further north) but against the curtain wall of the fortress and midway between two bastions. This attack was of course hopeless from the start, for the soldiers were shot down by a heavy crossfire before they could hope to reach the top of the wall; nevertheless they persisted for a long time and suffered hundreds of casualties before they finally withdrew temporarily to the shelter of a convenient mound. Fortunately Picton recovered fairly soon and seeing where the fault lay called for another effort further north. In spite of heavy casualties this appeal was at once answered.

During the time the 3rd Division was engaged in attacking the castle the two divisions detailed for the assault on the breaches had suffered the most appalling casualties without making any headway, and Wellington had eventually withdrawn them. Soon after this had occurred, Tyler arrived with the news that the 3rd Division had captured its objective, while simultaneously the sound of British bugles from the west announced the fact that the 5th Division had also been successful in its gallant attack there. The French then either withdrew or surrendered and the battered 4th and Light Divisions were thus spared the ordeal of a further assault. Instead they scrambled into the town through the silent breaches, which even without their defenders were rough enough to cause them some trouble.

The fall of the castle was due to a considerable extent to the persistent gallantry of Colonel Ridge, who was last met charging the French cavalry at El Bodon. The ladders, often rickety and made of green wood, had been badly knocked about, but three remained and these were eventually reared against the wall of the castle itself. Ridge was the first man up, closely followed by Lieutenant Canch of his grenadier company and his men, together with a savage and desperate crew composed of soldiers from half the regiments in the division.

Donaldson of the 94th, who took part in the attack, said that

> when the ladders were placed, each, eager to mount, crowded them in such a way that many of them broke, and the poor fellows who had nearly reached the top were precipitated a height of thirty or forty feet and impaled on the bayonets of their comrades below; other ladders were pushed away by the enemy from the walls, and fell with a crash on those in the ditch; while more who got to the top without accident were shot on reaching the parapet, and tumbling headlong brought down those beneath them. This continued for some time until at length a few having made a landing good on the ramparts at the expense of their lives, enabled a greater number to follow. When about a company had thus got collected together, we formed and charged round the ramparts, bayonetting the French gunners at their guns . . .

Once into the castle they met another body of Frenchman returning to the attack. These fired a ragged volley (which unfortunately killed the gallant Ridge) and were then swept away with the bayonet, after which there was no further resistance. Lieutenant McPherson of the 45th Regiment, who although wounded had remained in the forefront of the attack, then tore the Tricolour from the flagstaff and hoisted his scarlet coatee in its place, so that at first light it would be seen that the place was in British hands. After the battle he offered the flag to his divisional commander but Picton declined it. Instead he sent McPherson off to Wellington with a strong recommendation that he should immediately be given a company. All he got however was a cordial invitation to dinner, and it was not until 1814 that Picton, meeting the young officer by chance in London and finding him still unpromoted, carried him off then and there to the Horse Guards, where he demanded an interview with the Duke of York. As a result of this McPherson got his somewhat belated captaincy.

The 3rd Division, although firmly in possession of the castle, then found themselves unable to leave the place and break into town, although the reasons for this delay are not very clear. It may have been due to a very natural reluctance on the part of the British senior officers to let their men loose in the town in the dark and before the French had finally capitulated, or it may have simply been due to some lack of initiative. There was apparently no real difficulty in leaving the castle, since Fortescue gives a detailed account of French efforts to recapture it, and it is therefore permissible to suppose that if they could get in the British could get out. It is not known quite where Picton was at this time, for some would have him in the castle and some in the ditch; it seems however unlikely that a heavy, elderly man, suffering from the effects of a violent blow in the groin, could have been hoisted up a flimsy thirty-foot ladder, slippery with blood, in the darkness; and it therefore appears probable that he remained below in the ditch, at least until daylight, which, having regard to the difficulties of communication, would perhaps account for the apparent lack of drive.

Once the town was won things took their normal course and the soldiers, swarming into the place, indulged themselves in a prolonged orgy during which some ghastly horrors were perpetrated. These were chiefly directed against the unfortunate townspeople but even so a number of officers and men who had survived the assault were wantonly shot down by their drunken comrades, some at least while attempting to restrain their worst excesses. Much of the trouble was initially due to drink. Years later Sergeant Costello of the Rifles was to write:

It is to be lamented that the memory of an old soldier should be disturbed by such painful reflections as the foregoing scenes must give rise to; but it is to be considered that the men who besiege a town in the face of such dangers, generally become desperate from their own privations and sufferings; and when once they get a footing within its walls—flushed by victory, hurried on by the desire for liquor, and maddened by drink, they stop at nothing: they are literally mad and hardly conscious of what they do in such a state of excitement. I do not state this in justification; I only remark what I have observed human nature to be on these occasions.

153

The casualties had been horrifying; some 5000 officers and men had fallen, of whom over 700 had been killed outright, while hundreds more died either from neglect or under the knives of the overworked surgeons. So great had been the loss that on 9 April Picton found it necessary to explain to Flanagan that although he had intended to return to England for a visit at the termination of the siege, so many general and field officers had become casualties that he had felt it necessary to postpone the trip until the end of the campaign. He also commented in the same letter that when he had had occasion to visit Wellington on the morning after the assault the usually undemonstrative general had 'shed as copious a torrent of tears as any woman could have done'.

The whole plan of attack was crude in the extreme and deliberately so, for Wellington, before making it, had come to the conclusion that it was necessary to spend lives in order to save time; and once he had come to this conclusion it was then necessary to abandon the sure, well-tried rules governing the conduct of a siege and do the thing by brute force, simply spreading powerful attacks as widely as possible round the perimeter in order to confuse the French and make them overstretch themselves. Necessary or not, however, the assault on the breaches was a fearful waste of lives and difficult to justify.

Robinson was unable to find any letters of Picton's referring to the siege, and conjectured that they had contained such scathing references to its conduct that they had been burned, presumably either by their recipients at Picton's request, or later by some horrified executor as being near-treason. Nor is this conjecture wholly unreasonable, for although Picton had a high regard for Wellington's ability, and from their first contact went out of his way to praise him in his letters home, this would not have stopped him from delivering what he considered to be a fair critiscism. Wellington was never at his best in the conduct of formal siege operations and Picton, a well-read soldier with some pretensions to military knowledge, must have realised this. The only comment of his that is still on record is in his letter of 9 April, just quoted, where he noted, perhaps ironically, that 'military reputation is not to be purchased without blood, and ambition has nothing to do with humanity.' In spite of all his doubts, however, he was justifiably proud when he heard that Lord Liverpool had made a glowing reference to his part in the capture of Badajos in the House of Lords on 27 April 1812.

It was three full days before the fearful saturnalia of Badajos ended, and even then they seem to have petered out chiefly because of the extreme exhaustion of the participants.

That this terrible aftermath dimmed the glory of the siege somewhat is undeniable; yet even so it must for ever remain one of the most remarkable feats of arms ever achieved by the British army. If anyone should doubt this, let him go to Badajos and see for himself. The ramparts where the breaches were made have been cleared to make way for a new road into the town but the old castle stands much as it did. Even on a peaceful summer's evening the walls rise from their steep rock base like a cliff so that a modern soldier, highly experienced though he may be, can only wonder how the thing was done.

The French reaction to the loss of Badajos was of course considerable. Soult may have got some slight satisfaction from being able to say, 'I told you so', but was quite unable to do anything constructive, for his available troops were fully occupied either with the siege of Cadiz or in guerrilla hunting and he had none to spare for any operations further north. Fortunately Marmont was in a somewhat better position to act; he was not strong enough to tackle Wellington directly, but he was able to menace Ciudad Rodrigo to such effect as to cause Wellington to march north and drive him away. The French general then very sensibly withdrew before him and placed his army in cantonments round Salamanca where Wellington, satisfied with having driven him from the Portuguese frontier, made no further attempt for the moment to molest him. Instead he placed his own army into rather scattered cantonments round Fuente Guinaldo and contented himself with sending Hill off on a raid to destroy the bridge over the Tagus at Alamaraz.

This bridge, which was strongly protected at each end by permanent works, was an important point on the line of communication between Marmont and Soult, and Hill's successful capture of it on 19 May thus forced the French to communicate via Toledo, much further east. Nor could they do anything to restore it, for their only pontoon bridge had been captured in Badajos. This move southwards of Hill's was at first interpreted by Soult as being the beginning of an attack on Andalusia and caused him much worry until it eventually became apparent that this was not so. Wellington, being for the moment untroubled by the French, was able to start making preparations for his eventual move into the heart of Spain. The fact that he had both the great frontier fortresses firmly in his possession made it possible for him to move his bases and supply depots well forward while at the same time he had considerable work done on the roads, rivers and bridges between the frontier and Lisbon so as to improve his communications with the coast.

He then decided to move again against Marmont; the Spanish authorities rather objected to this, for they were anxious for him to drive the French out of Andalusia, but he decided against this course for two reasons: firstly because the siege of Cadiz and the guerrillas tied down between them a very considerable force of French; and secondly because if he spent too long in the south it would allow time for the harvest to ripen in the north and so enable Marmont, his chief opponent, to collect enough food to allow him to embark once more on offensive operations.

Wellington's planning was helped very much (although even he, with his excellent intelligence service, can hardly have realised quite how much) by the almost constant dissent amongst the French generals. King Joseph was theoretically in supreme command, with Jourdan as his chief of staff, but as the other French generals all declined firmly to obey his orders (unless it happened to suit them to do so) it cannot be said that he exercised much effective control over them. Napoleon was far too busy with his Russian campaign to spare much time for the Peninsula and his generals (who feared him but no one else) had thus come to look upon themselves as virtually independent rulers who might co-operate with each other by mutual agreement but could not be compelled to do so.

As soon as Wellington's preparations were made he set off to find Marmont and on 22 July the two armies met in a natural amphitheatre a few miles south of Salamanca. The battle ended in a victory for the British and it was the 3rd Division, falling like a thunderbolt on the over-extended French left wing which contributed largely to this great success. On that occasion they were however under a fresh commander, for a few weeks earlier Picton had finally been compelled by reasons of ill-heath to hand over temporarily to Major-General Edward Pakenham, elder brother of Hercules, his DAAG, and retire to his bed. He had not been well for some time and the combination of his eye trouble, several recurrences of Walcheren malaria, and the wound received at Badajos, had proved too much for him. He was then fifty-four and much of his life had been spent in unhealthy places at a time when medical science was still in its infancy, so it is not suprising that his constitution had been badly affected. Apart from his poor physical condition, he was also at that time very low and depressed and, although this is a common after-effect of malaria, it also seems possible that the appalling losses at Badajos worried him rather more than he cared to admit. So much so indeed that on 24 June he wrote to Marryat:

I am perfectly tired with the movements and fatigue of this unceasing kind of warfare, in a country where we are exposed to every kind of privation, and, I may almost say, want. I mean to make by interest, as soon as I find a favourable opportunity, for someone to succeed me in command of the 3rd Division.

He lay ill for some time in Spain and it was during this period (according to Robinson) that a young officer of the Rifles, on being allowed in at his own earnest request to see him, burst into unmannerly laughter at his gaunt, grey and woebegone face under its huge nightcap and had to be ushered out hastily before the weak but furious general could struggle to his feet and seize his sword. Three years later at Waterloo, this same young man (who had in the meanwhile risen by interest to the command of a battalion of Guards) attempted some civility to Picton and was very severely snubbed for his pains.

A little while afterwards he was sufficiently recovered to return to England, accompanied by Tyler, and take a course of the waters at Cheltenham, after which he retired to Wales. Here he busied himself with his estate and amongst other things sold a farm for two thousand pounds which he at once lent to Flanagan to enable him to overcome some financial embarrassment and continue his forensic studies, assuring him in the most generous way not to distress himself about the interest until the returns from his legal labours enabled him to do so without inconvenience. He also visited Ishcoed, once the seat of the family, which he described as being 'certainly one of the most beautiful places in the Principality; combining all the advantages of wood, water and diversified scenery'. He went on to say that 'the house is a mere shell and will require very considerable repairs before it will be inhabitable'. It is apparent from his letters that he was quite prepared to carry out any necessary work.

It looked for some time as though he had finally decided to abandon his military career but presently, as his health improved, he began to think again about returning to Spain. On 1 February 1813 he was summoned to Carlton House and there invested with a Knighthood of the Bath in the most handsome manner by the Prince Regent; they must have made an odd couple, the fat, witty poseur and the gaunt, austere general, but apparently Prinny turned on his famous charm, for almost immediately Picton, now the proud possessor of the 'Red Ribbon' which he had earlier affected to despise, applied to return to the army in Spain.

Much had happened there in his absence. Wellington, after consideration of the several courses open to him after his success at

Salamanca, eventually decided to march to Madrid and on 12 August 1812 entered that city, King Joseph and his army having withdrawn. One of the results of the British move was that Soult, acting, though reluctantly, on Joseph's orders, raised the siege of Cadiz and withdrew northwards to Toledo, thus finally leaving Andalusia in the hands of the guerrillas.

Wellington then advanced and laid siege to Burgos, but although the place was weak he was unable to take it; he was short of siege guns and his men were exhausted after months of hard work. On 22 October 1812 he raised the siege and withdrew. He was at once pursued by Clausel, who had reinforced and reorganised his army, and simultaneously the combined forces of Joseph and Soult advanced on Madrid. Hill, who had been left in command in the capital, was too weak to resist them and therefore withdrew north-west to rejoin Wellington near Salamanca, thus leaving the unfortunate city of Madrid again in the hands of the French. Wellington, having been rejoined by Hill, offered battle near Salamanca but the French, very sensibly, preferred to manoeuvre against his line of retreat, as indeed Wellington had done against Masséna in the pursuit from Torres Vedras the year before.

Wellington conducted the retreat with his usual great skill. His reputation stood him in a good stead, for the French had developed a healthy respect for his ability and seemed content simply to shepherd him out of Spain. This was just as well, for the British were short of rations, exhausted by their exertions and harassed by bad weather, and in these conditions their discipline began to fail as it had done in Moore's army some four years before. Fortunately as it turned out, conditions on the retreat did not compare in severity with those experienced by Moore's army and by 19th November the British, less it must be said a disgracefully large number of stragglers, were safely behind Ciudad Rodrigo, upon which the French withdrew and both sides presently went into winter quarters.

The British retired to their old familiar billets along the Portuguese border, where they settled down to the rest and refit which they needed so badly. Their magazines were full, stores of all sorts (including wine) were plentiful and they seem to have enjoyed themselves thoroughly. The French occupied cantonments round Valladolid and it is to be feared that they were not as comfortable as their enemies, for they were short of supplies of all kinds, their generals were at daggers drawn with each other, and they were practically cut off from France by the operations of the guerrillas, who, sensing that the war was at last going against their hated enemies, had become more active.

CHAPTER 12

VITORIA

When Picton rejoined the Peninsular army in the early spring of 1813, it had fully recovered from the hardships of 1812, and the long spell of rest, recreation, and training had had a most beneficial effect on it, so that it is no exaggeration to say that when it set off a few weeks later for the campaign of 1813 it was at the peak of its efficiency. Not only was it strong in numbers but the quality of its men had also improved. The various measures to stimulate recruiting had on the whole been successful, and in particular many militiamen of good type had enlisted. This is not simply to imply that the soldiers were all angels. They still needed a very strong hand and this they were given. The disciplinary system was ferocious enough, for it was based on death, long imprisonment or the lash, but as this ferocity was much on a par with that of the punishments meted out by civil courts in England few people worried about it. Indeed the better type of soldier welcomed it as being the only thing likely to save him from the worst excesses of the criminal fringe. It must also be remembered that on the whole discipline was administered sensibly. Plenty of men were hanged or flogged, but it was usually for murder, rape or other serious offences against their officers, their comrades, or the inhabitants of the country. The great bulk of crime was of a petty character, and was dealt with adequately by either company commanders or regimental courts martial which administered rough, but on the whole equable, justice.

A great deal of crime was caused by drunkenness. Most Englishmen drank copiously in those days, and in a country where brandy was very cheap and wine virtually to be had for the asking it was impossible to prevent it.

The terrible excesses in Ciudad Rodrigo and Badajos and the heavy loss of stragglers in the retreat of the previous autumn had all been largely due to drunkenness, and there were many men in the army, good enough soldiers otherwise, who would commit any crime from

selling their necessaries to highway robbery for the sake of a few pence
to buy a drink. They had little in the way of other amusements, for
the bleak villages along the Portuguese border offered few amenities,
and although many of the more enlightened regimental officers
encouraged them to dance or play games it is certain that the chief
enemy of the soldier was boredom.

Food played a considerable part in their lives; basically it was very
simple, for the rations consisted of a pound of beef, usually off some
muscular bullock which had marched many miles behind the army,
and a pound of either bread or biscuit. There was sometimes an issue
of a few vegetables or some rice to thicken the soup, and occasionally
coffee was issued to men on particularly arduous duties. That was all,
at least officially, although the soldiers had by then become adept at
discovering ways and means (usually illegal) of supplementing their
rations. In winter quarters there were usually hares or rabbits to be
poached, or pigs or sausages to be stolen from the long-suffering
inhabitants, while in the summer fruit and vegetables were often
available to supplement and vary the diet. On active operations there
was also the chance of looting a French convoy.

In appearance the men had practically ceased to look like soldiers
and had become a strictly 'operational' army, round-shouldered, ill-
shaved, and slouching about in ragged, faded uniforms; they were
however fit and hard and confident and their muskets at least were
always clean and in good order. They never did perhaps quite reach
the excellent standard of marching of the French but much practice
and their series of successes had given them the ability to manoeuvre
with freedom and confidence. The infantry were almost certainly the
best in Europe; the cavalry, although not always well led, were a
formidable, well-mounted body and the artillery were excellent, while
behind the fighting troops there was an extremely well-organised
commissariat system, efficient, flexible and capable of answering any
call made upon it. The famous Doctor McGrigor had done much to
improve the medical system and thereby saved many lives. There
were of course no antiseptics and no anaesthetics; wounds in the
body were frequently fatal, while those in the limbs were often dealt
with by amputation to avoid the spread of gangrene, so that after a
battle the whereabouts of the surgeons could often be ascertained
by the piles of amputated limbs littering the ground around them.
There was no finesse; the patient was thrust on to an impromtu
table, perhaps a door resting on casks, and the limb cut off, and
although the weaker brethren had sometimes to be held down most
men seem to have suffered stoically, chewing a piece of rifle sling or a

bullet to stifle their cries and curses. It says much for their constitutions that many survived, to draw their pensions to a ripe old age and get drunk regularly on the anniversaries of the various great battles in which they had taken part.

The divisional system, although only some four years old, was so highly developed by 1813 that divisions had become almost miniature armies, with a proper proportion of all arms except cavalry. They usually consisted of two British and one Portuguese brigade and two batteries, with a proportion of engineers, medical services, ambulance wagons and commissariat. Every division had its own characteristics and its own nickname (the 3rd bore the proud soubriquet of 'The Fighting Division') and the divisional and army spirit was strong; thus in a few years a loose collection of regiments had been welded into perhaps the finest army that Britain had ever had, and this chiefly by the genius of one man, Wellington.

Picton arrived back with the army in Portugal in the spring of 1813, and if we can believe Robinson the men of the 3rd Division came swarming out to meet him as soon as the news of his approach spread abroad. This may well have been so; 'Old' Picton, as he was always known in the division, was not a man to inspire much love, but he was a just general who did all he could for his men and they appreciated it. He was rough and occasionally severe and he had a splendid flow of language, but they were rough and foul-mouthed themselves and so did not resent it. Perhaps the chief qualities which appealed to them, however, dyed-in-the-wood professional soldiers as they were, were his gallant leadership and his success; they had confidence in him and that was all that really mattered. The Light Division had had the same attitude to Craufurd; for that matter the whole army had that attitude towards Wellington—he beat the French, and that was enough.

After some unavoidable delays the British finally moved off in the third week in May 1813. Wellington's plan was to move his army in two main bodies, one advancing direct in a north-easterly direction upon Burgos and the other making a wide outflanking movement to the north. He himself planned to travel initially with the force moving direct, for he knew that the French would concentrate their attention wherever he was, and thus perhaps not at once appreciate the strength of the northern outflanking wing under Graham. By these means he hoped to press the French steadily backwards, threatening their right flank each time they attempted to stand, from which it will seem that his plan did not differ in essence from the one he had adopted against Masséna in the great advance from Portugal two years before.

Graham's left wing, of which the 3rd Division formed a part, crossed the Douro in Portugal and struck off into the broken, trackless country of Tras-os-Montes; this area had previously been considered as impassable except possibly to bands of lightly equipped guerrillas, but Wellington's army already merited his later description of one which could 'go anywhere and do anything', and all the problems were overcome.

In the meanwhile Wellington moved off towards Salamanca (where Hill joined him from the south) and, as he had hoped, his presence there distracted the attention of the French from the menace of Graham's movement. The French at once began to withdraw under this double threat.

On 3 June 1813 Wellington and Graham joined forces again at Toro, and King Joseph on hearing this news at once began to despatch large convoys of baggage from his headquarters in Valladolid so as to disencumber himself for the battle which he saw would sooner or later be inevitable.

On 4 June the British moved off again, Wellington and Graham being together, with Hill moving to the south of them; and on that day (although of course he did not know until later) Picton became a lieutenant-general in the army; previously he had held local rank in Spain and Portugal only.

The French were, as usual, very short of rations, and because of this were unable to take more than momentary advantage of a number of strong positions which successively presented themselves to them on their line of withdrawal. Even the allied commissariats noticed the considerable strain of the steady movement on their resources, and Wellington was soon compelled to halt for a day or two in order to let his supplies catch up with him. A certain amount of food was available locally but not very much, for the harvest was not yet in so far north. The standing grain luckily provided forage for the animals of the army, but the British soldiers, ever wasteful of other people's property, destroyed much of it unnecessarily so that on 9 June 1813 Mr Larpent, the Judge Advocate, noted with judicial approval in his diary the fact that he had that day seen General Picton preparing to execute a little summary justice on a number of culprits in this respect from his division. Picton had, as always, been particularly careful to guard the interest of the unfortunate inhabitants of the Peninsula against unnecessary depredation, even at the expense of the backs of a number of his more unruly soldiery, and this policy, although not always enforced by other divisional commanders, had the full approval of Wellington; indeed it was only the latter's later rigid insistence on its enforcement that made possible his later invasion of France without the inhabitants of that country rising against him.

Meanwhile the steady move north-east continued and the French, too dispersed and too short of rations to risk a battle, eventually blew up the fortress of Burgos which had given Wellington so much trouble a few months before, and continued their retreat to Vitoria.

It was during the course of this march that Picton lost his temper with Wellington's butler. The headquarter's baggage always considered that it had priority on whichever route it happened to be moving and the butler, confident no doubt in the strength of his position, rashly attempted to remonstrate when ordered to clear the way for the 3rd Division, upon which Picton spurred his cob forward and beat the unfortunate servant severely about the head with, of all things, an umbrella. His reason for carrying such an unmilitary piece of equipment was of course the continued weak state of his eyes which were particularly badly affected by the brilliant sunshine, and although this is understandable he must nevertheless have presented a slightly peculiar figure, even by the lax standards of the Peninsula. Umbrellas were not altogether uncommon there (although not perhaps such an everyday item as some writers would have us believe) and Wellington did not appear to be unduly worried about them within reason, although Captain Gronow records that when the commander-in-chief saw a Guards battalion, in line and under fire, in which almost every officer had an umbrella up, he at once sent an ADC galloping over to tell them sharply not to make themselves ridiculous. He subsequently issued one of his terrible reprimands to its colonel in which he said that 'the Guards may in uniform, when on duty at St James's carry them if they please; but in the field it is not only ridiculous but unmilitary'.

The whole incident of the butler is really little more than light relief except that it does offer yet another unedifying example of Picton's occasional furious outbursts of uncontrollable anger. The butler was presumably a foreigner, since it is improbable that any superior British private servant would have tolerated such treatment as this one apparently did, consoling himself no doubt with the widely held belief that all Englishmen of position were a little mad. Ward, in his *Wellington's Headquarters*, gives a list of the personnel of the head-quarters in October 1813; the name of Wellington is followed by those of Bonduc and Smiley, together with a variety of unnamed footmen and grooms, so it is possible that Bonduc, a French-sounding name, was the individual concerned. Wellington's reaction to the episode, if indeed he ever heard of it, is unknown.

At Palencia, Wellington swung his army northwards off its direct route and into a wilderness of rock and hill; here progress was slow, for the slopes were so steep and rocky that for much of the time the guns and wagons had to be manhandled by the sweating infantry who strained away at the dragropes for hour after hour, tearing the flesh off their hands and the soles from their boots in their efforts to move and control their unwieldy loads.

This departure from the main axis puzzled the French, who for some time lost contact with the British, and at one time King Joseph believed that Wellington might be moving on Bilbao; presently contact was regained and it was then clear that his immediate objective was Vitoria.

Joseph was now in a difficult situation; he had summoned Clausel and his Army of Portugal to join him at Vitoria from Pamplona, and he dared not retire before his arrival lest Clausel should march straight into the arms of the British. In addition to this worry, Vitoria was packed with convoys of loot, baggage, and francophile Spaniards, and Joseph was most reluctant to abandon them; he therefore decided, although not without serious misgivings, to fight a delaying action, and having reached this decision at once placed his army in a strong position a few miles west of the town. Judged as a rearguard position the ground on which the French stood was strong and their dispositions good, but it suffered from the disadvantage that it was overlooked from further west by some high ground held by the British, so that Wellington was able to make a fair assessment of the opposition from long range before committing any of his troops.

The French occupied a bend in the river Zadorra which covered both their front and their right or northern flank, while their left was to some extent protected by a ridge of high ground known as the heights of Puebla. The river was in fact little more than a fast-flowing mountain stream, fordable in many places and crossed by a number of intact bridges, so that its real value as an obstacle was not as great as it first appeared.

The forward French troops occupied some high ground running northwards from the heights of Puebla to the Zadorra, the centre of this particular position being the village of Subijana de Alava, while behind them stood a second line on a second piece of high ground, roughly parallel to the first, on which stood the village of Ariñez; and behind this position was yet a third one, centred on the village of Zuazo. The French were somewhat inferior in numbers to the allies but were unusually well equipped with artillery.

164

Wellington spent 20 June in closing up his troops ready for an attack on the 21st; his plan, based on close observation, was to threaten both flanks of the French and then attack their centre and with this object in view he formed his army in four columns. In the extreme north Graham, with two British divisions, two Portuguese brigades, two cavalry brigades and a considerable force of Spaniards, was to move wide round the right flank of the French and come in almost behind them from the north, while at the same time Hill was to attack their left on the heights of Puebla with his division and Morillo's Spaniards.

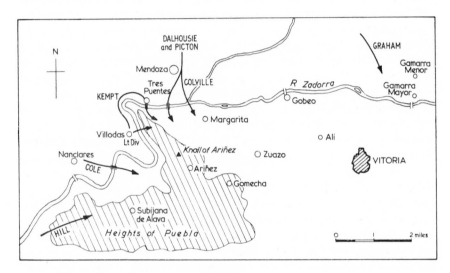

Vitoria

On the left centre of the British attack the 3rd and 7th Divisions under Lord Dalhousie (who normally commanded the latter) were to cross the river and attack the right of the French second line, while on the right centre Cole, with the 4th Division and the bulk of the cavalry, was to turn the left of the leading French troops. In view of the wide frontage on which the British attack was to be launched, co-ordination and control were certain to be difficult so Wellington decided to remain in the centre (whence he could also to some extent control Hill) leaving it to Graham, whom he trusted, to do the best he could on the left.

The first British to be engaged were troops under Hill, who crossed the river at about 8.0 am on the morning of 21 June and at once opened their attack against the French left. Hill's Spaniards assaulted the crestline of the heights while his own 2nd Division advanced against the village of Subijana de Alava on their northern slopes and for a while both parts of his force met heavy resistance until they were finally held about a mile west of the village. The comparative inaction of the rest of the British at this time puzzled Joseph who, in the absence of any positive information, first strengthened his left against Hill. The latter however also brought up his reserves and presently, after more heavy fighting, succeeded in taking the village.

By mid-morning the Light Division was at Villodas, Cole was at Nanclares and Picton with his 3rd Division was at Mendoza, but the 7th Division was delayed for some reason and had not yet reached its appointed position. Presently a Spanish peasant reported to the Light Division that the bridge at Tres Puentes, a couple of miles further north round the bend in the river, was unguarded, whereupon Kempt's brigade was at once sent off to investigate. The statement of the peasant was found to be true and Kempt promptly pushed his brigade across the river with no more opposition than a few random cannon shot (one of which killed the unfortunate Spanish guide) and was soon established unseen in a hollow almost in the centre of the French position where he was quickly joined by the 15th Hussars.

While these operations were in progress Picton, apparently forgotten, was waiting at the head of his division north of the river. He was fuming with impatience and his unfortunate horse stirred restlessly under the ceaseless tapping of his stick on its neck.

Eventually, just as the furious general was remarking to his staff for the dozenth time that Lord Wellington must have forgotten them, they saw a staff officer galloping past in a cloud of dust. He was clearly not interested in the 3rd Division but the great voice of its commander brought him abruptly to a halt. When asked his business the staff officer said that he had a message for Lord Dalhousie to cross the bridge, adding worriedly that he had so far been unable to find him; upon this Picton took these orders upon himself and at once led his leading brigade (Brisbane's) across the bridge of Mendoza while Colville and his men forded it a little further up-stream. Dalhousie then arrived but having lost his place in the order of march was fain to follow on behind the eager Picton.

The French made some effort to oppose this crossing, but were promptly taken in flank by Kempt's riflemen and forced to retire. Simultaneously Cole crossed the bridge of Nanclares quite unopposed and the French, seeing that the line of the river was irretrievably lost, at once started to retire under cover of a strong rearguard posted on the knoll of Ariñez just north of the village of that name, their movement being covered by the fire of no less than sixty guns. The situation then became rather confused and divisional order was to some extent lost, for Dalhousie, with Colville's brigade, was drawn into an attack further north near Margarita while Wellington himself led Picton with Brisbane's brigade of the 3rd Division and Kempt's brigade of the Light against the knoll.

This attack was met by tremendous artillery fire but pressed on gallantly, for it was the sort of uncomplicated fighting which Picton understood and enjoyed. Young Kincaid, a rifleman of Kempt's brigade, later described him as riding at the head of his division wearing a blue coat and a round hat and swearing as roundly all the way as if he had been wearing two cocked ones. There was at least one shothole through the skirt of the blue coat before the day was over.

At last the French began to give way, and presently a charge by the 87th Regiment finally cleared the village after some severe close-quarter fighting in which the British captured three guns; the French made a gallant counterattack to regain them but were unsuccessful.

One interesting aspect of this particular part of the battle is that it was fought over the very ground on which a detachment of an earlier British army had also gained distinction. In 1367 the Black Prince had been pursuing a Spanish army along the same road as the one on which Wellington was pursuing the French (although in the opposite direction) and in order to harry his enemy had sent out small companies of irregular horse to attack him whenever opportunity offered. One of these companies under Sir Thomas Felton made such a nuisance of itself to the Spaniards as they were crossing the Zadora that the latter turned back several thousand men to deal with it. It is not clear whether Felton's company was cut off by this surprise move or merely disdained to retreat, but what is certain is that this handful of a hundred or so Englishmen fought and died with great gallantry on the very knoll of Ariñez taken by Picton 446 years later.

While Wellington's attack on the knoll was in progress, the French further south were also driven back as far as Zuazo, where they turned yet again and fought back fiercely. During these operations in the centre Graham had made his wide outflanking movement to the north and was now pressing the French at Gamarra. There was here, as elsewhere, very severe resistance and for the moment the British made no progress. The attack on Zuazo by the 3rd Division was also held up at first, chiefly by artillery fire, but then Cole brought up his division (which had not been seriously engaged) on Picton's right and together they thrust the French back a further two miles.

Dalhousie and the bulk of the cavalry then rode past the northern flank of this part of the French army and attacked the left of the troops who were holding up Graham. This movement was decisive, for although there was a good deal of scattered, disorganised fighting further east the battle was won; the French contrived to withdraw most of their troops, although they were compelled to leave behind some splendid trophies in the shape of 151 cannon—virtually their entire artillery, for they only succeeded in saving two pieces. There was nearly a spectacular finale when a troop of the 18th Hussars actually made a dash at King Joseph himself, but that unfortunate monarch was just able to elude them by leaving his carriage and galloping away on a horse belonging to one of his staff. The hussars, though they had lost the King, made the best of things by looting his carriage, and it was there that they acquired his silver chamber-pot which is now one of their most cherished possessions.

The French fought extremely well at Vitoria, although they were by no means well handled and their omission to destroy the Zadorra bridges was a remarkable one. They were, it is true, inferior in numbers to the allies but they had a considerable preponderance in artillery, an arm which they habitually used to great advantage, and were in possession of some remarkably strong ground. It seems probable that Graham's attack on their right flank and rear finally demoralised them, but it is difficult to see now why this attack was not successful earlier.

The British were held up for a long period in the area of Gamorra Mayor, and it was not until the defenders there were taken in flank by Dalhousie's division and the cavalry that their resistance collapsed. It is of course very easy to be critical over 160 years later; nevertheless it is interesting to consider that if Graham's force had burst across the river earlier and continued its southward thrust to Vitoria a great part of the French army must inevitably have been captured.

There was no immediate pursuit after the battle, chiefly for the reason that a considerable part of the British army at once dispersed amongst the great convoys in search of plunder. There was a great deal to be had, and something for all tastes. There were carriages full of wives, of mistresses, and of other young women euphemistically described as actresses, so many of the latter indeed that a bitter French officer described Joseph's army as 'un bordel ambulant'; there were wagons full of food, wine, gold and jewellery, and there was load upon load of books, pictures, statuary and rich clothing of all descriptions.

The British soldiers naturally made the most of it; first they plundered the food and wine and sat down to rich and impromptu meals amongst the wreckage and then, having satisfied the inner man, they went off purposefully in search of some more durable souvenirs of the great day, of which there were plenty. Wellington later estimated that about a million pounds went into the pockets of the soldiers; and although Robinson makes him say kindly that they deserved it, it seems unlikely judging from his subsequent fury, that he ever uttered such a remark.

Some men did particularly well; Costello of the Rifles admitted that he was able to load a mule with gold and silver doubloons to the value of £1000 and bring it safely back to camp (after threatening one or two would-be sharers with his rifle). There he left it in the charge of the quartermaster of his battalion, who can hardly have believed it to be anything other than loot.

Some regiments tried to regularise the position by pooling all loot and then making an equitable distribution and Kincaid, with his usual sense of the ludicrous, recounts how his brigade assembled for such a share-out of a number of pleasantly heavy boxes, only to find that they contained hammers, nails and horseshoes.

A few officers joined in the scramble and one at least had a stand-up fight with a private in the German Dragoons who used the most abusive language in the secure knowledge that the officer had, by his own conduct, forfeited any right to take official action against him. Generally speaking, however, officers contented themselves either with food or wine or, at most, a genuine souvenir of the great day, although one or two of the more sophisticated succeeded in acquiring young women, lately the property of the French, who preferred to remain with their new protectors rather than be returned to their original ones. Surtees, a most respectable quartermaster of the Rifles, later commented tartly that 'such is generally the fidelity to be expected from that sort of people'. Genuine wives were treated civilly and sent off as soon as possible after their retreating husbands, indeed one of the peculiar and more pleasant aspects of the orgy of looting was the extremely good-natured way in which it was carried out.

That evening the army held an impromptu market, and as many of the soldiers were wearing magnificent captured French full-dress uniforms, and their wives and followers were similarly decked out in the most splendid dresses, the effect, by torchlight, must have been remarkable.

On 22 June Wellington, having collected his army again, sent Graham off on a wide sweep north while he himself marched for

Pamplona; but the French had had a good start and the British, gorged with food, loaded down with loot, and probably mostly suffering from considerable hangovers, were unable to catch them.

When Wellington reached Pamplona he left Hill to besiege that fortress while he himself marched southward to intercept Clausel; that general, having been unable to reach Vitoria in time for the battle, was marching furiously to avoid being cut off, and this he finally succeeded in doing by swinging far to the south of Zaragoza before striking north again. As soon as Wellington realised that Clausel was beyond his grasp he abandoned the pursuit and returned to Pamplona.

The 3rd Division took part in this march and during the course of it Picton had yet another brush with the Light Division; fuel was scarce, not an unusual thing in parts of Spain, and a party of the Light Division had been authorised to pull down a house in Sangüesa for the sake of the wood used in its construction. This operation had been completed and the party was returning to camp with its load of timber when Picton rode up and in his usual direct way said to the subaltern in charge, 'Well, Sir, you have got enough wood for yours and my Division. I shall have it divided, make your men throw it down. It is a damned concern to have to follow. You sweep up everything before you.' Fortunately for the officer concerned General Alten, commander of the Light Division, then arrived and having had the matter reported to him at once remonstrated forcibly with Picton for interfering with one of his officers in the course of his duty. The argument doubtless grew heated and while it was going on young George Simmons, the subaltern in command of the fatigue party and as shrewd and sensible an officer as ever wore the green coat of the Rifles, quietly ordered his men to take up their loads again and move on, so that whatever the final outcome of the dispute between the generals the Light Division got its full share of firewood.

There was a good deal of manoeuvring for a few days after this but finally the French were able to establish themselves along their own frontier with their right resting on the sea. For once they seem to have had fairly adequate supplies of food, for the Royal Navy was so weak on the Biscay coast that it was quite unable to prevent French supply ships from sailing in. Ironically enough, there were no wagons or pack animals with which to distribute it, so that in spite of relative plenty on the coast there was still much hunger a few miles inland and mobile operations were impossible.

As soon as Wellington received information that the French really were immobilised for lack of food he turned his attention to San Sebastian, a fortress standing on a small peninsula jutting into the Bay of Biscay, which the French withdrawal had left isolated. The siege opened on 12 July and at first sight there seemed to be no reason to suppose that the place would give much trouble. Operations were however indifferently planned and an attack on a barely practicable breach by the 5th Division a fortnight later was beaten back with heavy loss. Wellington was furious about this failure which he attributed, somewhat unfairly, to misconduct on the part of the 5th Division, and announced that when the siege was resumed he would carry out the assault with parties of volunteers from the rest of the army who 'would show the 5th Division how to mount a breach', a remark not calculated to endear him to the members of the formation concerned. In the meanwhile he was constrained by lack of ammunition for his heavy guns to convert the siege into a blockade.

The battle of Vitoria had a considerable effect on the affairs of Europe: it left France open to a possible invasion from the south and it encouraged the other European powers, notably Russia, Prussia and Austria, to ally themselves once again in a last great effort to overthrow their common enemy. Napoleon was greatly put out by the news of his brother's defeat and his first action was to send Soult off as fast as he could post 'to re-establish the Imperial business in Spain'. He then sent orders for Joseph to relinquish his command and remain under what was virtually arrest, and also removed the unfortunate Jourdan from his post as chief of staff. Joseph, not unnaturally, objected so strongly to this indignity that Napoleon gave him leave to retire privately to France, leaving Soult in supreme command of the French forces in the Peninsula. It was by no means a bad choice, for Soult, although a surly, uncouth individual, was a very fine organiser; he was moreover one of the few French generals with previous service in the Peninsula who had not been beaten by Wellington, so that psychologically too the appointment was a sound one.

On his arrival in Spain, Soult at once set about reorganising the French forces there: this in itself was no mean task, for the soldiers as a whole were thoroughly tired of the hunger and hardship of the Peninsula and would have been delighted to be quit of the place for good. Everyone from marshal to private foraged and looted as best they could as a mere matter of survival. One of the most heartening aspects of the matter as far as Wellington was concerned was that even when the French were within their own borders, they still continued this course of conduct and pillaged French villages with as much enthusiasm as those in Spain. Hitherto for many years they had conducted their operations outside their own country, and had made war pay for war without much direct detriment to their own people. Now the case was altered, and the ordinary people of France were at last given a sample of the conduct of their previously popular army, an example which they disliked intensely.

Wellington's reaction to this was to stiffen even more the discipline in his own army, particularly as regards offences against the civil population, and to impress continually on all ranks the necessity for restraint when they finally entered France, so that they might be welcomed by the inhabitants as a pleasant change from their own brigand-like soldiery. If they behaved, if they paid their way and respected the property and people of the country, all would be well. If they behaved badly then the end might be disastrous. Wellington had seen in the Peninsula the effect that guerrillas could have, and he knew only too well that if the people of France rose spontaneously against him all might be lost.

The British for the moment remained stationary, assembling ammunition for the renewal of the siege of San Sebastian and taking other steps in preparation for a resumption of the offensive; amongst these latter was the handing over of the blockade of Pamplona to the Spaniards on 17 July, thus freeing more British soldiers for future operations.

During this period of comparative inactivity, Picton amused himself by composing long letters to his regular correspondents and on 26 July he wrote a particularly scathing one to Flanagan on the subject of the Vitoria despatch which he had just seen. He considered it to be 'like most of the despatches of the noble Marquis, . . . anything but a correct likeness of the event it purposes to relate', his chief objection being that it attributed the success of the action too much to combination and manoeuvre (which he allowed to be excellent) and not enough to hard fighting. The common subject of all his letters was however his eyes and he much feared that the trouble 'from its long continuance, was becoming chronical'; to his old friend Marryat he wrote sadly that 'I must give over the business after the campaign, or it will give me up, which I must not run the risk of'. and it was by then obvious that he had but little hope of a cure.

CHAPTER 13

ACROSS THE PYRENEES

Soult continued his reorganisation of the demoralised French army behind the great mountain barrier of the Pyrenees while Wellington remained inactive on the Spanish side of them. The British general was in a difficult situation, for although the simplest answer to his problem might have been to break Soult's line on a narrow front and invade France, a task within the capacity of his army, there were certain serious objections to this. Militarily he was reluctant to continue to advance with the fortresses of San Sebastian and Pamplona still untaken behind him, or before he had had a proper chance to establish a new and shorter line of communication through a Biscay port; while on the purely political side he feared that current negotiations in Europe would end in an armistice between France, Russia and Prussia which would result in Soult being heavily reinforced to the stage where he could begin a successful counter-offensive. A few months earlier Wellington could have dealt with this in his usual way, but by the end of 1813 things were changing. The Spaniards were delighted that their country had finally been cleared of the hated French, but being natural isolationalists they were by then beginning to show an almost equal dislike of the British. So apparent was this that Wellington believed that if he invaded France and was repulsed, he might find it difficult to withdraw into Spain.

The initiative for the moment was thus with Soult, who could assemble his army anywhere along the line of the Nivelle and thrust back into Spain along several possible routes. The first ten miles or so of the frontier running south from the sea were easily passed; then came the huge natural barrier of the Rhune mountain, after which there were three practicable routes available. The first and most westerly of these was the valley of Baztan, the second the valley of Baigorry and the third and most easterly the road by the valley of Carlos and the pass of Roncesvalles.

The roads on the French side were relatively good but on the

Spanish side they were bad, and there were few lateral communications, those that existed being little better than goat-tracks, so that Wellington was compelled to extend his army along a front of some forty miles of difficult country in order to cover all the possible French lines of advance into Spain. He knew that by doing so he ran the risk of defeat at a certain point but saw no alternative, so on 17 July he handed over the blockade of Pamplona to the Spaniards and having thus freed as many reliable troops as possible for active operations he proceeded to dispose them along the line he had selected.

On the extreme right or southern flank Byng with his brigade of the 2nd Division was in position just north of Altobiscar with a flank guard of one Spanish battalion at Orbaceita; next to Byng's brigade to the north was Campbell with a Portuguese brigade at Aldudes; and further back in reserve at Viscarret was the 4th Division under Cole, who also commanded the whole force.

In the right centre the valley of Baztan was guarded by the remaining British brigades of the 2nd Division, with the cavalry and some Portuguese watching various lesser passes further north, the whole being commanded by Hill. Picton with the 3rd Division was in general reserve to this part of the line, his headquarters being at Olaque.

In the left centre the Light Division was at Vera and the 7th at Echellar, the 6th being in reserve behind them at Sanesteban, while the extreme left was held by Graham, with the force blockading San Sebastian and Longa's Spaniards.

Wellington placed his own headquarters at Lesaca, well towards the north, because he appreciated that Soult's first effort would be directed to the relief of San Sebastian and he therefore wished to be close to the main threat.

Soult's plan however, as it turned out, was to attack Wellington's right to relieve Pamplona, and then to manoeuvre the British out of Navarre by threatening their line of communication through Vitoria; by these operations he reckoned that he might compel the British to fall back to the Ebro, a move which would automatically relieve San Sebastian. In order to distract attention away from his true point of attack he made arrangements to have a pontoon bridge prepared near the coast; this deception succeeded, for Wellington wrongly dismissed the correct reports of a southward concentration as a feint and remained convinced that the main French effort would be made in the north.

Soult's plan was therefore well conceived, but it proved more difficult to put into operation than he had anticipated; this was partly due to the exceptionally bad weather which hampered movement and partly, perhaps chiefly, to the usual weakness of the French, the lack both of supplies and a train to transport them. The French indeed were so hungry and so used to taking what they wanted that when a large number of draught animals were assembled with much difficulty to drag their heavy guns over the pass of Roncesvalles, the hungry soldiers at once fell on them and butchered a number before being driven off by force. It was not an auspicious beginning to Soult's campaign.

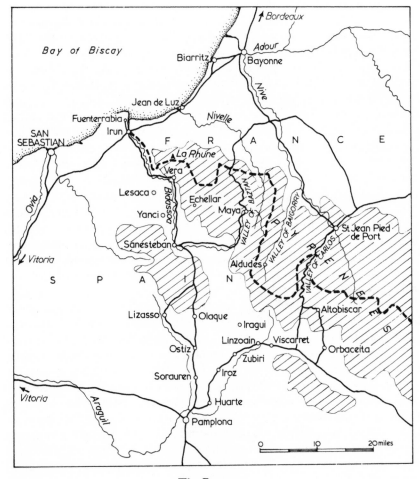

The Pyrenees

Eventually all was finally arranged and on 25 July the French army began its offensive. In the south Reille, with three divisions and some mountain guns, pressed southwards down the ridge of high ground separating Valcarlos and Aldudes, while part of Clausel's force attacked Byng's brigade just north of Altobiscar. This brigade fought with great gallantry but was presently forced to retire to Altobiscar where it again took up a defensive position in the face of the advancing French. The remainder of Clausel's force simultaneously attacked Orbaceita, whereupon Cole, who had of course gone forward to see what was happening, decided that it was necessary to retire to avoid being outflanked. While this was going on Reille had thrust as far south as Lindux, but the crest along which he was moving was narrow and hampered his movements, so that presently the head of his column was fiercely counter-attacked by a bayonet charge of the 20th Regiment of Ross's Brigade and the whole brought to a halt. Captain John Kincaid, the Rifle Brigade diarist, later described this attempt as one of the most brilliant feats of the war. It was delivered by a single company some seventy strong and led by Captain George Tovey, and that officer later recounted that he had lost eleven killed and fourteen wounded of this gallant little force but had destroyed many Frenchmen with the bayonet. The spirit of the affair was well illustrated by one soldier who, retiring after the charge with only the blood-stained socket of his bayonet left on his musket, remarked that he had 'killed away until his bayonet broke'.

By this time it was late afternoon and a heavy fog descended and stopped the fighting; the French then bivouaced where they stood, while Cole retired his force to Linzoain; it is difficult to blame him for this, for he was heavily outnumbered and his right flank had been completely turned. Nevertheless Wellington later censured him for withdrawing prematurely.

In the left centre the French had done well. When the firing started in front of Cole's position in the morning, Stewart, who commanded at Maya, decided for some remarkable reason that he would not be attacked and having withdrawn most of his men from the pass, rode off to see what was happening on his right. As a result, D'Erlon's attack on the position was at first opposed only by the outlying pickets and the light companies of the brigade and these, although fighting furiously, were eventually pressed back by the superior numbers of the French. The remainder of the British scrambled uphill into the fight as best they could, but their efforts were uncoordinated and the French continued to gain ground, although at great cost. At this point Stewart returned and ordered a withdrawal to another position a few miles further back; there he was reinforced by Barnes's brigade of the 7th Division, which delivered a fierce charge and brought the French progress to an end. Wellington later reproved Stewart very sharply indeed for his unwarranted absence at the critical moment and the reproof was well justified, for had he been there to take immediate command in person it is probable that he would have held the French at Maya.

At the end of the first day's fighting Soult was by no means dissatisfied with the overall progress he had made, although in some respects he had not done as well as he had anticipated. He had for example hoped that the threat to the British right would induce Wellington to reinforce it from his centre, that is from the troops at Maya, thus reducing resistance there to a point where D'Erlon could break through. Had this happened he had anticipated that D'Erlon and Reille would then be able to meet somewhere north of Pamplona to concert further plans, but this hope did not materialise. Nevertheless his thrust at Pamplona bid fair to succeed, and with that fortress in his hands he could then, he hoped, roll up the British northwards.

As late as the evening of the 25th, Wellington was still very much in the dark as to what was happening, for the front was a long one and lateral communications on it were bad. He eventually decided to move his headquarters further south to Almandoz, and having sent a message to Picton that come what may he must stand and fight at Zubiri, he rode off southward to see for himself what was happening.

On 26 July the French resumed their attacks and Cole, hard pressed, continued to withdraw to Zubiri where he placed his division in a defensive position; there he was joined by Picton, who as senior officer at once assumed command. Picton did not like the position, and nor for that matter did Cole, but the latter produced a report by one of his staff that there was no other suitable rear-guard position between there and Pamplona.

In spite of this Picton decided to withdraw; he had not received Wellington's message and was extremely afraid that the right wing of the army might be cut off and destroyed. He said later in justification that 'superior numbers made resistance almost hopeless' and this may have been so; it was, nevertheless, unfortunate that the order to fight had not reached him, for it is improbable that Picton would have disregarded it. He was not the man to shirk a battle, but having no broad outline of Wellington's intentions on which to base his own operations he was presumably reluctant to take any action which might prejudice the main plan. It was a well-known weakness of

Wellington that he was always reluctant to tell his generals more than the minimum necessary, and although (in view of their letter-writing propensities) this may have been wise as a general rule, it made it very difficult for them to make any independent decisions when, as was the case here, they were widely spread and faced with a series of rapidly changing circumstances.

Whatever the reasons, the retreat continued with the French in pursuit and there were several partial rearguard actions, notably one at Iroz. Robinson assures us that 'the skill and judgement of Picton stopped every attempt of the enemy to throw him into confusion'; and this, combined with the difficult country, was probably so. The French nevertheless had some reason to be confident, for they found themselves in the most unusual position of driving two British divisions before them without any serious resistance, and soon began to be hopeful that they would relieve Pamplona without a serious fight.

When Picton reached the Spanish outposts blockading that fortress he decided that he had retreated far enough and must stand and fight. His reasons for this sudden decision are not very clear; it may have been that the sight of the Spaniards suddenly brought to him the fact that he, the fighting general, was deliberately abandoning them, or it may have been that he had had the particular position which he eventually chose in mind from the start as a result of some previous reconnaissance of the area. The position he chose was at Huarte, where the two valleys of Baztan and Carlos came together and could thus be covered by a single force; Cole was in position on his left and about a mile forward of him, so that at last the continued withdrawal was over and a battle imminent.

The French then came up opposite Cole, whose position on a piece of high ground just south-east of Sorauren was a particularly strong one; both his flanks were covered by deep valleys while a third also protected much of his front, so that the only practicable approach to his position was by a narrow neck of land on his right, and even this was fortunately occupied by two battalions of the Spanish blockading force, which, having been there for some time, were very firmly established.

Clausel, contemptuous of the Spaniards, at once attempted to force their position with a detachment, but this being sharply driven back he then formed his whole army opposite Cole and prepared to deal with him, having first seized the village of Sorauren and sent off a couple of regiments under Foy to occupy the high ground opposite Picton.

Wellington received no firm news until he got as far south as Ostiz, where he heard that Picton and Cole had retired at least as far as Huarte; he at once sent back orders to halt the troops following him until the situation became clearer, and having done this rode off southwards again as fast as his excellent horse could carry him. By the time he reached Sorauren he was alone except for Lord Fitzroy Somerset, the only member of his staff and escort who had been able to keep up with him. He at once sent this officer back northwards with a message to his Quartermaster-General to push on the 6th and 7th Divisions by a more westerly route and then, quite alone, put his horse at the steep slope which led up to Cole's position. Even as he did so a French cavalry patrol caught sight of him and gave chase, but their ill-fed troop horses were no match for this thoroughbred, tired as it was, and he easily outdistanced them.

His arrival at Cole's division evoked a storm of cheering, for although by no means a popular commander he was a successful one and the men were delighted by his dramatic appearance at the eleventh hour. This uproar did not escape Soult, who was only a few hundred yards away to the north, on the opposite side of the valley, and there was no lack of Frenchmen able to identify for him the cocked-hatted, frock-coated figure which had caused it. The French marshal, although a fine organiser and tactician, was never at his best on the actual battlefield; the unexpected stand of the British had already disconcerted him somewhat, and now, faced with the unpalatable fact that he was about to cross swords with Wellington in person, he deferred his attack until the next day; and even then he made no movement until midday, when the sight of the leading elements of the 6th Division arriving to reinforce Wellington induced him to attack while he still had superiority of numbers.

The attack, when it came, was a complete failure, for although the French advanced with great gallantry many of them were so weak and hungry that they had not the strength to scramble up the steep slope. Those who succeeded in reaching the summit were at once charged by the British and, after a short but fierce fight, sent tumbling down the hill again with heavy losses. By 4.0 pm the battle was over, and the French decisively defeated.

The 3rd Division took no part in this action except for some skirmishing between their outposts and those of Foy, but although the French regiments opposite them were far too weak to attempt anything more than a feint, they did succeed in occupying the attention of the 3rd Division while the main battle was fought out to the north-west.

After the battle of Sorauren, Soult gave up any idea of relieving

Pamplona; he had been fairly beaten by an army numerically inferior to his own, and his troops, whose morale had not been fully restored after the shattering blow of Vitoria, were extremely discouraged as a result. In spite of this he believed that he might yet save something from the wreckage of his original plan by striking boldly across country in an attempt to relieve San Sebastian.

He was chronically short of rations and transport, but in default of any acceptable alternative he was prepared to pin his faith on the known ability of French troops to cover ground swiftly while living on practically nothing. As a preliminary to this new plan he directed D'Erlon (who had just arrived at Ostiz down the valley of Baztan) to move to Lizasso and reconnoitre northwards from there, while to Reille he entrusted the delicate task of masking the withdrawal of the French still facing the British across the deep valley at Sorauren.

The latter movement was a remarkably dangerous one to attempt, since in practice it amounted to making a flank march across the front of a confident and recently victorious enemy. The unfortunate Reille, driven in desperation to try it, was detected in the middle of the movement by Wellington, who promptly launched his troops at him. Picton and his division thrust up the valley of the Arga against the original French left and Cole demonstrated against their centre, while the 6th and 2nd Divisions pressed on after the head of the column. These operations were all successful and the French, almost surrounded, were hustled unmercifully until formation after formation abandoned all semblance of order and fled northwards as best they could, mere crowds of fugitives. They were in such disorder that they took the wrong route and, veering eastwards off their true line, made for St Jean-Pied-de-Port, still pursued by the 3rd Division.

In the meanwhile Soult, on the 30th, found Hill just to the west of him in a rather isolated position and concentrated against him, but with little success. Then having wasted a day and neglected the remainder of his army, he finally retreated again up the valley of the Baztan. The whole front was now in such wild confusion that Wellington was at first unable even to ascertain the exact route by which the French were retreating; he therefore sent Picton and his division off towards Roncesvalles followed by the 6th, while he himself with the rest of the army made for Sanesteban, following what was in fact the main French line of retreat.

The pursuit continued on 31 July and Soult hurried on with his dispirited troops up the valley of the Bidassoa; he had no alternative to this scrambly retreat, for his army was so disorganised that it was quite impossible for it to offer any serious resistance to the British.

By the early days of August, the French were back in their original positions along their frontier; the operations had been disastrous for them, for they had lost some 13,000 men and a great quantity of stores without achieving anything more than the complete exhaustion and discouragement of their army. The truth was of course that in spite of Soult's boasts the French had never recovered from Vitoria, and at long last Soult realised this and decided that his only chance was to remain on the defensive and hope for the best.

The line he took up was a strong one but was too extensive for the numbers of men he had, with the result that his whole army was strung out along the front in a series of strong earthworks leaving few reserves available. Wellington realised this fundamental weakness of the French position but being still reluctant to attempt an invasion of France he merely fortified a line of his own facing the French and then resumed the siege of San Sebastian. That fortress fell after much hard and costly fighting on 31 August and the British soldiers, once in, gave themselves up to a savage orgy which made their earlier efforts in the frontier fortresses seem tame by comparison.

On the very day that San Sebastian fell, Soult made one last effort to relieve the place, but his efforts, which were in any case too weak to have much chance of success, were additionally hampered by fog, and on 1 September 1813 he retreated, having lost some 4000 men and achieved nothing. The chief interest of the operation therefore is that it marked the last real attempt at any offensive action (except for purely local counter-attack) on the part of the French for the remainder of the Peninsular War.

About this time the gratifying news of the various French defeats in Germany reached Wellington, who nevertheless still believed that Napoleon might yet snatch some last-minute advantage from his adversaries and force a peace upon them. In view of this he was still understandably reluctant to commit himself and his army too deeply into France, but confined himself to forcing a crossing of the Bidassoa, a strictly local operation designed to give the British possession of the high ground east of that river. The operation was completely successful and on 9 October, after three days' fighting, the French withdrew to the line of the river Nivelle. Picton's division took no direct part in these operations, having been sent off to the south as a flank guard.

As soon as these operations were over Picton left Spain for England taking Tyler with him. On 19 March 1813 he had been elected as a Member of Parliament for Pembroke Borough in the Tory interest, the vacancy having occurred through the decision of the previous member, Sir John Owen, to sit for Pembroke County. He was returned unopposed (the seat being a pocket borough) and wished to take his seat in the House of Commons, and it is also probable that he intended to get further advice and treatment for his eyes, which were still causing him much inconvenience and some pain.

On 11 November 1813 he took his seat in the House, where he also received the thanks of Parliament for his recent services in Spain. He seems to have been genuinely overcome at his honour and replied with difficulty. His speech opened with the memorable 'Being entirely unaccustomed to speak in public . . .' but it is not very clear whether the phrase was even then a cliché or whether, solemn thought, Picton can be claimed as its inventor. Whichever the case the sentiment, although quite genuinely expressed, came oddly from a general whose speeches to his division were famous throughout the army and whose voice had sounded 'with the power of twenty trumpets' above the uproar of Ciudad Rodrigo; this sort of performance however clearly bore no connection in the General's mind with public speaking in the sense of addressing the House of Commons. In spite of his apprehensions he nevertheless managed to say all the proper things and seems to have impressed his fellow-members, although many of them must still have had unfavourable recollections of the Trinidad affair.

Having by now achieved a considerable degree of fame, he was of course much exposed to requests for favours of various kinds, not least of which were for places in the army and in particular on his staff, for protégés. One of these at least was successful, for on 18 November 1813 he wrote: 'In case of any vacancies upon my personal staff (which consists of two ADCs only) I have long since been engaged three deep; but if Sir William Garrow is desirous that his young friend, Captain Chambers, should have an opportunity of seeing what is going on with the Army in the Peninsula, and can obtain the Duke of York's consent, I shall have great happiness in meeting his wishes. . . .' It can be assumed that the commander-in-chief *did* consent, for young Chambers accompanied Picton back to the Peninsula and stayed with him for the few months remaining to both of them.

By the end of 1813 it was fairly clear that Napoleon must soon fall and Picton, obviously and understandably anxious to be in at the death, did not linger in England. On 21 December 1813, he embarked at Portsmouth and ten days later was at St Jean-de-Luz; he had had an uneventful trip but it was otherwise for Tyler who, travelling on a different ship with the horses, 'experienced a most miserable voyage and did not arrive at St Ander until two days after, having lost one of the horses, and otherwise in miserable plight . . .' It must have been an appalling voyage to have upset the large and placid Tyler.

Before leaving England, Picton had been offered command of the Army of Catalonia and on his arrival at Wellington's headquarters at once sought the advice of the 'Marquis', who advised him against accepting. The force concerned was a somewhat mixed body of troops, British, German, Sicilian and Italian, operating in conjunction with a body of Spanish guerrillas, and the command had become vacant as a result of the misconduct of its previous commander, Murray (who was subsequently court-martialled). Although the offer gave him an unusual chance of virtually independent command, Picton, who looked disdainfully on the Army of Catalonia as being little more than a guerrilla force, soon decided to accept Wellington's advice, and a day or two afterwards wrote to his friend Flanagan to that effect, adding that he had therefore, 'with the approbation of the Marquis', determined to resume command of his old 3rd Division.

In spite of the season there had been a certain amount of activity along the Spanish/French frontier during Picton's absence. The fall of Pamplona on 30 October had left Wellington free to force a crossing of the Nivelle, which he had done with no great difficulty, for the French, as at the Bidassoa, were so over-extended as to be unable to concentrate at the vital points. As a result of this operation the British were much better situated, for they had come down from the exposed mountain-tops onto the plains of southern France and were thus able to establish themselves in reasonable comfort for the winter.

The British troops behaved well in France and the inhabitants, relieved from the depredations of their own bandit-like soldiers, welcomed them rather as deliverers than conquerors. The Spaniards however took a different view; the French had been living in their country by extensive plunder for six years and now that the tables were turned they were not unnaturally determined to have their revenge. Nor was the situation improved by the fact that their commissariat was in any case so bad that they were practically compelled to live off the country as the only alternative to starvation. Wellington was understandably furious about this; he had disciplined his army rigidly with the eventual invasion of France particularly in his mind, and he therefore decided that rather than spoil everything by the indiscipline of the Spaniards he would send them back to their own country. This he did, and although it weakened him at a critical juncture he felt, rightly, that it was better to accept that than to provoke a national rising against him, for such a rising might have been fatal. The French were a people trained in arms and the Basques in particular were a brave and warlike race who had already shown their mettle by combining together to drive off various bands of marauding Spanish guerrillas, to the great surprise of the latter and the barely concealed joy of Wellington.

The British government then ordered Wellington to continue his advance into France, so as soon as the weather cleared up he crossed the Nive, not without heavy fighting, and advanced to the line of the Adour. He was still distrustful of the capacity of the allies finally to deal with Napoleon, and was moreover short of money and clothing for his army, but by the early days of 1814 the situation had improved and he was thus able to make plans for a further advance into the heart of France. The French by this time were in no state to offer any really effective resistance, for Napoleon had been withdrawing troops steadily from the southern front to bolster his armies on the Elbe, and had also found it necessary to disarm some of his foreign troops because of their disaffection, with the result that the unhappy Soult had no option but to remain on the defensive and parry the British blows as best he could.

The next move of the British commander was to cross the Adour, and his plan, which took full account of the over-dispersion of the French in their entrenchments, was to strike at their left and, simultaneously, pass a considerable part of his army over a bridge of boats which he proposed to have built near the mouth of the river. He therefore set about collecting boats and making other arrangements and on 12 February 1814, everything being ready and the weather suitable, he set his troops in action.

Picton's 3rd Division formed part of a force under Hill destined to turn the French left, and on 14 February this force advanced upon the French under Harispe and after some fighting, which continued on the 15th, drove it back towards St Palais; during these operations the 3rd Division had a good deal of fighting against a division under Villatte.

On the night of 15 February 1814 the French withdrew across the Bidouze by the bridge of St Palais, which they blew behind them, so that the British were compelled to spend much of the 16th repairing it. On 17 February however they pressed on eastwards again after the French and at Rivareyte had the good fortune to capture the bridge there intact; this was important, for the country east of Bayonne contains river after river, almost all flowing north-west and all therefore admirably suited for successive rearguard actions by an army retreating into France.

On 24 February the British opened their attack on the French line behind the Gave d'Orloron, the 3rd Division having the task of seizing the important bridge at Sauveterre; the French pickets resisted obstinately, presumably while the bridge was being prepared for demolition, for it was presently blown up in the faces of the British. Fortunately a ford had been found in the meanwhile, a little way downstream by a mill, and Picton at once ordered Keane to start crossing his brigade over at this point. The crossing was a difficult one for the current, due to the mill-race, ran very swiftly over slippery rounded stones; nevertheless Keane pushed his light companies over and presently these were able to line a wall on the east bank with a view to covering the crossing of the remainder of their brigade.

Donaldson of the 94th (whose light company took no part in the operation) explained that the initial crossing was covered by a party of the 7th Hussars, and although the meaning of 'covered' is not very clear in his narrative it seems probable that the cavalry were actually used physically to help the infantry through the difficult ford. The horsemen then withdrew to the west bank and the right battalion of the brigade (the 1st/5th) had just begun to cross when Villatte's division counter-attacked with great spirit. The light companies, heavily outnumbered, were driven back in confusion down a narrow lane to the water's edge. There a few succeeded in scrambling back across the difficult ford, while a number more (most of whom were drowned) took to the deeper water; the bulk of them however formed up with their backs to the river and prepared to fight, although their chances of success were very slight and they had every prospect of being either bayoneted or captured by the advancing French.

Fortunately at this stage Picton in person brought up a battery of nine-pounders which unlimbered in the open on the west bank of the river and opened such a fire of grape at short range that the French were fairly brought to a standstill, and presently withdrew. Picton then bought the survivors of the light companies back across the river and bivouaced his division on its west bank; the next day the engineers put a bridge of boats across the river and the 3rd Division at once continued the pursuit with the rest of the army to the river Gave de Pau, where Soult had taken up a position at Orthez.

The light companies of Keane's brigade lost fairly heavily; Napier, who commented that the operations were not very happily executed, put their losses at about ninety (including thirty prisoners), which must have been almost a third of the force engaged, but it is probable that in the circumstances the attempt was justified. The ford was indeed a difficult one but the French were in full retreat and Picton obviously thought, and thought rightly, that it was his business to keep hard on their heels, by forcing a crossing as quickly as possible.

He had apparently taken all reasonable steps to cover the operation (for the battery he brought up must have been pre-positioned well forward for that very purpose) so that its failure may be put down more to the fortune of war than to any lack of judgement. It must also be said that another contributory factor was the remarkable quality of the French defence, which says much for the particular spirit of Villatte's division.

One interesting aspect of the operation was Keane's use of the massed light companies of his brigade to act as a spearhead in a difficult task, for although the practice had been common enough in the eighteenth century it had latterly fallen into disuse. Picton however at least permitted it and perhaps even favoured it, for it will be remembered that he massed his light companies at Bussaco and Fuentes d'Onoro; it had earlier been a favourite system in the West Indies, so it is possible that he had seen it there and approved of it.

While these operations were in progress Hope, on the extreme left, had begun his crossing of the Adour near its mouth and by the end of February had passed all his troops over the boat bridge and had laid siege to Bayonne. In the south the main body of the army under Wellington simultaneously came up to the Gave de Pau and by 27 February most of it was on the French bank. The enemy position was a strong one and the French were moreover numerically superior to the British. In spite of this Soult's dispositions were made chiefly with an eye to retreat, for he was rapidly losing confidence in his ability to hold Wellington in check.

The French right flank, which was about two miles back from the river near the village of St Boes, and part of their right front were covered by difficult, broken country including a good deal of marsh; their centre was strongly posted on a bare, heathy hill which offered no covered line of approach to the position, while their left rested on the village of Orthez; this flank of the position was covered by a stream running south-west down a narrow valley until it joined the main river half a mile or so east of the village.

Wellington's plan was the usual one against a rearguard, namely to envelop the flanks while also pressing against the centre. The 4th and 7th Divisions were directed to drive in the French right flank, while Hill was given the task of crossing the river well to the east of Orthez so as to be in a position either to attack the French left flank or cut their line of retreat according to circumstances. The 3rd and 6th Divisions were ordered to demonstrate against the French centre, while the Light Division was held in reserve under Wellington's hand on the British left.

On the left the 4th Division (for the 7th was delayed) opened its attack upon the village of St Boes from the west, but the French under Taupin resisted desperately and held firm for several hours, after which Wellington pushed forward the Light Division from the south-west to try to relieve the pressure on the 4th Division by an attack on Taupin's left.

In the centre the 3rd and 6th Divisions moved against the French and drove in their outposts under a heavy fire of artillery. They then halted for a time in accordance with the original orders not to become seriously engaged, until Wellington, seeing that the attack on the French right was making no progress, ordered them to attack in earnest. Picton's main body was on the left but one of his brigades (Wallace's) had been detached temporarily to the 6th Division and was leading the attack on the right, so that the first brunt of the fighting fell wholly upon the 3rd Division. The fire, particularly that of the French artillery, was very heavy, and Donaldson noticed that several men in his brigade were decapitated by chain shot, an unusual projectile in a land battle although common enough at sea, where it was used to cut rigging. Eventually General Foy was wounded and his division broke and fled soon afterwards, pursued by the 6th Division which was still led by Wallace's brigade. Picton at once brought up a battery to harass the French retreat and to prevent their reforming, upon which Soult, who was directing operations opposite, ordered a squadron of Chasseurs to charge it. The order was an astounding one and can only have been given either in error or because the British guns were causing such havoc that some desperate expedient was necessary to silence them, but whatever the reason the French cavalry responded gallantly. Their charge started well, for the first British they met were leading companies of the 88th, which being somewhat disorganised by their dash after the French infantry presented an ideal target for cavalry. A considerable number of the foremost of the scattered Irishmen were quickly and ruthlessly cut down, but before the Frenchmen could reach the guns they galloped in the excitement of the moment into a sunken road, both sides of which were lined by the remaining companies of the 88th. The result was inevitable; the French were caught like rats in a trap and were shot down mercilessly by the angry Irishmen who spared neither man nor horse. It is a pity from the historian's point of view that Grattan, the faithful chronicler of the old Connaught Rangers, was no longer with them to record the bloody scene.

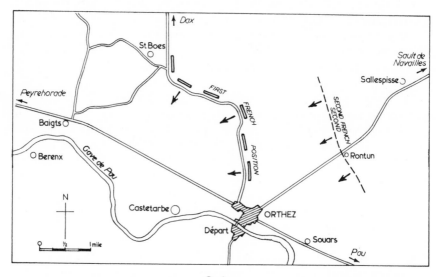

Orthez

Picton, having seen the French cavalry disposed of, then advanced the battery again, presumably to soften up the French second line, but this attempt was met by such heavy fire that he was for the moment brought to a standstill. Presently however the attack by the Light Division on the left, and Hill's wide outflanking movement on the right, began to take effect; the French centre then finally broke and the British advanced all along the line, forcing their opponents back to Sault de Navailles, where they crossed the single bridge under cover of guns posted on the high ground to the north. The British pursuit was not continued beyond this point and Soult was thus able to extricate the bulk of his army from a potentially unpleasant situation.

The French fought stoutly at Orthez and it was not until their line of retreat was menaced that they finally broke; their numerous and well-served artillery in particular were responsible for holding up the British for long periods and inflicting heavy casualties. Captain Parker of the Royal Engineers, acting on that occasion as ADC to Sir Thomas Picton, was killed close to him by a roundshot, while the general himself later told Flanagan, in a letter of 4 March 1814, that the entire gun detachment of one of the battery of nine-pounders which he himself had brought forward to harass the French had been killed near him by a single French salvo. The total losses of the 3rd Division amounted to 700, which gives a fair indication of the severity of the action.

In the opening stages of the battle Picton yet again found time to have one of his famous brushes with the Light Division. The reasons for it are by no means clear but Sir Harry Smith tells us that as the Light Division

> were moving on the right of the 3rd Division, Sir Thomas Picton who was ever ready to find fault with the Light, rode up to Colonel Barnard. 'Who the devil are you?' knowing Barnard intimately. 'We are the Light Division.' 'If you are the Light Sir, I wish you would move a little quicker', said in his most bitter and sarcastic tone. Barnard says very cool, 'Alten commands. But the march of the infantry is quick time and you cannot accelerate the pace of the head of the column without doing injury to the whole. Wherever the 3rd Division are, Sir Thomas, we will be in our places, depend on it.'

This incident was presumably provoked partly by Picton's impatience to get into action, but largely by his chronic inability to resist a dig at the Light Division under any circumstances. Barnard, as it happened, was by no means a man to be intimidated and appears to have given as good as he got, a fact which Picton probably appreciated.

CHAPTER 14

PURSUIT AND ARMISTICE

On 28 February 1814 Wellington, having reorganised his army after
the battle of Orthez, resumed his pursuit of the French who were
withdrawing towards Grenade. Their situation was by then almost
hopeless, and it was clear that the end was nearly in sight, so that a
few days later on 4 March even Picton, by no means a natural optimist,
was writing cheerfully to Flanagan:

> I believe I shall see the end of this eventful war—and then-what then?
> Why, after the example of Pyrrhus sit down and drink good wine! But
> you may rejoin with that King's minister, why not do so at present?
> Because after all the fatigue of joining in the chase it would not be
> decorous to be thrown out at the death'.

This comparison of the campaign at that stage with a hunt was apt
enough; the whole British army felt it (and so of course did the
French), but Soult was doggedly determined to see the thing out to
the end, being perhaps still hopeful that some eleventh-hour stroke
on the part of his Emperor would restore the balance of things to the
French advantage.

The French general calculated that Wellington's next objective
would be either Bordeaux or Toulouse, and reckoned that Aire offered
him a good central position whence to strike at whichever flank the
British offered him, but although this was sound enough in theory he
was not strong enough or sufficiently well supplied to make it possible
in practice. Wellington, who appreciated this perhaps better than
Soult, did not hesitate, for having despatched Beresford with a force
towards Bordeaux (which was showing every disposition to declare for
the Bourbons) he attacked Soult at Aire on 2 March and drove him
back across the Adour. The French were again saved by the presence
of an effective water obstacle, for they blew the one remaining bridge
at St Sever after crossing it and were thus able to retreat unmolested.

Soult then decided that he must abandon Bordeaux completely and operate to cover Toulouse, and at once changed his line of withdrawal towards that town. There was a partial engagement at Vic-en-Bigorre on 19 March where the 3rd Division was heavily engaged, and again at Tarbes where the French were skilfully manoeuvred off the direct route to Toulouse. As it was essential for Soult to reach that town, which was well fortified and supplied with munitions and stores of all kinds, he was thus compelled to hurry his exhausted soldiers forward at such a speed and on such a bad by-road that almost all order ceased, and the French infantry was reduced to little more than a vast mob of stragglers. Fortunately the French cavalry, who from the nature of the country had been but little engaged, were in fairly good shape and Soult was therefore able to employ them effectively on the flanks and rear of his army, partly in a protective role but largely as drovers to keep the discouraged foot soldiers moving in the right direction.

Wellington followed on, but with great caution, partly because he was still by no means convinced that Napoleon would finally be beaten but mainly because it was essential that supplies should keep pace with his army. This involved building or rebuilding bridges, repairing roads, and buying draught animals, but it was nevertheless essential, for as long as he could keep his army well fed he could ensure that it remained in a compact, disciplined body and did not disperse to plunder. In this he was entirely successful; the French civilians, who were tired of war (and particularly tired of being plundered by their own countrymen) were delighted with this strange phenomenon of a well-disciplined army which paid promptly and generously in gold for everything it required. The frugal peasantry were only too pleased to provide them with every sort of supply which they had been at pains to conceal from Soult's hungry soldiers, and so the advance continued. Inevitably it took a few days to gain the confidence of the local inhabitants and this delay allowed the French marshal just enough time to shepherd his weary men into Toulouse, where he collected some reinforcements and at once set about re-equipping his army from the considerable resources available there. He realised that any further attempt to continue the withdrawal would inevitably mean the complete dissolution of his army and considered that his best course was to shut himself and his troops up in a strong, well-supplied town and await events.

Toulouse stands in a convex bend on the east bank of the river Garonne, with the suburb of St Cyprien on the opposite side, the two being connected by a bridge. A canal runs along the north and east sides of the town and just to the east of the canal there is a ridge of high ground running north and south for about four miles. East of this high ground again there is the river Hers, flowing from south to north and crossed by a number of bridges.

In 1814, the country to the north was fairly open, but to the south it was enclosed and full of small streams. The town, including the bridgehead of St Cyprien on the west bank, was strongly fortified and contained a well-stocked arsenal and considerable quantities of provisions and warlike stores, and thus offered an excellent refuge to the French. The possession of the bridgehead was a particular advantage to them since it meant that any attempt Wellington made to cross the Garonne, which he had had to do to get at the town, would offer Soult an excellent chance to attack him with a concentrated army while the British were divided by the river.

Wellington was well aware of this advantage to the French, but by now he felt able to take liberties with Soult; on 30 March therefore he built a pontoon bridge across the Garonne some four miles south of the town and the next day Hill crossed it with 13,000 men with orders to make his way eastwards, if possible to the highroad running northwards to Toulouse. Wellington would have preferred to approach the town from the south because it was the only side unprotected by a major water obstacle, but after forty-eight hours Hill was quite unable to find a practicable route through the maze of streams and therefore recrossed the river on the night of 1 April. The bridge was then taken up and the British army marched off northwards to see what could be achieved below the town; as soon as this happened Soult, who now saw from which direction the blow was likely to fall, at once set about strengthening the fortifications on the north and east sides of the town and also caused a series of redoubts to be constructed on the ridge of high ground to the east.

On 4 April 1814 the British bridge was again in position, this time some twelve miles north of the town, and that night the 3rd, 4th and 6th Divisions crossed it together with some cavalry. Unfortunately, heavy rain then fell, the Garonne rose rapidly and the bridge had to be dismantled, so that for some days the troops on the east bank were dangerously isolated. Picton, who commanded the force, took steps to fortify his position as strongly as possible, but the French made no move. The reasons for this inactivity are not altogether clear but it is more than probable that their morale was so low that Soult was simply not prepared to commit them to an offensive battle, even though the odds should be greatly in his favour. By 8 April the bridge was again in position, more troops then crossed,

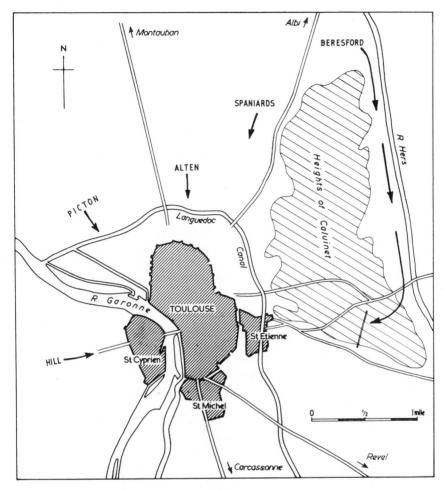

Toulouse

and the whole force advanced southward upon Toulouse with a flank guard of cavalry over on the east bank of the river Hers.

Two days later, after some delays due to moving the bridge further south towards the town, the British were ready to resume operations. Wellington's plan was complicated and potentially dangerous, even against a comparatively inactive enemy, for he intended to occupy the defenders on the north side of the town by a series of feint attacks by the 3rd and Light Divisions while the bulk of his army under Beresford made a difficult march southwards between the high ground and the Hers as a preliminary to turning westwards and

193

assaulting. Hill, who remained on the west bank of the river, was given the task of delivering a feint attack against the bridgehead of St Cyprien.

The operations which opened on 10 April started well; on the west bank Hill's thrust against the bridgehead was enough to drive some of the French thence in disorder, after which he contented himself with a series of spirited demonstrations to keep the remainder occupied. In the north, Picton's division drove the French skirmishers and outposts back across the canal and the Light Division made similar progress on their left, while the Spaniards made their preparations for a thrust from the north-east.

Beresford's move, which constituted the main effort, went slowly because of the appallingly bad going in the low ground by the river, and Soult was thus given plenty of time to reinforce his threatened eastern face; the Spaniards, whose attack from the north-east was supposed to be delivered simultaneously with that of Beresford, then unfortunately attacked prematurely, and were repulsed with heavy losses, leaving the British to continue alone.

Beresford eventually got his infantry to the point where they were due to wheel westwards, and having beaten off a local French attack formed them up in readiness for their advance; very sensibly however he made no attempt to advance until his artillery, still struggling through the heavy mud, could get into positions whence it could support him up the long, bare slope in front of him.

All activity on the eastern side of the town thus ceased and to Picton this seemed ominous; he had seen from afar the summary repulse of the Spaniards, and having then heard the firing die away on Beresford's side he seems to have come to the rather hasty conclusion that the attack had failed on all fronts. He therefore decided to convert his own feint into a real assault, in the hopes that he might break into the town and save the day, and there can be little doubt that in making this decision he was deeply influenced by the memory of his earlier, dramatic success against the castle at Badajos when all had otherwise seemed lost. He therefore brought up two guns and under cover of their fire launched Brisbane's brigade straight at the powerful works covering the northern end of the Jumeaux bridge over the canal. This first attempt was a complete and utter failure. No previous reconnaissance can have been made, for even Robinson admits that 'it was not until the counter-scarp had been gained that General Picton discovered the formidable nature of the defences', and it is obvious that even the best infantry, launched in daylight against such works and supported by only two guns, were bound to fail, even against relatively moderate resistance. Picton nevertheless persisted stubbornly in his attempts and two more equally hopeless and bloody assaults were made before he finally ordered a withdrawal, having achieved no more than to give the French a heartening little success when they sorely needed it. He never subsequently offered any reason for his rashness on this occasion, but it is probable that he wished to gain just a little more glory for himself and his division before the French finally collapsed.

This very unfortunate affair ended the day's fighting round the town; nor could it be resumed on the 11th, for the British had expended great quantities of ammunition on the first day and Wellington was therefore compelled to halt the operations until more could be brought up. The British cavalry however continued to press southwards down the line of the Hers and soon threatened the road leading south out of Toulouse to Carcassonne, and as this was the only line of retreat left open to the French Soult, worried by the possibility of being cut off, withdrew by it on the night of 11 April leaving the town of Toulouse to the British. The next day Wellington received the news of the abdication of Napoleon, and did not therefore pursue the French but merely forwarded the information to Soult under a flag of truce.

Apart therefore from a sally from Bayonne on the night of 14 April (which provoked a savage, inconclusive, and quite unnecessary fight) there was no fighting after Toulouse, for on 18 April Soult signed an armistice and the war was over.

Almost immediately Wellington's splendid army began to disperse; the cavalry and artillery marched off across France towards the Channel ports, while the bulk of the infantry embarked at Bordeaux, many en route for the war in America. The Spanish and Portuguese troops then returned to their own countries taking with them hundreds of unfortunate Spanish and Portuguese women who, having attached themselves to British soldiers and followed them faithfully, sometimes for years, were now arbitrarily ordered to be cast off. A few, it is true, were permitted to marry their protectors but the bulk of them had no option but to return to the Peninsula, and as many had either lost their families or been disowned by them as a result of their attachment to the foreign heretics they had little to look forward to there. There were many wild scenes of grief as the final partings came; it is but fair to the soldiers to say that many of them looked upon these women as their wives and their children as their legal offspring but this was no help, for they had no funds with which to buy their passage home and had perforce to abandon them.

The 3rd Division dispersed with the rest, and with profound regrets, for five years of warfare had welded its units into a fine fighting machine; Picton went off fairly soon, for he was by no means well and his eyes were still troubling him, so that he took the first opportunity he could to bid farewell to his troops and sail for home.

The officers of the 3rd Division subscribed almost sixteen hundred pounds for a service of plate for their old general, as a mark of their esteem and a souvenir of the many experiences they had shared, but even this event was marred by the flat refusal of the officers of the 88th Regiment to subscribe a penny towards it. The reasons for this have perhaps already been made clear; Picton had made an unfortunate first impression in the far-off days of 1810 when he had first assumed command of the 3rd Division, and although there is no doubt that he looked upon the Connaught Rangers as one of his finest fighting regiments (as indeed they were) it is also certain that he regarded them off duty as a wild, ill-disciplined corps much given to looting, an opinion which again had much truth in it.

The Connaught Rangers, for their part, had a considerable regard for the fighting qualities of 'Old Picton' but they felt, rightly or wrongly, that he never gave them enough credit for their conduct in action, and discriminated against them unfairly in the matter of promotion and honours. Whatever the circumstances of the case, it must for ever remain a pity that they found it necessary thus to cast a slight on the commander of the 'Fighting Division' in which they had been proud to serve.

Picton's first acknowledgement of the gift was short to the point of curtness but he later made amends in a longer letter in which he pleaded ill-health for his earlier abruptness.

Soon after his return to England the award of a number of peerages for services in the war was announced but Picton, to his great disappointment, was not included amongst them. This omission caused much feeling among his friends and supporters, controversy raged in the press and elsewhere, and the whole case was argued and re-argued *ad nauseam*. In view of the heat engendered over the affair it may perhaps be as well to examine the claims of the actual recipients of peerages, particularly since Picton's exclusion from the list was more or less explained officially by the fact that he had never held a 'separate command'. The claims of Generals Hill and Graham are so well founded that they cannot be denied by even the most biased critic, while Beresford, although certainly no great commander in the field, had achieved such success in his reorganisation of the

Portuguese army that it is difficult to deny him his place on the list. Hope, it is true, had only joined Wellington in the Peninsula after Vitoria, but had certainly had a 'separate command' (which he had handled very skilfully) in the operations on the Adour and round Bayonne, and also had earlier claims for his good service under Moore. The weakest claimant on the list was clearly Cotton, who commanded the cavalry with no great distinction and who can hardly have been said to have had a 'separate' command in the sense that the word separate in this context clearly implied. He did however have influence, which was almost as valuable as ability.

Picton himself, to his credit, kept out of the controversy as much as possible although he is said to have remarked privately to friends: 'If the coronet were lying on the crown of a breach, I should have as good a chance as any of them.' This remark, if true (and it is very much in character), was unfortunate and somewhat unfair, for the qualities needed to storm a breach were not necessarily those which make a great general. In those days, when commanders led from the front, it was rare to find any leader without a fair share of physical courage and undoubtedly all the recipients of peerages were well enough endowed in this respect, whereas the exercise of an independent command required other, and possibly even greater, qualities of knowledge, judgement and moral courage. It is certain, whatever the cause, that Picton's only essay in separate command during the early operations in the Pyrenees did not end very auspiciously.

It is probable that had he accepted the command of the Army of Catalonia it would have given him an undeniable claim to the honour of a peerage, and had he survived Waterloo it is virtually certain that he would have received one; as it was, he was appointed a Knight Grand Cross of the Bath when the Order was reformed in 1814 and thereafter announced his intention of retiring permanently from the army. He then settled down in his country seat (interspersed with spells of duty as a Member of Parliament, whose official thanks for his services he had just received for the seventh time) and there, had things been different, he might have ended his days quietly. After a slow start and some serious setbacks in his earlier military career he had achieved a considerable amount of fame and glory, and although the faint shadow of the Trinidad affair was still occasionally apparent, he had otherwise caught the fancy of both the army and the public. Anecdotes about him were legion, and many who had barely heard of Graham or Beresford knew (or thought they knew) all about the fighting general; his stolid courage, his blue frock coat, his civilian hat, his cane, his cob and his astounding flow of strong language had all become legend.

Not a great deal is known about his activities for the first few months after the end of the war, but during that period England, and indeed much of Europe, gave herself up to a round of gaiety and relaxation and it is probable that the general followed suit in his rather solemn way; he was not a 'fashionable' man and seems to have shunned London society, much preferring the more restricted life of a Welsh country gentleman and quietly enjoying his fame and the local society. His letters of the period are full of details of country pursuits; thus on 5 September 1814 he wrote:

> I have not yet taken the field against the Partridge, although report makes them rather abundant. My gun case has not yet arrived from France, though it was entrusted to an Officer of my Regiment; but as the harvest (generally a good one) will not be completely over before the 10th or 12th of the month I shall, probably, be in a state to take the field by that time.

The reference to his gun is faintly ominous and one cannot help but feel that the unfortunate officer entrusted with it may have been given a mild sample of the general's vituperation for the time he had taken to get it home.

A few months later he was out after woodcock, which he had earlier described as 'the great diversion of this country', but noted with regret on 7 December 1814 that he had 'as yet been able to bagg [sic] but one solitary woodcock'. This failure was however apparently softened by the fact that the parson, who had been shooting with him, had had no better success.

Like many other distinguished soldiers he also tried his hand at farming; he was fully aware of the possible consequences and was quite prepared to pay (although he hoped not too severely) for his amusement; he wrote to Flanagan in the autumn of 1814 of his need for an experienced person to assist him—'a useful working bailiff; a plain kind of man on whom I can rely during my unavoidable absence . . .' . Inevitably he missed the excitement of campaigning and was even, on reflection, a little disappointed with Iscoed in spite of his earlier enthusiasm; his explanation of this was that 'I discover that my disposition has undergone a considerable revolution and that these tame appeals to the senses have but little amusement for one who has been habituated to scenes of more distinction and interest'. In a word, he was bored.

Much of this feeling must have been due to loneliness; he had always been rather a solitary man and had by 1814 reached the age when he looked with some envy on the peace and domestic comfort enjoyed by his married acquaintances. He practically admitted as much to a correspondent when he remarked, 'I don't think wine drinks well by one's self whatever the quality of it may be'.

He seems also to have been much affected by the sudden death of his brother, who had just retired from the East Indian Company's service as a major-general and settled near him, and after describing him as a man of independent principles said sadly that having been parted when young he had lost him at the moment when they were just becoming acquainted.

It is just possible that he may even have contemplated matrimony, although there is no direct evidence of it. He was not, apparently, averse to female company and (in a way not perhaps unusual for men of his age) seems to have shown some preference for the younger members of the opposite sex; Stanhope tells us that when Sir Lowry Cole once announced to the Duke of Wellington in Picton's presence the fact of his intended marriage to a lady of mature years and stated somewhat pompously that he thought he was not being imprudent, Picton quickly deflated him by saying in his rough, jesting way, 'Well, when *I* marry I shall do a damned imprudent thing, for I mean to marry the youngest tit I can find'. This remark, which scandalised the prim Cole but made Wellington roar with laughter, was of course made in jest but there may nevertheless have been some significance in it.

During the first few months after the end of the war the capitals of Europe had an air of permanent holiday; even in Paris, technically the capital of a conquered country, the people, heartily sick of war (or at least heartily sick of unsuccessful defensive war within their own frontiers) rejoiced that it was over and welcoming their conquerors as friends joined them in their pursuit of pleasure. Although much of this feeling on the part of the French was quite spontaneous, it was further fostered by Talleyrand who said, shrewdly enough, that the best hope of a lenient peace was to impress upon the allies the fact that the French were at bottom a gay, peace-loving, people and that their long history of aggression had been due to the evil influence of one man only; Napoleon Bonaparte their erstwhile Emperor. The latter had by this time abdicated and having also renounced all claims on the part of his descendants, had been banished to Elba, leaving the way open for the return of a King.

Britain, Russia, Prussia and Austria, who had formed a military alliance to keep France in her place, then concluded a most generous treaty with her which restored her original frontiers of 1792 and which demanded no indemnity for the years of suffering she had brought upon Europe. Later in the year a great Congress of the Allies assembled at Vienna to confirm this treaty amid much rejoicing and elaborate festivities.

On the surface therefore everything seemed to be settled, and it looked as though Europe was about to enjoy a long spell of peace, but unfortunately all was not as well in France as it appeared to be. A great many people, hard, ruthless, ambitious individuals, had been compelled to retire from public life in favour of Bourbon nominees, and in addition the country was full of thousands of half-pay officers and abruptly discharged soldiers, who having been reduced from positions of honour and affluence to near-beggary, could hardly be expected to join in the general rejoicing. Even in the few regiments which had been kept in being most of the old, battle-tried officers of the Revolution had been replaced by aristocrats whose haughty incompetence infuriated their soldiers. All the conditions for a further explosion of feeling in France were thus present, and it could only be a matter of time before it occurred.

CHAPTER 15

NAPOLEON'S RETURN

By the beginning of the new year the leaders of the French discontent, the violent Jacobins, judged that the time was ripe, and on 1 March 1815 Napoleon (who had of course been kept fully informed of all the intrigues in France), landed in the Gulf of St Juan with a few hundred of his infantry from Elba and a handful of dismounted cavalry, and marched forthwith upon Paris.

As was to be expected this event caused great consternation among the allies; the Congress of Vienna at once declared Napoleon to be an outlaw and then, in terms of their earlier treaty, began to assemble troops to deal with him. Strangely enough one of the few people in high places who at first misjudged the gravity of the situation was Wellington himself; he was offered and accepted (subject to the consent of the Prince Regent) the command of the allied armies in Europe, but declared that the whole affair was a flash in the pan and that the forces of the King of France would be more than sufficient to suppress what he judged to be no more than a minor insurrection. Herein he was wrong, for the troops despatched by the French King all joined their old general as soon as they met him, so that on 20 March he was able to enter Paris and resume control of France amid the wild enthusiasm of thousands of his old soldiers, who came flocking back to their colours. In a few weeks he had raised and equipped a powerful army and was ready to undertake active operations.

Wellington, by then fully convinced of the gravity of the situation, left Vienna on 29 March, and by great exertions reached Brussels on 4 April; there he took over command of the Anglo-Dutch Army from the eager but inexperienced Prince of Orange who, having served as an ADC to Wellington in the Peninsula, fancied himself as a master of war. The situation was by no means a comfortable one, for there were but few troops available, and although there was a Prussian army within striking distance, the bulk of the allies, the great armies of

Russia and Austria, were several weeks' hard marching away from the vital point. It was therefore in Napoleon's interest to deal with the British as soon as possible, to dispose of them before he was called upon to face the great mass of his enemies, and with this in mind he began to concentrate his army as soon as it was ready.

The British element of the allied force of which Wellington took command in April 1815 differed greatly from the fine army which he had left in the south of France only a few months before, particularly as regards the infantry. A number of the best battalions had been sent across the Atlantic to fight the Americans, and a great many individual soldiers who had enlisted in response to Windham's appeal in 1807 had been discharged as time-expired, while some units had been disbanded completely. Fortunately the cavalry, not being required in America, were available in fair strength, while the horse artillery was in its usual high order; a number of troops of the latter had moreover just received nine-pounders in place of their old light six-pounders, and although this had a slightly adverse effect on their mobility, it increased their firepower very considerably. The field artillery (to use a term not then in use but which will be readily understood) was however very short of both horses and drivers.

In spite of these shortcomings, the British troops were nevertheless still a formidable body. The battalions available were in many cases under strength, but most contained a high proportion of old, tried, Peninsular veterans; it is true that they also contained a fair proportion of young recruits, but this was of course also the case in the Peninsula, where it had been caused by the steady replacement of casualties. The army also included the King's German Legion, which had already served under Wellington for six years with much distinction, and although its units were also under strength they were all composed of excellent soldiers.

The staff situation was also by no means bad and although the Duke subsequently complained that he had had no hand in their selection this seems unreasonable. It would have been unfair in the extreme, and indeed extraordinarily difficult in the short time available, to have arbitrarily replaced the bulk of its existing members with Wellington nominees, but as far as was possible the Duke of York and his staff at the Horse Guards supported Wellington loyally, and a steady stream of officers acceptable to him began to flow towards Brussels soon after his arrival there.

Wellington's complaint therefore that he had an 'infamous Army, very weak and ill-equipped, and a very inexperienced Staff' is not entirely a fair statement of his situation as regards the British element.

It is well known however from other sources that he was not altogether above exaggerating his difficulties in order to highlight his subsequent successes, and this may be a case in point. At the same time it is true that the foreign troops in his army were extremely poor; the Dutch and the Belgians were newly raised, ill-trained, and ill-led, and as a great many of them were also better disposed towards the French than the British their military value was obviously very limited. Wellington tried hard in the short time available to persuade the Portuguese Government to send him a few thousand of the troops whom Beresford had so painstakingly trained to such a high standard, but in this he was unsuccessful.

One of the chief difficulties which faced him was that no one in England was prepared to define the country's current relationship with France, so that when a Member of Parliament asked bluntly whether it was 'Peace or War?' no one in authority could answer him. The Royal Navy, with its highly developed tastes for prize-money, had already started seizing French ships with great enthusiasm, but on land Wellington felt it necessary to be more cautious, and as a result he was severely handicapped. In the Peninsula, he had had a highly organised system of intelligence based on information from the guerrillas, from the inhabitants (whose goodwill he had enjoyed), from his own military patrols, and from reconnoitring staff officers, but in Belgium he had no chance to organise a local system, while his reluctance to cross the French frontier prevented him from employing even the most elementary military methods of reconnaissance. The French, who had numerous agents and sympathisers in the Low Countries, laboured under no such difficulties; indeed, after their situation in Spain, they must have rejoiced that the boot was at last on the other foot. Wellington thus faced his enemy blindly, while of course continuing to make such dispositions as his scanty information indicated to be desirable; apart from the purely strategic aspect these dispositions included the careful intermixing of the various troops under his command, so that the strong might support the weak, and the good counterbalance the bad.

In the meanwhile Napoleon was still busy reorganising his army; his return was not really very popular with the French people as a whole, but he reckoned that a sweeping victory or two would quickly set him up again in his old place. He had no great difficulty in obtaining men, for his veterans came back in great numbers; nor were there any problems of equipment, for France was full of military stores. His chief worry was in selecting reliable leaders, for most of his old marshals and generals had declared publicly and actively for the Bourbons, while others remained firmly on the fence. The fact is that they were almost all tired of war, and having done well enough financially over the previous twenty years were more than content to make the most of their acceptance by the new regime. Nevertheless something of Napoleon's old magic remained, and a number were persuaded or cajoled into joining him. They did so with some foreboding since the Bourbons, if successful in regaining power, would hardly be likely to treat them generously a second time.

By the beginning of May the French army was almost ready to open operations against the British and Prussians and, although Napoleon had no more than 115,000 men against a combined Anglo-Prussian strength of 150,000, this did not apparently worry him. He was confident that he could outmanoeuvre the allies and thus beat them in detail, for he had beaten the Prussians before, and although he had little experience of fighting the British it is quite clear that he thought that his marshals much overrated them as soldiers.

While all these preparations were made on both sides of the French frontier, Sir Thomas Picton remained quietly in England; he was still eager for a little more distinction and therefore very willing to see another campaign, but he forebore to ask for an appointment until he was absolutely certain who was to command the allies. He had a real and abiding regard for Wellington but was by no means anxious to serve under any other British or continental general, particularly, it seems, the Prince of Orange, whom he regarded (and perfectly correctly) as a mere novice from a military viewpoint.

The Duke however very soon asked for him and towards the end of May the summons reached him in Wales, when he at once started making is arrangements for a campaign. On 26 May he wrote to Tyler to tell him the good news and to arrange for him to warn his other ADCs, Chambers and Price. He also bade him look out for some 'active horses not above fifteen hands'; he had, he wrote, 'the old horse and the mare and another in London', and supposed that three more 'would be about his mark'.

He set his affairs in order particularly carefully before his departure, and it has been said that he had a strong presentiment that he would not survive the campaign, but although this may be so it seems likely that his care was no more than might have been expected of a middle-aged soldier who had seen too much of war to take any chances. We are told one rather macabre story of how, while walking past a cemetery with some friends, he leapt into a freshly dug grave and, lying down in it, remarked that it was just his size; not unnaturally this strange behaviour distressed the ladies of the party considerably, and was doubtless much discussed afterwards as an example of premonition, but may have been no more than a joke.

When all was ready, he moved to his house in London and it was during a round of farewell dinners that he met a young Guards officer to whom we are indebted for much information on the general's last days. The Guardsman, whose name was Gronow, had seen some service in the Peninsula with the 1st Guards and was extremely anxious to take part in the operations which were obviously imminent across the Channel, but had the bad fortune to be at that time posted to a battalion destined to remain on London duties. Being a self-confident young man, however, he quickly seized the opportunity to press his case with Picton and, as he was both a friend of Chambers *and* a countryman of the general's, the latter soon agreed in the most genial way that he might accompany him to the Low Countries as an extra ADC. The promise was of course made subject to Gronow's being able to obtain leave.

Gronow was highly elated by this, but being chronically short of money he had first to raise sufficient to outfit himself, to use his own words, 'in a manner worthy of the aide-de-camp of a great General'. His first actions were simple and direct (and have been copied by many officers since) for they consisted simply of visiting Messrs Cox and Greenwood, 'those staunch friends of the hard-up soldier', and borrowing from them the sum of two hundred pounds. This sum, although generous enough by the standards of the time, was not apparently enough to equip a young guardsman with expensive tastes, so Gronow at once repaired to a gambling house in St James's where, his luck being as good as his nerve, he succeeded in trebling it. Thus equipped he made numerous purchases, including two excellent horses from Tattersalls which he at once sent forward to Ramsgate, and by Saturday 10 June 1815 he himself was bowling off to the same destination in company with his friend Chambers and in the latter's carriage. Either from lack of time or, most probably, from a certainty that it would be refused, he had not bothered to apply for leave, but nevertheless set off confidently in the hopes that he could fight a battle and be back in London before his next turn for guard came round.

Picton travelled down with Tyler and having dined at the Fountain tavern in Canterbury went on to Ramsgate, where the rest of the party joined them. They spent the night of 11 June there and next morning embarked with horses, grooms, servants and baggage on a vessel specially hired for the purpose.

The party reached Ostend the same afternoon and stayed the night there in an hotel in the square where Picton, to the surprise and obvious admiration of his new ADC, at once started a flirtation in excellent French with the very pretty maid who waited on them. The general of course travelled in plain clothes which Gronow describes as 'a blue frock coat tightly buttoned up to the throat; a very large black silk neck cloth, showing little or no shirt collar; dark trousers, boots, and a round hat'. Now this is the very same clothing that he wore a day or two later at Quatre Bras, and although Gronow puts that fact down to the non-arrival of his baggage it is probable that it was more a matter of taste than necessity, for it was also the type of dress which he had habitually worn on campaign for several years.

The general and Tyler then went on to Brussels (having sent young Gronow on ahead to book accommodation) and arrived there in time for breakfast on 15 June. In the middle of this meal Colonel Canning of Wellington's staff arrived to inform Picton that the Duke wished to see him immediately, upon which he at once left the table and accompanied Canning to the park where Wellington was walking. The meeting was brief and oddly cold; Gronow says:

> Picton's manner was always more familiar than the Duke liked in his lieutenants, and on this occasion he approached him in a careless sort of way, just as he might have met an equal. The Duke bowed coldly to him and said, 'I am glad you are come, Sir Thomas; the sooner you get on horseback the better; no time is to be lost. You will take command of the troops in advance. The Prince of Orange knows by this time you will go to his assistance.' Picton appeared not to like the Duke's manner; for when he bowed and left he muttered a few words which convinced those who were with him that he was not much pleased with his interview.

Robinson, as is perhaps to be expected, says that Picton was greeted with 'friendly warmth', but on balance it seems reasonable to accept Gronow's account which is first-, or at least second-, hand and which is in accordance with the facts known from other sources. Even Robinson, elsewhere in his book, quotes his anonymous staff officer (who has already been identified as Hercules Pakenham) as saying that he readily believed that there was some lack of smoothness between the Duke and Picton 'from the habitual frankness with which Sir Thomas would offer his opinion without respect to persons'. Many years afterwards Wellington himself said, in reply to a direct question on the subject, that he did not recollect 'even a difference of opinion, much less anything in the nature of a quarrel' between them, but while this may well have been true in a general sense, enough has perhaps been said to make it clear that there was no warmer link between them than a firm mutual respect based mainly on military ability. Many years later the Duke, when discussing Picton with Stanhope, described him as 'a rough foul-mouthed devil as ever lived', but added that 'he always behaved extremely well; no man could do better in the different services I assigned to him', and we may perhaps safely accept this as being Wellington's final assessment of him, socially and professionally.

The 'troops in advance' turned out to be the 5th Division and they were a particularly fine body, comparable with the best that any Peninsular division could have produced, which is not surprising when it is noted that all eight of the British battalions in it had served there under the Duke. It was composed as follows:

8th Bde (Major-General Kempt)   1/28th, 1/32nd, 1/79th, 1/95th
9th Bde (Major-General Pack)   3/1st, 1/42nd, 2/44th, 1/92nd
5th Hanoverian Bde (Colonel V. Vincke)   4 Landwehr Battalions
One British and one Hanoverian battery

In spite of the Duke's admonition of 'no time to be lost' Picton did not leave Brussels until the early morning of 16 June. On the night of 15 June, the Duchess of Richmond held her famous ball and it is very probable that Picton attended it, although there is no evidence as to this beyond the fact that he was on the invitation list. None of his ADCs appear to have been invited, but they doubtless managed to amuse themselves in such a place as Brussels; Gronow makes no mention of his own activities but as he admits that the next morning he was compelled to mount his best horse and ride hard to catch up his general it is probable that he at least found some agreeable way of passing his last evening there.

Picton had arrived in Belgium only just in time, for Napoleon had made such good progress with the formation of his army that by mid-June he was ready to move. His concentration had been successfully concealed from the allies, whose reluctance to enter France had left them with little information other than the wild rumours and deliberately false reports spread by the numerous French agents and sympathisers in the Low Countries.

These latter had also of course kept Napoleon well informed as to the allied positions, so that he knew that Wellington's troops were widely cantoned over a front of a hundred miles to the west and south of Brussels, and that Blücher's army was similarly extended over a front of fifty miles a little further east. The allied cantonments were thus in the form of an irregular V pointing south, the junction of the two armies being just above Charleroi, and it was at this point that Napoleon planned to strike; he well knew that the junction between two armies was always a weak point, and reckoned that a sudden thrust on his part would place him in a most advantageous position between the allies. He also calculated that once separated the British and Prussians would concentrate on their centres, thus drawing even further apart and leaving him a clear line of advance into Brussels, the capture of which would strengthen his prestige with his own people and with the Belgians, and have a correspondingly bad effect on allied morale. He went even further than this, for he also thought that a sufficiently violent blow might cause the allies to make considerable withdrawals, the British westwards upon their ships, and the Prussians eastward along their lines of communication.

The French army actually crossed the frontier on 15 June; its staff work was faulty, as was understandable in such a hastily raised force, and there were many hitches, but it made progress nevertheless and soon passed northwards through Charleroi, driving off a Prussian force at Gosselies, while simultaneously a strong detachment was thrust up the road to Quatre Bras.

When this news reached Blücher he decided to concentrate his army near Sombreffe but, owing to some lack of communication between the allies, Wellington did not receive any detailed information of this until some time later; although he was therefore aware that the French were across the Sambre in force he was still undecided as to where he should concentrate. By the evening of 15 June he had fortunately received enough information to be able to order his army (which had previously been warned to be ready to move at short notice) to concentrate on the Brussels–Charleroi road just south of the Forest of Soignies.

The situation on the evening of 15 June thus favoured Napoleon, for his strategy had been successful and the British and Prussians, still widely dispersed, were trying desperately to concentrate while he was between them with his army compact and ready to fight. There is no doubt that he had achieved a considerable measure of surprise and, although this was in part caused by the remarkable respect with which the allies had treated the French frontier, it was also due, to some extent, to over-confidence on their part. Their minds had been set on invasion as soon as their government should have decided that such a move was politically permissible and they were clearly disconcerted by the fact that the French had taken the initiative.

Early on the morning of 16 June Wellington heard at the Richmond Ball that the French cavalry had reached Quatre Bras, but that they were for the moment being held by a brigade of Nassau troops which fortunately had happened to be in possession of that place. He at once ordered Picton's division southward to support the Nassauers and then, having briefed his senior officers (most of whom were at the ball with him), retired to bed for a few hours. History does not record whether Sir Thomas followed his example but we do know that soon after dawn he and his staff were cantering down the pavé to overtake his marching battalions.

On the same morning Napoleon decided to attack the Prussians

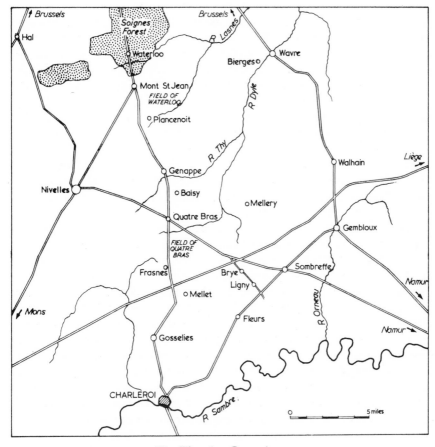

The Waterloo Campaign

with his right wing while Ney pressed on up the Brussels road with the left. The Emperor had no great regard for the Prussians as soldiers, and reckoned that he would have no difficulty in driving them off eastward in defeat and disorder, after which he would march north-west again and rejoin Ney for their triumphant advance on Brussels. These plans, as it happened, were based on a set of circumstances which did not in fact exist, for he imagined that his defeat of the Prussian detachment at Gosselies on 15 June had been enough to cause both armies to retreat, whereas in fact the Prussians were in position and ready to fight at Ligny, while the British were advancing southward upon him with all speed.

Wellington left Brussels at about the same time as Picton but soon turned off by a more easterly route towards Ligny, where he had a brief meeting with Blücher whom he promised to support 'if not too heavily attacked himself'; he then rode off to the north-west towards Quatre Bras, where he arrived about midday. At about 3 pm Napoleon attacked Blücher and, although the Prussians were in greater strength than he had anticipated, he advanced confidently; in order to make his victory complete he had ordered Ney to wheel eastwards from Quatre Bras and fall upon the right flank and rear of the Prussians and although Ney (for reasons which will become apparent later) was fully occupied with his own operations, Napoleon still achieved a considerable victory. After several hours of severe fighting the Prussians were compelled to retreat towards Wavre and once this retreat had started, Napoleon, confident that he had finally knocked them out of the war, made no effort to pursue them but turned again towards Brussels and bivouaced for the night.

Ney arrived in front of the Nassauers' positions at Quatre Bras at about midday and at once prepared to attack them with the troops he had in hand. In this he was undoubtedly right, for the position was but weakly held and one good thrust in the French manner must have broken through without much trouble. His staff on the other hand were much more cautious, for having seen a few redcoats (who were in fact staff officers) opposite them they hastily concluded that this was a typical Wellingtonian defensive position and that any serious attack would be met at the proper time by a previously concealed British line. They therefore prevailed on Ney to delay his attack until more troops could be got up and this delay, which is attributable to nothing but Wellington's Peninsular reputation, was just long enough to allow Picton's leading battalions to arrive on the scene.

CHAPTER 16

WATERLOO

Quatre Bras, as its name implies, stands at the point where the Brussels–Charleroi road is crossed by the Nivelles–Namur road and in 1815 consisted of a small group of buildings only. On the eastern side of the Charleroi road the ground falls away gently southwards for about 1200 yards to a shallow valley (along which runs a stream) before rising again to another low ridge.

The western flank of the position was then covered by the thick Bossu wood, which ran south-west from the crossroads for about a mile and a half and which was of an everage width of 7–800 yards, while the eastern side was similarly flanked by the Hutte wood; the whole position, much of which was covered in tall rye, was very enclosed.

On 16 June the position was at first held by ten Nassau battalions, a total of some 7000 men, and 16 guns. One battalion was extended along the line Grand Pierrepont–Gemioncourt–Pireaumont, six were either in or just south of the Bossu wood, and the remaining three were écheloned back along the road from Gemioncourt to Quatre Bras.

When Ney arrived, confident in the knowledge that some 35,000 infantry, 2000 cavalry and 6 guns were close behind him, he at first resolved to attack at once but was, as already seen, dissuaded by his staff. At about 2.0 pm, however, he finally moved forward with 6000 infantry and all his available cavalry and guns, and the Dutch skirmishers, hard pressed (and if truth be told not over-enthusiastic) were pushed back rapidly. Almost simultaneously Wellington arrived from Ligny and Picton came down the Brussels road with his division behind him and the two forces meeting head on, at once began what was virtually an encounter battle.

Wellington's first action was to send Picton's leading battalion, the 1/95th Regiment, off to seize Pireaumont to keep open his communications with Blücher, but it was strongly held by the French so the riflemen occupied Cherry Wood as an alternative, whence they gradually extended eastwards to Thyle. He then halted and reformed the retreating Nassauers and persuaded them to move southwards again to try to recapture Gemioncourt, supported by the 28th Regiment. This renewed effort of the Nassauers was however a very half-hearted one and made no progress, upon which the 28th, seeing that there was nothing to be gained by supporting such timid, unenthusiastic gentry, returned to the Namur road.

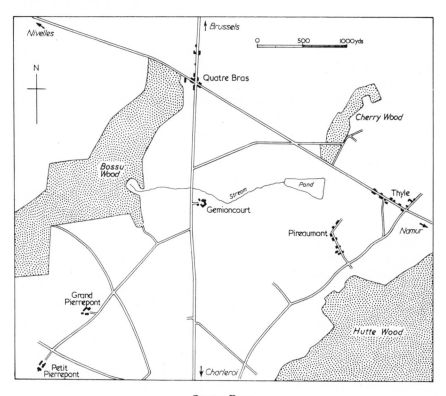

Quatre Bras

As the remainder of Picton's battalions came up, their commander formed them facing south along the general line of the Namur road; the leading unit, the 92nd, had its right actually resting on the cluster of buildings at Quatre Bras, and the other British battalions took up their ground successively further east as they arrived on the field. Picton's Hanoverian Brigade stood in reserve behind his main line while some Brunswick infantry who arrived next were sent off to occupy the northern end of Bossu Wood.

Ney then launched a full-scale infantry attack, supported by artillery, along his whole front; it was promptly counter-attacked in the centre by Kempt and his brigade, who brought the advancing French to an abrupt halt, but it made considerable progress against the now discouraged Nassauers in Bossu Wood. Wellington then pushed a force of Brunswickers, both infantry and cavalry, southward down the Charleroi road to support them, but these were promptly charged and dispersed by the powerful French cavalry and their commander, the Duke of Brunswick, was killed. After this success the French horsemen pressed on northwards and at one stage got so close to Wellington (well forward as usual) that he had to leap his horse over the heads of the 92nd, who were lining a ditch, to avoid them.

Although Wellington's particular pursuers were soon dispersed with a volley or two, the bulk of the French cavalry succeeded in passing the crossroads, where they turned eastwards and rode along the rear of the British line before swinging in right again to attack it. Their first blow fell on the 42nd and 44th Regiments, both of which were some distance south of the road; the former was actually caught in the act of forming square but the men, veterans as they were, stood firm and quickly drove off the French, while the latter simply turned about in line and met the charging horsemen with a single decisive volley, which drove them back with a heavy loss.

Ney's first great attack had thus achieved little; his infantry had indeed made appreciable progress on their left and had also succeeded in driving the British riflemen out of Thyle, but that was all; while his cavalry, after their initial success against the Brunswickers, had been bloodily repulsed at all points by the British battalions of Picton's division. Incredible as it may sound, Ney then decided to renew his cavalry attacks, and at once ordered Kellerman (who had just arrived with his heavy cavalry) to charge the British centre. The French horsemen again advanced gallantly, their first objective being, as before, the 42nd and 44th Regiments, which were somewhat in advance of the rest of the British line; but these two regiments were both firmly established in square, and although unsupported received them as before with steady musketry and broke their first attack with heavy losses. The French then withdrew to reform and having done so again rode desperately at the stolid red squares, but the latter were by then surrounded by such heaps of dead horses that the impetus of the French charges was lost before they fairly started, with the result that they made no impression.

The enemy horsemen, still reluctant to retire, continued to mill aimlessly round the squares on their exhausted horses so that at last Picton, despairing of the arrival of any allied cavalry to drive them off, decided to do so with infantry. He therefore formed the 1st and 28th into a single column of companies at quarter-distance (this being the formation from which square could most quickly be formed) on the Namur road and forthwith marched southward with it into the midst of the astonished French cavalry until he was level with the 44th Regiment when he halted, formed square, and at once opened fire. He was promptly followed in succession by the 32nd and 79th Regiments which both formed battalion squares next to him.

The French cavalry at once accepted the challenge of this new row of squares; their horses were exhausted and the rye so high that it became necessary for a few bold spirits to ride forward and drive their lances into the ground as markers for their comrades to charge on, but although they never wavered their attempts were all completely unsuccessful. They then again withdrew a little way and were replaced by French light infantry who crept up through the high crops and fired away at the huge targets presented by the squares, well knowing that the latter dared not adopt a thinner formation because of the menace of the hovering cavalry. The British light companies ran out to deal with this new and dangerous development but being both outnumbered and short of ammunition were soon driven back, whereupon the French cavalry attacked yet again. They seemed not to have been discouraged by their former failures for they came on with such determination that at one stage Picton's square was attacked simultaneously from three sides by angry Frenchmen determined to break it; there was a breathless pause as the French horsemen approached until Picton, sitting composedly on his cob, roared out in his hoarse voice '28th – remember Egypt'. Then the muskets came up, the volleys rolled out, and the galloping French squadrons dissolved into a bloody shambles of dead and wounded men and horses.

Picton's allusion to Egypt was appropriate; he was referring to the famous occasion near Alexandria in 1801 when the 28th, attacked simultaneously from front and rear, had coolly turned its rear rank about and dealt with both assaults. The episode had already taken its place in regimental tradition, and it is possible that a few survivors of the earlier battle were present at this greater one. Certainly the behaviour of the 28th (now the Gloucestershire Regiment) was exemplary on both occasions.

This was the end of the cavalry charges, which had achieved little except their own destruction, and although one must admire whole-heartedly the splendid spirit which made the French cavalry continue to press their attacks, it seems clear that Ney, who had had some experience of British infantry in defence, had blundered badly.

Kincaid of the Rifles, who watched Picton's first advance from Cherry Wood, said that 'this was a crisis in which, according to Bonaparte's theory, the victory was theirs by all the rules of War, for they held superior numbers both before and behind us', but goes on to comment with great admiration that

> the gallant old Picton, who had been trained in a different school, did not choose to confine himself to rules in these matters; despising the force in his rear he advanced, charged, and routed those in his front, which created such a panic amongst the others that they galloped back through the intervals of his division with no other object in view but their own safety.

There was then a short lull in the battle during which two more allied brigades arrived on the scene; of these Picton directed one, a British brigade under Halkett, to reinforce the few Nassauers remaining in Bossu Wood, and sent the other (of Hanoverians) to help the Rifles on his eastern flank. Halkett's brigade had formed a line of battalion squares near the north-east corner of the wood when the Prince of Orange, a gallant and enthusiastic young man but no general, galloped up to the nearest battalion, the 69th, and ordered it to form line. His reasons for this are by no means clear, and it is very probable that the commanding officer had the gravest doubts as to the wisdom of the move. Nevertheless discipline unfortunately prevailed and the movement was completed, upon which the French cavalry charged and broke the unfortunate battalion. Much elated with their success they then turned their attention to the next regiment, the 30th, but this time they caught a tartar for the 30th was still in square, and although composed almost entirely of recruits it received the French onslaught with great steadiness and drove it off with considerable loss.

The French, passing on, next attacked the 33rd Regiment and here they had more success, for the young soldiers wavered and broke before the terrifying onslaught of the enemy horsemen, and ran for shelter to the wood with their pursuers slashing furiously amongst them. The situation on the western flank had thus suddenly become serious, for two out of three of Halkett's battalions were out of action and the French infantry, who were making good progress northward through the Bossu wood, thus had every prospect of being able to turn the British right. Fortunately a battalion of the 1st Guards then arrived and plunging into the trees soon brought the French to a halt. One small enemy column did succeed in leaving the wood close to the north-east corner but this was quickly driven back by the 92nd Regiment.

By nightfall the Guards had cleared the wood and Halkett's brigade had rallied just to the east of it, so that that flank was secure; Picton's division still stood steadily in the centre, while on the left the 95th and the Hanoverians were well established in Cherry Wood. The French had thus made no perceptible progress after hours of heavy fighting and Ney withdrew discouraged; both sides were completely exhausted and bivouaced as quickly as they could, the British on the field itself and the French a little to the south of it.

The battle had been an exhausting one, both for commanders and troops, and several times the British had been on the verge of losing it; Wellington and Picton, however, by hard riding, gallant leadership, and the judicious use of the successive reinforcements as they arrived down the Brussels road, had succeeded in holding their ground. The chief interest of the action is perhaps Ney's persistent employment of cavalry against formed British infantry, for he had served in the Peninsula and must have realised what the result would be; he had of course achieved some initial success against the Brunswickers by this means and had also roughly handled two of Halkett's battalions. But this latter achievement was due in the one case to faulty handling by the Prince of Orange and in the other to the unsteadiness, pardonable but disastrous, of a battalion of young recruits and thus does little to excuse Ney's gross tactical error. It was one which he was to repeat two days later with even more calamitous results for the unfortunate French horsemen.

The fighting of the 16th had appreciably worsened Napoleon's position. It is true that he had driven off the Prussians in some disorder but he had counted on Ney's blow on their flank and rear to make this defeat decisive and this blow had not fallen.

He had moreover deluded himself that the Prussians were withdrawing eastward and had sent Grouchy off with thirty thousand men to shepherd them on their way. The bulk of the Prussians had in fact gone north but, unfortunately for the French, one corps had retreated eastwards with the result that Grouchy followed them confidently and was thus not available for the decisive battle on 18 June.

Picton spent the night of the 16th in considerable pain and discomfort, for at some stage of the battle he had been wounded. It is difficult to determine the exact circumstances under which this occurred for the general, realising full well that a second and greater battle was imminent, resolutely refused to go to the rear and concealed the fact of his injury, or at least its gravity, from all but his personal servant. It seems probable however that both he and his horse were struck by a discharge of grapeshot at extreme range, but that after the first shock he was able to continue in action. The projectile did not penetrate and in the excitement of the battle it is possible that he did not at once realise quite how serious a blow he had received. It is known that at some stage of the action he remarked to Tyler, 'I shall begin to think I cannot be killed after this'; and it seems at least possible that this was said when he realised, after the first stunning shock, that the ball had not in fact entered his body. It was almost certainly a grapeshot rather than a bullet which struck him, for the blow broke two or three ribs and caused heavy bruising and some internal injuries, all of which indicates a heavier projectile than a spent musket ball.

On 17 June Wellington, having at last received reliable news of the movements of the Prussians, decided to retire to Mont St Jean where he proposed to stand and fight, provided that Blücher could support him with one corps. He was by no means seriously pressed during this retreat, for Napoleon had halted to reorganise after Ligny while the bulk of Ney's troops, ill-supplied and but sketchily disciplined, had dispersed to seek food.

The British infantry marched off northwards at about 10.0 am, but it was midday before the French cavalry, urged on by Napoleon, began to follow them. As soon as this forward movement was apparent Wellington himself rode away, leaving Lord Uxbridge to cover the retreat with his cavalry and horse-artillery. There was heavy rain for most of the day, which largely confined the horsemen of both sides to the roads, so that a close pursuit was out of the question; the Horse Guards had a brisk little fight at Genappe but otherwise operations were confined to skirmishing, as the total casualty list (which was under a hundred) attests. Uxbridge himself called it 'the prettiest field of cavalry and Horse artillery that he ever witnessed', and this perhaps sums it up.

Sir Thomas Picton accompanied his division back. Although he had strapped and padded his injuries the night before as best he could with the help of his servant he must have been in considerable pain. Nor can his discomfort have been reduced by the fact that he was riding a troop-horse, for his own mount had either died or at least become unserviceable as a result of wounds, and his grooms with his other horses had temporarily gone astray in the confusion. Robinson also says that Picton had no saddle, but this is rather unlikely. There was no great urgency in the retreat and, although it was quite common for even senior officers to ride troop-horses in an emergency, it is hard to believe that a lieutenant-general would have been reduced to riding bareback. By a coincidence Tyler was also riding a borrowed pony and as he too (and perhaps more credibly) is also said to have been without a saddle, there must have been some frantic searching for the missing grooms.

The position chosen by Wellington near Mont St Jean was only eight or nine miles north of Quatre Bras, so that the withdrawal was soon complete and by the late afternoon of 17 June the bulk of the army was in bivouac on the ground which it was destined to defend the next day. In spite of his wounds, Picton carried out a detailed reconnaissance of the new position soon after his arrival; in the course of it he stopped to speak to Captain Mercer, whose troop of horse artillery was firing at the French as they arrived on the opposite slope, and that officer (who had not served in the Peninsula) was so misled by 'the shabby old drab greatcoat and rust round hat' that he treated him very brusquely in the belief that he was 'some amateur from Brussels'.

Having ensured that all was ready for the morrow, Picton retired to the cottage in which he had been billeted and there re-dressed his wounds, after which he lay down to rest. It is at this stage that Gronow gives us his last piece of information. Having finally caught up with his commander on the morning of the 16th, he had remained with him until they arrived at Mont St Jean on the evening of the 17th; at that stage however his friend Chambers who knew (what Picton did not) that Gronow was technically an absentee, apparently began to have qualms of conscience and terminated his short tour as supernumary ADC abruptly with the words: 'Now Gronow, the loss has been severe in the Guards, and I think you ought to go and see whether you are wanted; for as you really have nothing to do with Picton you had better join your Regiment or you may get into a scrape.'

The young guardsman, having achieved his main object of being present at the scene of the battle, accepted this arbitrary dismissal with good grace and rode off to find his regiment. He was somewhat apprehensive as to the sort of reception he was likely to get; nor was he disappointed, for the colonel's first words were 'Get off your horse and explain how you came here'. Even a guards colonel, however, could hardly be seriously angry with such a fire-eater; besides, he had other things to think about, so that when the adjutant, Gronow's friend, suggested that there was plenty for him to do he acquiesced readily enough. Upon this Gronow, having sold his horse on the spot to Captain Stopford, at once resumed his proper place as a subaltern in a company. That evening he was invited to dinner by Chambers and says that as he passed the room where Sir Thomas lay he heard him groan from the pain of his wound; it is not however clear whether he was genuinely one of the few who knew of the wound at the time, or whether this passage in his reminiscences was written in the light of later knowledge.

The British position at Mont St Jean (now better known as that of Waterloo) was one well suited to the type of defensive battle which Wellington had in mind and of which he was such a master. The allied army was formed up facing south on the reverse slope of a long low ridge running east and west, across which passed the Brussels–Charleroi road, its position being further strengthened by the occupation of three strong outposts.

On the right or western flank, covering the shallow valley along which ran the Nivelles road and which offered a covered line of approach to the main position, was the farm of Hougoumont; in the centre, on the Brussels road, was the farm of La Haye Sainte; and on the left were the groups of buildings of Papelotte, La Haie, Smohain, and Frischermont; all these posts were strongly garrisoned. The position taken up by the French was on a second and parallel ridge about twelve hundred yards further south.

The morning of 18 June 1815 broke heavy and overcast after a night of rain and the British were early astir in their comfortless bivouacs; there was a great bustle as the men dried themselves as best they could round their cooking fires, after which they ate a meal and having cleaned and carefully loaded their muskets, fell in in preparation for the forthcoming battle. The total strength of the allies was some 63,000 men of whom 21,000 were British; of the remainder, 5000 were of the King's German Legion, 11,000 were Hanoverians, 5,500 were Brunswickers, while the remaining 20,000 were assorted Dutch and Nassau troops. Their quality varied considerably but broadly speaking the British and King's German Legion were good and relatively experienced, the Hanoverians and Brunswickers were good material but very raw, while the Dutch and Nassau troops were poor in every respect. The army was supported by 156 guns. The French mustered some 70,000 troops, the bulk of them experienced veterans, and 266 pieces of artillery.

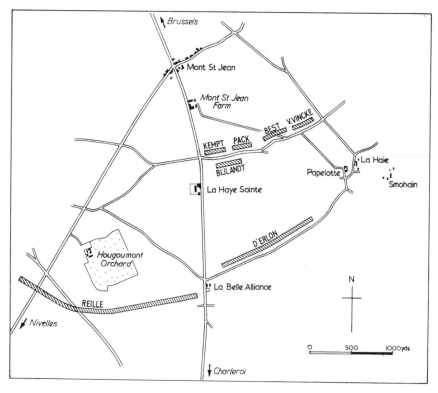

Waterloo

Picton's division formed with the right of its right-hand battalion (of Kempt's brigade) resting on the Brussels road. Next to Kempt, in pursuance of Wellington's policy of mixing the good with the bad, stood a brigade of Dutch troops under Bijlandt who, having presumably misunderstood his order, had formed his line well forward of the others on the crest of the ridge. Next to him, but back in line with Kempt, stood Pack's brigade, then there was a Hanoverian Landwehr brigade under Best and then Picton's own Hanoverians under Von Vincke. Two companies of the 95th had been detached from Kempt's Brigade and were occupying a gravel pit between the main position and La Haye Sainte, which was held by a force of Brunswick riflemen.

Picton, having supervised the forming up of his division, then posted himself near Kempt's Brigade; although he must have been in considerable pain he apparently showed no signs of it but sat composedly on his horse amongst his staff, a conspicuous and striking figure in a blue frock coat and low-crowned beaver hat. Fortunately his grooms had turned up earlier with his spare horses so that he was at least comfortably mounted. The commanding officer of the 52nd Regiment, who happened to pass the group at the time, heard Picton say that he had just galloped the whole length of the line, a remarkable feat in his condition. The old general added, caustically but very characteristically, that he had never seen a worse position, which was the sort of remark not calculated to improve his relations with Wellington.

Napoleon, still certain that the Prussians were fleeing eastwards in irretrievable confusion, was very confident that he would beat the rather heterogeneous army before him. He had intended to open his attack early but was compelled to postpone it, partly because many of his units had dispersed to plunder but also because the ground was so wet in the early morning that his mounted troops would have been seriously hampered in their movements. His plan was simplicity itself; there was to be no complicated manoeuvres, he would simply hammer his opponents with artillery, attack them with cavalry to make them reveal their positions and then, when he was certain of the exact location of the British, he would destroy them with his Guard. After which the remainder would run away and the battle would be over. Some of his generals tried to impress on him the fighting qualities of the British, of whom (unlike Napoleon) they had had much experience, but Napoleon simply told them insultingly that they only thought Wellington a good general because he had beaten them. After this there was little else to be said and it must be assumed that the conversation languished.

At about 11.30 am Napoleon ordered an attack on Hougoumont with the object of distracting Wellington and causing him to weaken his centre, where the main blow was to fall, by sending his reserves prematurely to the threatened flank. This attack, as is often the case with diversions, quickly developed into a serious affair and Napoleon's brother, Jerome, who commanded it, was soon pouring in infantry in a series of desperate but unavailing attempts to capture the place.

By about 2.0 pm Napoleon was ready to launch his main attack and presently his guns opened a tremendous fire along the whole length of the allied line, under which heavy columns of French infantry formed up on both sides of the Brussels road and began to move forward. He had apparently abandoned for the moment his intention to attack first with cavalry to make his enemies show themselves, presumably because he thought he knew where the British were.

The French columns came on with great gallantry and in spite of the heavy return of fire from the allied artillery they were soon close to Wellington's line. During their advance they attacked La Haye Sainte briefly, but being unable to take it, they simply by-passed and isolated it, and prepared to fall on the main allied line. On Picton's front, Bijlandt's brigade, which by then had been withdrawn to its proper position, soon began to waver and on the close approach of the French fired one wild volley and turned and ran. Picton, who had earlier observed the unsteadiness of the Dutch, was apparently expecting something of the sort for he at once deployed Kempt's brigade to fill the gap, which they did very quickly. By then the French were only thirty of forty yards away, and the British, having fired one terrible volley, did not wait to reload but at once charged with the bayonet and drove the French back in confusion. Picton rode beside them, urging them on with word and gesture, until a bullet, fired at random by one of the retreating enemy, struck him in the head and he slumped forward in his saddle. His horse, excited by the noise of the battle and bewildered by the sudden slackening of the rein, stirred restlessly as the shouting infantry swept by it, and was only prevented from bolting by a wounded man in Kempt's brigade who caught its bridle and brought it to a halt. Tyler, riding close behind his general, flung himself from his charger and lifted Picton to the ground, but he was already past help for the ball had passed through his brain, killing him instantly.

EPILOGUE

Tyler left the body of his commander at the foot of a conspicuous tree close by, so that he could find it easily when the battle was over and then, conscious that there was still much to be done, he galloped off to find Kempt who, as next senior, automatically assumed command of the division.

The remainder of the battle can be dealt with briefly. Pack also charged with his brigade but was so greatly outnumbered that after the initial shock he could make no headway against the French but was driven back. Fortunately at this most critical moment the Union Brigade of cavalry charged with great success and, driving the French off in confusion, restored the situation.

After this there came a succession of great French cavalry attacks launched by Ney, apparently in the mistaken belief that Wellington's withdrawal of his line further behind the crest to avoid the French artillery fire presaged a general retreat. In this he was sadly mistaken for although some of the allied units dissolved at the first onslaught, the British squares stood firm, the story of Quatre Bras was repeated on a larger scale, and the French horsemen eventually withdrew, having suffered horrifying casualties to no purpose.

These attacks were followed by a renewal of infantry assaults and La Haye Sainte eventually fell but Wellington was still able to keep his line intact. By then it was 6.0 pm and the Prussians were getting close; Napoleon therefore strengthened his right to hold them off and immediately launched the Middle and Young Guards at the right centre of the British. This attack was repulsed, the Guard retreated, the Prussians closed in, and at last the British line advanced with a roar of cheering and drove the French from the field.

As soon as the fighting was over Tyler rode back to find the body of his old general and having done so, he obtained the services of a party of the 5th Division to carry it off the field. Several regiments claim to have provided this party but it seems probable that it came from the grenadier company of the 32nd of Kempt's brigade.

It is an indication of the severity of the battle that at the end of it Tyler was the only officer of Picton's personal staff on his feet; Langton had been hit at Quatre Bras and Price had sustained terrible wounds of which he later died. Chambers, Gronow's friend and ally, was dead too, killed while taking part in a gallant but unsuccessful attempt to recapture La Haye Sainte, while even Tyler had not escaped unscathed for his horse had been killed under him by a roundshot and he himself, in the very act of falling, had been struck by a bullet, fortunately spent.

When Wellington first heard the news of Picton's death he merely said after a pause, 'I'm sorry Picton's gone' and at once returned to the business of winning the battle, but although they had never been close personal friends he must have been more affected than he showed at the death of an officer who had served him loyally for so many eventful years. He was, however, engaged in the greatest battle of his career and officers and men were dying round him in horrifying numbers so Picton was, for the moment, no more than one further addition to the list.

When the battle was over the Duke sent Tyler off to England with the body, and it was not until it was being laid out in preparation for this journey that the full extent of the wounds received at Quatre Bras became known. Although there was no post-mortem, the surgeon who examined Picton's body gave it as his opinion that they might in themselves have proved fatal and it is a measure of the general's fortitude that he had been able not only to remain on his feet with such wounds but actually to command his division in a great battle.

The news of the death in action of Sir Thomas Picton had gone ahead of the cortège, and as the boat carrying his body sailed into Dover the warships there lowered their ensigns and fired minute guns in his honour. The party spent the night at Canterbury and by a melancholy coincidence, the body was laid for the night in the very room in which Picton had dined on his way to the campaign only a few days before. The next day they reached London where the body was taken to the general's town house at 21 Portman Square.

There was a strong suggestion from many quarters that Picton should be buried in St Paul's Cathedral but this was not proceeded with and on 3 July he was buried at St George's, Hanover Square. A memorial to him was however erected in St Paul's in the north-west transept and later a much more elaborate one was built at

Carmarthen by public subscription, the list for which was headed by the Prince Regent with a donation of a hundred guineas. This was unveiled in the presence of a great crowd of friends, constituents, countrymen and old soldiers, all of whom had assembled to pay their final respects to one of Wales' great soldiers.

It is difficult to make a really full assessment of Picton's character, because remarkably little information is available regarding his private life. He was never a 'fashionable' man, he is rarely mentioned in the numerous gossipy memoirs of the period, except in those dealing specifically with the campaigns in which he took part; his name was never linked with that of a woman and he fought no duels. His interests, apart from his military ones, were in general those of a country squire; he loved his hunting, shooting, and later his farm, but none of these naturally ever brought him into prominence. Virtually all the available information deals with his military career, and thus no really balanced portrait of the man is possible.

It is not difficult to picture the soldier of the Peninsula and Waterloo: hard, stern, foul-mouthed, solidly brave in action, and usually ready to seize every advantage offered—only 'usually' because, on occasions and particularly when in positions of semi-independent command, he was shown to be oddly hesitant. His lack of initiative at Foz d'Aronce was understandable for he was relatively inexperienced and perhaps also influenced to some extent by the incompetent Erskine, but his precipitate retreat almost to Pamplona in the campaign of 1813 was oddly out of character. There is little doubt that it surprised Wellington and later may even have influenced him in his advice to Picton not to accept the Army of Catalonia, although if this is true it is a little unfair, for there is no doubt that much of the hesitancy of Wellington's generals stemmed from his own insistence on their obedience to instructions, even when changes of circumstances made this difficult and even dangerous.

In this connection, however, it is but equally fair to say that some other generals rose above this disability, for Hill, Graham and (within the scope of his more limited opportunities) Hope all showed considerable powers of leadership and decision when in independent situations.

One can visualise also the earlier administrator; here the main characteristic is a remarkable amount of confidence, and a certain bluff denial of any real freedom or self-determination to his subjects; in short, a benevolent dictator but with at least a suggestion of more sinister undertones to darken the picture. It was of course difficult for

225

an officer of any standing to vary very much from this pattern, for the squire/tenant relationship led easily enough to the officer/man relationship and after many years of this, it was perhaps natural for even the kindest and most liberal-minded senior officer to feel that he knew best what was good for those under him. Yet all Peninsular writers deny most emphatically any suggestion of tyranny on his part, and his relationships with his brother-officers, although rarely close, were usually good.

A good indication of his political views was given in a letter he wrote to Marryat in July 1811 in which he said:

> You know I was always against puppet-show legislature in the Country, and I have hitherto seen nothing to make me change my opinion. Generally speaking, and with few exceptions, it is a society composed of materials unfit to be trusted with the important power of legislation. It will be enough to give them good laws, and respectable, responsible people to execute them with impartiality.

There speaks the old, autocratic (and perhaps the true) Picton of Trinidad, who readily decided what was best for people without much regard to the wishes of the people themselves.

The real character of the man is still difficult to assess at all accurately; was he perhaps, like Wellington, a rather shy youth who had deliberately cultivated a hard shell round him but who (unlike Wellington) had received in his maturity a shock to his self-confidence, the Calderon affair, from which he never really recovered? Or was he from the first a hard, assertive thruster, soured by the Trinidad business and its blow to his self-pride, and furious that anyone dare question his conduct?

There is little doubt that he was always a lonely man; he appears to have had few close friends and his only regular correspondents during the war years were Colonel Pleydel, Mr Marryat, and Lewis Flanagan; even to them his letters, although long and informative, were formal in the extreme, except for one or two to Flanagan offering shrewd, concise (but possibly not always palatable) advice on his private affairs.

At the same time he was prepared to offer more practical assistance too, for he cheerfully sold a farm in order to be able to lend Flanagan £2000 to enable him to continue his legal studies. Even Napier, no great admirer of Picton, admitted freely that he had been most generous, in the short time left to him, to the widows and other dependants of members of the 3rd Division who had fallen in the Peninsular war.

No woman's name is ever mentioned in connection with him, although his tastes in that direction appear to have been normal, if possibly a little underdeveloped by the standards of his age. It may perhaps be inferred too that in later life he had a slight preoccupation with younger women, but this is hardly uncommon by any standards. His general attitude to the sex could well have been influenced by the Trinidad affair, for it received such a great deal of unpleasant publicity that it may have left him with the secret feeling that decent women looked upon him as a cruel, inhuman monster. One story current at the time had recounted how the general had personally stripped Luise Calderon naked and then flogged her almost to death; and although there is not a scrap of truth in the story its strong sadistic undertones may have made it remembered long after the legal aspects of the affair had faded from memory.

As was natural from his forthright character, a host of stories were, and still are, told about him; more probably than about any other general of his time, save only Wellington himself. The oldest of these is the story of how he threatened to hang a commissary and how that individual (who had appealed indignantly to Wellington himself) was advised to do as he was told as the only means of saving himself. This however is a standard 'soldier's story' of the Peninsula and has been told of several other generals, so that it is by no means authentic. His complete disregard for the niceties of dress on campaign, his conduct in action, and his remarkable powers of invective all lent themselves to numerous good anecdotes. It was later said that he was 'Wellington's right-hand' (which he emphatically was not), and even that after Waterloo a secret commission was found on his body appointing him to the chief command should anything happen to Wellington; but in view of the presence of Uxbridge and Hill this seems to be highly unlikely.

Robinson related a strange little story of how Picton was quite unable to watch a celebrated gymnast perform a somersault over a line of soldiers with fixed bayonets, but covered his eyes saying, 'a battle is nothing to that', which in view of his own undeniable physical courage is interesting. Many years afterwards, in 1835, Wellington told Stanhope:

In France Picton came to me and said . . . 'My Lord, I must give up. I am grown so nervous that when there is any service to be done it works upon my mind so that it is impossible for me to sleep at nights. I cannot possibly stand it, and I shall be forced to retire.' Poor Fellow! He was killed a few days afterwards.

Now this is hard to believe, and it is almost certain that the old Duke, speaking many years afterwards, was mistaken as to time, or misreported. It is known that towards the end of the Peninsular War Picton's health had deteriorated, his morale perhaps lowered accordingly, and that he did in fact go home in order to recuperate so that if one reads 'months' for 'days' the remark makes sense. As it stands, however, it is clearly not a recognisable description of the general who boldly marched a column of infantry into the midst of the French cavalry at Quatre Bras and who, although desperately wounded, led Kempt's brigade forward against the swarming French columns at Waterloo.

BIBLIOGRAPHY

Anderson, J. *Recollections of a Peninsular Veteran*, London 1913
Anglesey, Marquess of. *One-Leg*, London 1961
Aspinall-Oglander, C. *Freshly Remembered* (Sir Thomas Graham) London 1956
Bell, G. *Rough Notes by an Old Soldier*, London 1863
Bell, D. *Wellington's Officers*, London 1938
Blakeney, E. (ed. Sturgis). *A Boy in the Peninsular War*, London 1864
Bruce, H. *Life of Sir William Napier*, London 1864
Bunbury, H. *Passages in the Great War in France*, London 1927
Butler, W. *Life of Sir Charles Napier*, London 1890
Chad, G. *Conversations with the Duke of Wellington*, Cambridge 1956
Cole, J. *Distinguished Generals during the Peninsular War*, London 1856
Cooper, J. S. *Rough Notes of Seven Campaigns*, Carlisle 1914
Costello, E. *Adventures of a Soldier*, London 1852
Craufurd, A. *General Craufurd and His Light Division*, London 1891
Creasey, E. *Fifteen Decisive Battles of the World*, London 1893
Delavoye, A. M. *Life and Letters of Sir Thomas Graham, Lord Lynedoch*, London 1868
Donaldson, J. *Eventful Life of a Soldier*, Edinburgh 1827
Draper, Lt-Col A. E. *An Address to the British Public on the Case of Brigadier-General Picton*, London 1806
Fortescue, J. *Wellington*, London 1925
—— *History of the British Army*, London 1910
Fraser, W. *Words on Wellington*, London 1889
Fullarton, W. *A Statement, Letters, ad Documents Respecting the Affairs on Trinidad*, London 1806
Fuller, J. *Sir John Moore's System of Training*, London 1924
—— *British Light Infantry in the 18th Century*, London 1925
Gleig, G. R. *The Subaltern*, Edinburgh 1845
—— *Life of the Duke of Wellington*, London 1899
Glover, M. *The Peninsular War*, Newton Abbott 1974
Gomm, W. *Letters and Journal of Field-Marshal Sir William Gomm*, London 1881
Grattan, W. *Adventures with the Connaught Rangers*, London 1902

Griffiths, A. *Wellington—His Comrades and Contemporaries*, London 1897
Gronow, R. H. (ed. J. Greco). *Reminiscences and Recollections of Captain Gronow*, London 1892
Guedalla, P. *The Duke*, London 1931
Harris (ed. Curling). *Recollections of Rifleman Harris*, London 1927
Hay, W. *Reminiscences under Wellington*, London 1901
Hooper, G. *Wellington*, London 1890
Howells, T. J. *A Complete Collection of State Trials* (Vol. XXX), London 1822
Kincaid, J. *Adventures in the Rifle Brigade*, London 1929
—— *Random Shots from a Rifleman*, London 1847
Larpent, F. *Private Journal in the Peninsula*, London 1854
Latham-Browne, G. *Wellington*, 1899
Lawrence, W. *Autobiography of Sergeant William Lawrence*, London 1886
Leach, J. *Rough Sketches of the Life of an Old Soldier*, London 1831
Leith-Hay, A. *A Narrative of the Peninsular War*, London 1834
Londonderry, Marquess of (with G. R. Gleig). *Story of the Peninsular War*, London 1827
Long, R. B. (ed. T. H. McGuffie). *A Peninsular Cavalry General*, London 1951
Longford, E. *Wellington: The Years of the Sword*, London 1969
McCarthy, J. *Storm of Badajos*, London 1836
Marbot, Baron de. *Memoirs of Baron de Marbot*, London 1907
Maxwell, W. *Life of Wellington*, London 1883
Mercer, C. *Journal of the Waterloo Campaign*, London 1927
Moore-Smith, G. *Life of John Colborne, Field-Marshal Baron Seaton*, London 1903
Naipaul, V. S. *The Loss of Eldorado*, London 1969
Napier, G. *Early Military Life of Sir George Napier*, London 1884
Napier, W. *History of the Peninsular War*, London 1882
—— *Battles and Sieges in the Peninsula*, London 1910
Oman, Carola. *Sir John Moore*, London 1953
Oman, Sir Charles. *History of the Peninsular War*, Oxford 1902
—— *Wellington's Army*, London 1912
Patterson, J. *Adventures in the Peninsular War*, London 1837
Petrie, C. *Wellington, a Reassessment*, London 1956
Roberts, F. *The Rise of Wellington*, London 1895
Robinson, C. *Wellington's Campaigns 1808–15*, London 1905
Robinson, H. B. *Memoirs and Correspondence of Lieutenant-General Sir Thomas Picton*, London 1836
Ropes, J. *The Campaign of Waterloo*, New York 1916
Ross-Lewin, H. *With the 32nd in the Peninsula*, London 1904
Rousseau, I. J. (ed.). *D'Urban's Peninsular Journal*, London 1930
Schaumann, A. *On the Road with Wellington*, London 1924
Sherer, M. *Recollections of the Peninsula*, London 1825
Sidney, E. *Life of Lord Hill*, London 1845

Simmons, G. (ed. W. Verner). *A British Rifleman,* London 1899
Smith, H. *Autobiography of General Sir Harry Smith,* London 1902
Southey, R. *History of the Peninsular War,* London 1832
Stanhope, Earl. *Conversations with the Duke of Wellington,* London 1888
Steevens, C. *Reminiscences of Colonel Chas. Steevens,* Winchester 1878
Surtees, W. *Twenty-five Years in the Rifle Brigade,* Edinburgh 1833
Thoumine, R. *Scientific Soldier* (Major-General Le Marchant), London
    1968
Tomkinson, W. *The Diary of a Cavalry Officer in the Peninsular War,*
    New York 1894
Ward, S. *Wellington's Headquarters,* London 1957
Warre, W. *Letters from the Peninsula,* London 1909
Wellington (ed. Gurwood). *Wellington's Despatches,* London 1837
Weller, J. *Wellington in the Peninsula,* London 1962
——— *Wellington at Waterloo,* London 1967
Wheeler, W. (ed. B. H. Liddell-Hart). *Letters of Private Wheeler,* London
    1951
Anon. *Military Adventures of Johnny Newcome,* London 1816

Other sources are the various letters and papers in the possession of the National Library of Wales, some of which were printed in volumes 13 and 14 of the Records of the West Wales Historical Association, and the Picton and Trinidad Papers in the Public Record Office.

ACKNOWLEDGEMENTS

Inevitably a good many people have given me much help of various kinds in the preparation of this book, and I am glad to have this opportunity of thanking them. Before mentioning them, however, I feel it very necessary to explain that a great deal of my original research on General Picton was done in the early 1960s; the project was then put aside for various reasons until now, almost twenty years (and six other books) later, it has finally come to fruition. This being so I can only apologize to those people listed below for the fact that my thanks have been so long in coming. This very long delay also makes it certain that most, if not all, of those listed will have ceased to fill the appointments attributed to them, while in some cases the nature and title of the appointments themselves have also changed. In the circumstances, however, I decided to make no alterations but to give them in their original versions.

I am most grateful to D. W. King, OBE, Librarian of the War Office Library and the unfailing friend and support of many writers on military subjects; E. D. Jones Esq, BA, FSA, Librarian of the County Library of Wales, who found a great deal of material for me; J. F. Mason Esq, Secretary to the Masters, Royal Courts of Justice; J. F. Jones Esq, BSC, Curator of the County Museum Carmarthen; Michael Lawrence Esq, Secretary to the Trustees of the History of Parliament; Lieutenant Colonel (retired) L. H. Yates, OBE, Librarian of the Prince Consorts Library; Lieutenant Colonel (retired) R. H. Hopking, Regimental Secretary 1st East Anglian Regiment (Suffolk Branch).

I must also thank Christopher Hibbert, who read the first typescript and offered some valuable suggestions regarding it; my old wartime friend Colonel (retired) D. G. Dickson, OBE, MC, TD, with whom I walked many of the Spanish and Portuguese battle fields which are mentioned in this book; my sister, Miss D. Myatt, who gave much help with the index, and lastly, but not least, my wife Liz who has lived with Picton (in the nicest possible way of course) for so many years that she, like me, may even feel a little lost once he has taken his proper place on a bookshelf instead of being littered all over the house.

INDEX